NINE LIVES
OF A BLACK PANTHER

A STORY OF SURVIVAL

NINE LIVES
OF A BLACK PANTHER

A STORY OF SURVIVAL

WAYNE PHARR

Lawrence Hill Books

Chicago

Copyright © 2014 by Wayne Pharr and Karin L. Stanford
All rights reserved
First edition
Published by Lawrence Hill Books
An imprint of Chicago Review Press, Incorporated
814 North Franklin Street
Chicago, Illinois 60610
ISBN 978-1-61374-916-6

Library of Congress Cataloging-in-Publication Data
Pharr, Wayne, 1950-
  Nine lives of a Black Panther : a story of survival / Wayne Pharr, with Karin L. Stanford.
      pages cm
  Includes index.
    ISBN 978-1-61374-916-6 (hardback)
  1. Pharr, Wayne, 1950– 2. Black Panther Party. Southern California Chapter—Biography. 3. Black Panther Party. Southern California Chapter—History. 4. African American political activists—California—Los Angeles—Biography. 5. African Americans—Civil rights—California—Los Angeles—History—20th century. 6. Political violence—California—Los Angeles—History—20th century. 7. Police-community relations—California—Los Angeles—History—20th century. 8. Los Angeles (Calif.)—Race relations—History—20th century. 9. African American youth—California—Los Angeles—Social life and customs—20th century. 10. Criminals—California—Los Angeles—Biography. 11. Los Angeles (Calif.)—Biography. I. Stanford, Karin L., 1961– II. Title.
  F869.L89N364 2014
  322.4′20973—dc23

                                        2014006732

Interior design: PerfecType, Nashville, TN

Printed in the United States of America
5 4 3 2 1

To the memory of my elders, who survived slavery, segregation, discrimination, oppression, and so much more . . .

Lucille "Nanny" Doxey
Namon and Effie Pharr
Felix Prescott
Edwin Prescott
and Lillian Brusard

CONTENTS

ACKNOWLEDGMENTS

Undertaking a book project is a formidable task, even when the topic is one's own life. Thankfully, I had the help of a community of people. I am grateful for the generous help of Karin L. Stanford, who believed in this project and stayed focused and committed throughout. I also thank James Simmons, Esq., whose legal expertise was invaluable; Michele Beller, whose creativity and editorial skills were paramount; and Thandisizwe Chimerenga, who provided editorial and research support. Several faculty, staff, and students at California State University, Northridge, brought enthusiasm and technological skills to this effort: Anita Hart-Simon, Aimee Glocke, Jeffory Alexander (rest in peace), Brandy Stone, and Samantha Waul. I would also like to acknowledge Ashley Jackson, who generously contributed to this book her ideas and technological abilities.

I am wholly indebted to Ronald "Baba" Preston, who was instrumental in giving this book direction and substance. I am also deeply thankful for the work of Gregory Everett, who kept alive the memory and history of the Southern California chapter of the Black Panther Party. Gregory opened up his home and resources for this project, and for that I am grateful. I also want to offer words of appreciation to Kathleen Cleaver for her unwavering support and for reaching out to me and my family in times of difficulty. For the generous use of photos, I thank Roz Payne of Newsreel and Kent Kirkton of the Institute for Arts and Media at California State University, Northridge. I also acknowledge and thank my editor at Chicago Review Press, Yuval Taylor, who provided encouraging support and an excellent vision, and without whom this project would not have come to fruition.

A special note of appreciation is extended to my comrades of the Southern California chapter of the Black Panther Party for Self-Defense, especially John Washington, Roland Freeman, and Ronald Freeman, whose help in filling in the blanks was invaluable.

To my wife, Carmen Pharr, whose patience and support has always been steadfast and invaluable, I thank you for believing in me. Without Carmen, this project would not have been completed. I also thank my children, Tammy Smith and Arron, Darron, and Dana Pharr, for nourishing my soul with their love. The same holds true for my grandchildren, Drew, Erin, Chayna, Chelsea, Yasmin, Dee-Dee, and AJ. The memory of my brother Druice Pharr sustains me. I thank him for reinforcing in me strong community and family values. I am deeply indebted to my mother, who gave me life and fought for me to stay above ground.

Most importantly, I acknowledge all the revolutionaries who have made their transition, are incarcerated, or are still facing the yoke of repression yet remain committed to the struggle. All power to the people!

1

SHOWDOWN AT SUNRISE

We were at Jerry's house, listening to 'Trane, smoking weed, and playing chess when I told my crew that G—Elmer "Geronimo" Pratt—had given me the go-ahead to implement a new tactic of defense. We needed to find more ways to protect the Los Angeles branch of the Black Panther Party from the Los Angeles Police Department and other forces waging war against us. I had been toying with the idea of plotting an escape route through the sewers from the Party's head-quarters on Forty-First Street and Central Avenue. The sewers could serve as a hiding place and even a point of attack if necessary. "I think we can go in on 120th and Central," I told them.

"Naw," said Baba as he inhaled a joint. "I know a way that's closer." He squeezed the answer out, exhaling the smoke through his nostrils.

Baba wasn't a Panther—he was a member of the Black Student Alliance, an organization of Black Student Unions throughout Los Angeles. He also belonged to the United Front, an umbrella organization with a black-socialist orientation. Ronald "Baba" Preston was one of the most intelligent people I'd ever met. He was tall and thin, a build that contradicted his athletic strength. Like many of us in those days, he had an Afro, mustache, and goatee. On this night, he had on his "movement uniform"—light brown khakis, an army jacket, and his dark brown socks, which were an exact match to the worn shag carpet in Jerry's house.

"We should go in by the L.A. River, over near County General Hospital in East L.A. It'll be closer," Baba proclaimed with assurance.

I turned and studied Jerry's face. "What you think?"

"Sounds cool to me," he nodded from the deep recline of his black leather La-Z-Boy.

Jerry, also a member of the Black Student Alliance, lived in a small cottage in the back of a bungalow on San Pedro and Fifty-Third Streets. His place was where lots of us—Panthers, BSA members, and even "nonaffiliated" folk—would meet and have political discussions. We took off our shoes at the door when we came in Jerry's spot. Posters depicting beautiful women with large Afros, political prisoners, armed resistance, and other manifestations of radical politics would shepherd our discussions. Folks would stop by at various times to share food, sleep on whatever was available, or just hang out after a long day of political work.

Jerry had a routine. He would lie all the way back in his recliner with his legs crossed, his hands in a lotus-like position on the armrests, and his eyes closed, as Coltrane blew from the speakers behind him. According to Jerry, it was "the proper way to listen to revolutionary music." But after I mentioned the sewers, Jerry's eyes opened; he sat upright in the chair and then stood up. One thing about Jerry: when he was ready, he was *ready*, and when it came to movement work he did not mess around.

"Let's go see," he said.

Baba and Jerry both knew, like all of us who were involved with the Black Panther Party in Los Angeles, that an escape route out of the headquarters was more than just a good idea; it was a necessity.

Julius Jones, a Vietnam vet, was hunched over on the edge of his chair, scowling fiercely as we played chess. He was a dark-skinned man, short and stocky, with powerful sprinter's legs. He had only been a sergeant in the army, but he played chess like a general, a tactician's tactician; even so, my intensity met his on the black-and-white squares of the chessboard, move for move.

"Come on, man!" Baba pressed.

We had decided that night to ride in Julius's Pontiac Grand Prix, so Baba was chiding him to get ready; Baba was ready to roll. I had been leaning on the edge of the couch focused on my next chess move, but I pulled myself up. Baba was right: it was time to take care of business. I grabbed my army boots and headed out the door, putting them on as I followed Jerry down the steps, Julius right behind me. I was wearing my army pants that night too—they had a pocket for damn near everything. But for some reason I couldn't find my knife—the main thing you carry in the pocket of army pants. For a moment I wondered if I should be concerned. *Never mind*, I thought to myself. I didn't expect anything major to jump off tonight.

It was around 2:00 AM on December 8, 1969, and the early morning air was cool as the four of us left Jerry's house. We started on San Pedro and then quickly made our way to Alameda Street, heading north through downtown. We were able to find a jazz station on the radio, which helped to keep our concentration on track. Other than the music, we rode in silence.

We parked near the L.A. River and entered through the storm drain. The sewer system was an underground labyrinth of tunnels and passageways to all parts of the city. It was muggy and steamy underground, and the smell was far from the sweet aroma of patchouli oil that had flowed through Jerry's house.

Heading south through the sewer, we made it to the Black Panther Party headquarters in about an hour. As we made our way, we looked for other exits, climbing up ladders to look out of the street gutters. Near the intersection of Hooper Avenue and Santa Barbara Boulevard, I came up one of the drains to see where we were. I noticed some police activity on the streets. I didn't think much of it, but I made a mental note.

As I climbed back down, my foot caught on the last rail of the rusted-out ladder, which sent my flashlight flying through the air as I scrambled to catch my balance. "Ain't this about a bitch!" I grumbled angrily, a little unnerved.

Laughter erupted all around me, and I realized the guys were stumbling all over each other, amused by my reaction to the near miss. It was obvious that we were still riding our high from earlier.

As we continued our investigation of the sewers, we periodically stepped into puddles of rippling water. We walked slowly, keeping watch for the sewer rats. When they saw us, the giant-sized rats ran from us. But, unavoidably, they eventually hit a dead end and turned and headed back. Soon, they were coming straight at us, eyes glowing an ominous bloodred as they leered at us in the dark. We were uninvited intruders, gate-crashers in their underworld kingdom. This effectively ended our reconnaissance mission for the night.

Hauling ass, slipping, laughing, and looking over our shoulders, we ran through the underground sewer tunnels all the way back to East Los Angeles, about two miles. I was trying to make it back to where we first entered the sewer, but Baba was in my way. Jerry was right behind me, laughing. The wet ground beneath us didn't help either.

But whatever we might encounter in the sewers that early morning would not stop us; we didn't think twice about operating in a space that most people wanted to avoid at all costs. The sewers were not our problem, but a possible solution. Our work that night was meaningful because we were united. We had forged a team committed to the idea that black people in the United States were an oppressed people, and we had a duty and a right to struggle for freedom from that oppression. We also knew that our survival depended on finding new ways to defend our community and ourselves. No, we didn't think twice.

I asked Julius to drop me off at the Black Panther Party headquarters on Central instead of at Jerry's house because I wanted to tell G what we had found on our underground scouting mission. For some reason, Central Avenue was eerily quiet, which was an uncommon occurrence—something was *always* happening on Central. But now, as Julius cruised toward Forty-First, it seemed almost like a ghost town. Momentarily, I flashed back to the earlier omen of my missing army knife; something wasn't right.

G was at the headquarters, looking out the front door when I got out of the car. Others in the two-story office building that night included longtime community activists Paul Redd, Renee "Peaches" Moore, Melvin "Cotton" Smith, and Robert Bryan, as well as Bernard Smith, one of the newest and youngest members of the Party. Upstairs were Roland Freeman, one of the first to join the Los Angeles branch, and Lloyd Mims, Will Stafford, Tommye Williams, and Pee Wee Johnson. Gil Parker, a foot soldier and stalwart of the Panthers' Free Breakfast for Children Program, was stationed on the roof.

As I came inside, G told me he was glad to see me. His contact in the police department had told him that they were getting ready to move against us. He didn't know when exactly, but he thought it was imminent. Like G, I knew it could be at any time, especially since the police had just ambushed the Illinois chapter a few days earlier, on December 4, killing two Black Panther Party leaders, Mark Clark and Fred Hampton, as they slept.

I said to him, "I just came from checking out the sewers again, and I found another route to access them from the headquarters." I also reported that the pigs were out in full force on Hooper Avenue.

"Right on. That's the kind of information we need. Especially now," G replied. He then told me who else was in the house that night.

"Cool," I said. "We have a serious crew with us tonight. If they come, we will be ready."

As we discussed the recent activity of the police, G walked me over to the gun room to familiarize me with the weapons at the headquarters. "Clean this and hold on to it," he said, handing me an automatic shotgun. He then disappeared into another part of the building. I took off my bush jacket, sat down in an old recliner in the corner of the gun room, and began to clean my weapon. Soon after I finished, I fell asleep with the gun across my lap.

The next thing I knew, I was yanked from my slumber by a thunder of activity and urgent voices. "Wake up! Wake up! They're out there!" Cotton ran into the room shouting; he grabbed a Thompson machine gun off the wall and ran back out.

"Who's out where?" I asked groggily.

It was around 5:00 AM. I shook off my sleep and stood up with the shotgun in my hands, walking quickly out of the gun room toward the front door. I had drifted off to sleep a mere two hours earlier, and now all hell was breaking loose.

Roland, Mims, Will, and Pee Wee had been asleep upstairs while Gil had pulled guard duty on the roof. But the cops had drawn down on Gil. They put a gun to his head and pressed it so hard that it left a dent. Then the pigs tied him up. Gil began to stomp his feet to signal that he had a problem. It was that commotion on the roof that Cotton had heard when he came to wake me up.

I was standing a couple of feet from the front door when suddenly—*boom!*—it blew open. I immediately jumped into a bunker we had built on the right side of the room as a uniformed blur of police officers stormed past me. Just then, Cotton opened with the machine gun, moving forward in the direction of the front door. *Bam! Bam! Bam!* I heard in rapid succession. My heart began to beat faster as the adrenaline raced through my body. The cops were stopped in their tracks; then they bunched up in the hallway trying to get back to the front door. As they moved back past my position, I let loose with the shotgun, catching the police in the side and front. Good thing for them they had on bulletproof vests. But now they had no choice but to withdraw. "They're shooting back!" a couple of officers yelled as they retreated, running and limping back out the front door.

I knew at least one had gotten shot; a trail of blood ran the length of the hallway. I was still in the bunker when Paul Redd jumped in next to me, shotgun in hand. Bernard fired his shotgun directly over our heads, out toward the front. The sound was like a thunderclap directly on top of me. "What the hell are you doing? Go upstairs and find a window to shoot out of!" I yelled at him.

The smell of gunpowder began to fill up the front of the building. It was dark, but there was no way we were going to turn on any lights. Robert Bryan came running from the back and took up a position behind the sandbags in the front office. Paul ran over to the left side of the building and hopped into a bunker over there. Cotton had been moving toward the front and got in the right bunker as I checked to make sure the rear of the building was secure. There was a ton of dirt piled up against the back door; this was where we had been digging a tunnel to the sewers below. Much of the dirt had also been used to fill the sandbags throughout headquarters and to fill the walls just in case the cops fired on us.

We were pretty secure downstairs. The dirt piled against the rear door made it immoveable. Outside, the downstairs door that led to our second-floor office had been reinforced and was also secure. In the upstairs office we had gun slats in the walls; the only problem was that once they were opened, the light would give away our positions. But the upstairs was still protected. There was a skylight in the center of the room, and because the pigs were on the roof, they had to walk over the skylight. We hugged the walls so they couldn't see us. The police had taken serious fire, so they hadn't tried to come up the steps. We had shot the cops out of our headquarters through the front door, their point of attack. To our credit, we had repelled the first assault by the police and secured the building.

Knowing the LAPD would need time to regroup, I went to the gun room and got the ammunition we needed to defend ourselves. Paul, who had a shotgun and a .30 caliber carbine, was reloading his weapons in the left bunker. When I returned to the front, I reloaded my M-14. Cotton reloaded his .45 caliber in the right bunker. I also passed out pipe bombs and Molotov cocktails, which we used to keep the police from sneaking up on us. As soon as we would hear movement outside, we'd signal for the bombs. This cleared the sides of the building so the cops couldn't rush through the front door again. A few of the pipe bombs landed on a car parked in front of the building, igniting it. The smoke from the fire, as well as kerosene and gasoline fumes, began to waft inside.

Soon, the police began throwing tear gas at the building. We had chicken wire around the upper windows, which blocked most of the incoming canisters, but the fumes still found their way inside, mixing with the cordite and gunpowder. My eyes began to tear up, but I didn't dare wipe them; we knew that the way to deal with tear gas was to keep our hands away from our faces so that we wouldn't accidentally rub the tear gas in our eyes and pores, where it would become more effective.

"Redd! You got some cigarettes?" I shouted. I was digging in my pockets looking for my pack of Kools, but they were nowhere to be found. Paul had taken some Lucky Strikes from his pocket and snapped off the filtered end, sticking them up his nose to keep the tear gas fumes out. He tossed me the pack; I did the same. I knew my other comrades would follow suit—our training required us to understand the dangers of tear gas.

Peaches and Tommye had been downstairs but needed to get to the communications room upstairs so they could notify other comrades, our families, and the community that the pigs had "vamped" on us. We knew the building like the backs of our hands. Every one of us was able to get through in the dark, but the pigs on the roof would be watching for movement of any kind. I escorted them both, covering them with the shotgun aimed at the ceiling, to the communications room where they manned the phones and called the local press and wire services. Though it seemed like an eternity, all of this activity had transpired thirty minutes after our initial contact with the police.

As we waited for the next round of attacks, we also waited for the cops to identify themselves as police and state that they had a search warrant or that we were under arrest. None of that happened—the pigs had just busted through our door. Basically, the police had launched a planned, unprovoked attack against us with the clear intention to kill. Again, we were able to survive because of our diligence and training. We had settled in to fight, and everybody handled their business. We fought back. No one thought of giving up.

■ ■ ■

Two hours passed. We were getting hit at various positions, and while the tear gas was having minimal success, the smoke was still drifting throughout the building. That's when the police decided to blow the roof off our headquarters.

It seemed like everything around us exploded, literally and figuratively. I looked up through the hole where part of our roof used to be and saw, with a note of irony, that the orange and red violence of dawn had swept the early morning sky, while the Panther headquarters had been covered with violent smoke from some serious munitions of the LAPD. The explosive charges they planted made a deafening noise, practically destroying Paul's eardrums. The hole in the roof was large, but the pigs didn't get the effect they had hoped for; the gaping hole allowed the tear gas that had collected inside to escape. Meanwhile, wood, composition tar paper, and all manner of debris rained down on us.

"I'm hit, I'm hit!" I heard Roland yell.

Tommye and Peaches came running downstairs, sweat and soot dripping from their faces. Roland had been wounded earlier when the pigs first came in, and he got hurt again when the roof blew. He came downstairs bleeding from his side, but the first thing he said was that he needed a gun; he didn't want the police running up on him with nothing in his hand. I went to the gun room to retrieve a .45 automatic pistol and gave it to him.

Snipers then became the central strategy of the police attack. The Panthers who remained upstairs were taking tremendous fire. "Duck, Wayne!" Pee Wee yelled out. "The bullets are as thick as donuts up here!"

He was right. I could hear the bullets whizzing by, hitting everything except my comrades. But even through the barrage of bullets, those still upstairs were able to hold on to one room for a good while.

During this time, I was holding fire with a sniper when he locked on my position. I could actually see the bullet coming at me in a straight line. I rolled out of the way, and it hit the concrete floor. Tommye, who was lying directly behind me, was hit twice, once in each thigh. Her blood squirted onto my ankle as the bullets tore into her flesh. My arm and chest suddenly felt as if they were burning, and that's when I realized that some of the bullet fragments had hit me in my left arm. I also took some shotgun pellets in my chest. Then I felt something warm and wet trickle down the side of my face; I don't know exactly when, but at some point a bullet had grazed my forehead.

Making matters worse, we had run out of .30 caliber ammo and shotgun shells. This was a serious blow because that's what most of our weapons needed. But we still had the Thompson .45, which Cotton was holding, and Robert and I had the two M-14s.

The pigs finally cleared us out of the upstairs space, so now everyone was downstairs. We could hear them talking from outside the building. We surmised that their next step in forcing us out would be to use a tank or armored vehicle. Based on this assumption, we finally began to talk about surrendering.

"I been shooting at the police for four or five hours, and I ain't about to go outside," I said defiantly. Some of the other brothers were in agreement, especially Paul Redd, who was adamant about not giving up. But as we were discussing the options, Peaches spoke up.

"I'll go out," she reasoned. We all got quiet. Peaches repeated herself. We finally agreed.

We had to cover Peaches as she went out. Cotton was in one bunker, Paul was in the other, and I had the M-14. Shortly before she left, I went back upstairs with the aim of starting a fire in our information room. But then I thought better of it once I got up there, because to do that, pulling down file cabinets and all, I would expose myself to police fire. Peaches went out waving a white rag.

Shortly after her, we all walked out, one at a time, in silence.

Paul, Cotton, and I were the last ones to leave the building. Cops were everywhere—on rooftops, the sides of the building, everywhere.

That's when I clearly saw that most of these guys weren't regular beat cops; they were the paramilitary Special Weapons and Tactics team, aka SWAT—the LAPD's newest weapon. The eleven of us were staring at about three hundred of them, face-to-face. They were dressed in all black from head to toe—black jumpsuits and baseball caps. The LAPD had thrown their best at us, yet none of us had died.

They herded us around the corner, where they got us down on the ground and tied us up with rope—no handcuffs. We knew they were purposely treating us like animals.

Roland, who was wounded, was lying on the ground when a paramedic came up and put a blanket on his head. He started wiggling and hollering, "I'm *not* dead!" This made the blanket fall off so that everyone could see his condition. Despite the violent and difficult circumstances we found ourselves in, we all found humor in Roland's actions.

The police put us all in squad cars to take us off to jail. Then my friend Erwin Washington, a reporter for the *Los Angeles Times*, broke through the police line. "Wayne! Do you have a statement?" he yelled.

"Tell Moms I love her and tell my Sharon I love her too," I said. I didn't think I would ever see the light of day again.

The cops put me in a squad car and rolled all the windows down because I was saturated with tear gas fumes. One of the officers asked me how we could take all that gas, and I told him about the cigarette butts. He looked at me incredulously; then he told me that their next move, had we not surrendered, was to bring in a tank and blow us out. As we headed out, one of the cops noticed I was bleeding from my forehead and my chest, so they took me to a hospital. It was the same hospital Roland had been taken to.

They put me in a bed near Roland. The cops had his bed surrounded and were gawking at his wounds when one of them noticed an old gunshot wound in his foot. When Bunchy Carter had been killed, Roland had been on a mission with a shotgun stuck in his pant leg. The gun had gone off and struck him in the foot.

11

"He probably shot himself in the foot," one of the cops quipped, just to make him mad.

Roland got pissed. It made me mad too. But there was nothing much I could do to come to the defense of my comrade. "Leave him alone!" I hollered in frustration.

That made the pigs turn and look at me. They came over to my hospital bed and grabbed my glucose bottles, rattling them to shut me up.

Later that night I was transfered to county jail. A nurse at the hospital, who was sympathetic to us, got word to my family that I was alive. I was only nineteen years old.

2

BACK HOME

I hadn't intended to disobey my mother.

"Wayne, go wash your hands and get ready for dinner," my mom called.

"Yes, ma'am!" I hollered back as I walked out of my room into the living room on my way to our bathroom, where I could run warm water and soap over my hands as I'd been taught to do. But on the way I stopped to flip on the TV and caught a glimpse of *The Cisco Kid*, one of my favorite shows. Instead of washing my hands, I sat down to watch.

A commercial came on, and I eyed the *Jet* magazine lying on our wooden coffee table. Enticed by the hope of catching a glimpse of the racy swimsuit model in the centerfold, I swiped the magazine. I glanced toward the kitchen, hoping that my mom wouldn't walk into the room, and then peeled back the cover. I looked down and saw the unexpected. The violence of the images hit me square in the chest; my heart started pounding and I couldn't breathe. I was looking at the gruesome pictures of Emmett Till. He was horribly disfigured.

His face was all bloated, with the left side of it crushed in, all the way to the bone. It was a lot to take in, especially for a five-year-old kid.

I closed the *Jet* magazine and sat on the sofa, frozen. My mother called again, asking me if I had washed my hands. I told her yes and joined her at the kitchen table. I didn't ask about the photo. I kept my silence, never forgetting the image. Even though the boy in the magazine was much older, I knew he was a black kid, just like me. *What happened to him?* I wondered.

Later I heard that Emmett Till was killed on August 28, 1955, at the age of fourteen, because he was flirting with a white woman. I couldn't stop rolling the idea around and around in my head. What kind of people would do that to a kid?

I was born in Berkeley, California, on August 25, 1950, to William and Evelyn Pharr. My father was from Gipson, Louisiana, and my mother's folks were the Prescotts from Bunkie, Louisiana. My parents moved to California during the 1940s, like a large number of African Americans who wanted to escape the racism and oppression of the South and build a better future. I was the only child of my father and mother. Dad had one other child, my half brother, who lived back in New Orleans.

Our family first settled in the Northern California areas of Vallejo, Oakland, and Berkeley. Wartime shipyards and factories beckoned newcomers, and the work was plentiful. While many of the men in my family had jobs in the factories, my father served as a merchant seaman in the navy. Dad was not physically imposing, but he was smart, especially when it came to generating income. Before joining the navy, he owned several small businesses, specializing in janitorial and plumbing work.

The women in my family did domestic work for wealthy white families. My grandmother's sister Nanny, an outstanding cook, was so respected among white folks that her referrals for domestic help could easily land someone a job. She was the lightest color in the family, with sparkling blue eyes. Actually, it was she who sent for my mother and persuaded her to leave Louisiana and finish high school in California. She hooked my mom up with a job while she went to school, working as a domestic, of course.

My mother was street-smart like my dad, but she was book smart too. She had earned the honor of class valedictorian at Vallejo High School, but it didn't mean much beyond the school grounds—she remained a domestic after graduation. But my mother was not going to let life's limitations stop her. She was hardworking and ambitious, and she created opportunities for herself. My mom and I favor each other physically—same caramel brown skin, same piercing eyes, and same distinctive nose.

My great uncle Edwin, one of my favorite relatives, introduced my parents to each other. Uncle Edwin was the color of shiny cocoa, with curly black hair and a big barrel chest. He was always nattily dressed in slacks and a shirt. He was also fond of leather coats. Edwin was a good hustler—I always admired that. He owned an after-hours nightspot in Oakland and a car wash too. As a kid, I was in awe of Uncle Edwin. He was flashy—he drove around in a Cadillac, and he even had a car phone back in the 1950s! It was a big, heavy, boxy thing, but who else had a car phone in those days?

My great-aunt Nanny (left) and my mother, Evelyn Dotson, sit together in the mid-1940s. Nanny brought my mother to California from Bunkie, Louisiana, to finish high school and to rescue her from the racism of the South. WAYNE PHARR COLLECTION

15

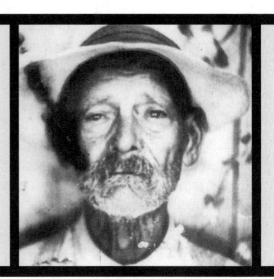

Felix Prescott was my great grandfather on my mother's side and the fearless patriarch of our family. He was born in Louisiana in 1868, three years after the Civil War ended. I admired him for refusing to let white folks bully our family. WAYNE PHARR COLLECTION

People saw Uncle Edwin as a renegade, notorious even, because he ignored societal norms about what was right or wrong. Nanny told me that Uncle Edwin got his personality from his father, who was my great grandpa Felix. Tales about Felix have been passed down through the generations in our family. He was considered a "bad nigga" who stood up to white folks. It might have been because he was half white himself, or, as my aunt Nanny put it, he was half crazy.

Being too much like Felix was the reason Uncle Edwin had to leave the South when he was young. I'm not sure what my uncle did, but Felix had to rescue him from a local white man who wanted to beat him. Felix told the family, "I ain't lettin' them white folks take Edwin!" When the white man came, Felix pulled him off his horse. After that, Uncle Edwin was put on a train and sent to live with Aunt Dovey in Oakland. Growing up, my cousins and I all wanted to be like Felix. My mother told me that my great grandpa picked me up and sat me on his horse when I was just a baby. He died in 1951.

Uncle Edwin played an important role in my life. He would give me bits of information on how to conduct myself so I could also be successful. "A man works for his money; it don't come to you. You go out and you get it," he turned and said to me one day.

I looked up at him and nodded, mesmerized by the baritone voice that boomed at me.

"You take care of yourself and you take care of your family. That's what a man does. You gonna be a man one day, so you gotta learn about the importance of family now, you hear me?"

"Yes, sir," I said, and I meant it.

"You got to keep yourself up; you can't go 'round looking like no hobo," he finished. I just smiled and thought to myself, *I will make this a part of my life.*

I learned from Uncle Edwin not just how to fight, but how to win. My aunt told me that one night some people tried to rob Uncle Edwin at his after-hours spot. He took a baseball bat and beat three of them up real bad. We talked about it one day, and Uncle Edwin told me that holding your fist up is just posturing; using the baseball bat was about winning. "A man ain't no man if he don't stand up for himself. You hear me, boy?"

"Yes, sir."

"You don't take no shit from nobody, and you don't run from nobody neither."

When I was fifteen, Uncle Edwin had a stroke and his speech became slightly garbled, but even then he still had that same personality. After the stroke, sometimes people couldn't understand what he said. One time I heard Uncle Edwin talking to one of his friends, who was having a hard time comprehending him. "If-i-hit-you-in-the-hey-wid-this-hamma-you-will-know-what-i-mean!" he slurred in frustration.

After that, I really tried to listen closely to what Uncle Edwin said, so he wouldn't hit me in the head with a hammer. Uncle Edwin was something else. I wanted to be just like him. I really valued the time I was able to spend with him, and he took special pride in knowing that he was partly responsible for my life.

About 1952, Nanny moved from Vallejo to Los Angeles and purchased a home on San Pedro Boulevard. Her brother, Fred Prescott, had been there for a decade, so Nanny already had family to welcome her to the city. My mother followed Nanny to Los Angeles after she and my dad separated. I never knew the reason for the separation; adults rarely shared those personal details with kids back then.

Always looking for a way to leave domestic work behind, my mother thought moving to Los Angeles would provide new opportunities, and her aim was to get a job working with the post office once we settled in. I knew I would miss my relatives in the north, but from the stories my mom shared, I was eager to meet my family in the City of Angels.

My mom started out as a domestic in Los Angeles, but around 1955 the postal service finally hired her. I was about five years old and had just started school. When my mom was at work, I would go visit other family members. Eventually, my mom was assigned to work the swing shift, and so she went to work at night. Of course, that's when I would sneak out of the house and go hang out with my relatives and friends in the neighborhood.

After my mom and dad separated, I did not see Dad much. He was often deployed, but he would send me gifts every now and then, like portable radios and the latest electronic equipment. When I was around ten, Mom took me up to Oakland to visit Dad, who at that time was living in a place called the California Hotel. It was a four-story brown brick building, and his space was quite small, with just a bed, a living area, and a kitchenette in one room. Because he was a navy seaman, he didn't bother with owning a home or even renting an apartment.

We had a pleasant conversation that day, but nothing earth-shattering. He called me Champ.

"How you doing in school, Champ?" He was looking at me with a smile.

"I'm doing well," I answered politely.

"Are you helping to take care of your mom?"

"Yes, sir, I am doing my best."

I was quiet and did not have much to say, but I checked out the environment, curious about how my dad was living. We talked a little bit more and then my mom and I left. That was it. Even though my mom and dad talked periodically, they didn't raise me together.

I loved living in Los Angeles. Holidays and regular weekends meant nothing but fun and family get-togethers. I had a large, close-knit family. Nanny's brother Uncle Fred had fifteen children, and they all had children, so I had a whole gang of cousins I could hang out with. My father's brother, Uncle Bill, lived in Los Angeles too. Uncle Bill's daughter, Doretha, worked in the undertaking business, which seemed like a gruesome line of work. But everywhere I looked in my family, I was able to gain insight into the importance of earning a living and eventually owning a business so that I could work for myself.

One day after school, I ran into the house excitedly. "Mama, I know what I wanna do with my future!" I could hardly wait to tell her my news.

"What you want to do, baby?" I could tell my mother was interested.

Kindergarten class photo of me at the age of five. WAYNE PHARR COLLECTION

"I want to establish my own business, like Doretha and Uncle Edwin. I want to start a car washing business."

I was excited and proud about my decision, but my mother's interest evaporated as quickly as it had appeared. "Wayne, no child of mine is going to wash cars! You will do better than that."

"But why not?"

"I'm not working as hard as I do so that my child can go clean somebody else's car! I don't clean other people's houses no more, and my child is not going to clean other people's cars . . . other people's *anything*!"

I was speechless.

Quietly, she mumbled, "I can even accept you running a gambling house. At least you would make a lot of money."

I barely heard that last declaration, but I wasn't surprised about my mother's under-her-breath statement about gambling, and I knew she was somewhat serious. My mother understood and appreciated hustling. The postwar years had brought opportunities for employment to low-skilled workers in Los Angeles, so everybody in my family was doing *something*—either working or hustling.

After a while my mother remarried. I didn't really pay attention to their courtship, but I thought that her new husband, Mr. Oscar Morgan, was a fine gentleman. Mr. Morgan was tall and had kind eyes. There was an important air about him, and he was always well dressed in a suit or shirt and slacks. He was a college-educated man, a member of Kappa Alpha Psi fraternity, and he taught junior high school math. Soon after they married, Mr. Morgan and my mother bought a house on Eighty-Third Street and Avalon and I started going to South Park Elementary School. I had happy times with Mr. Morgan as my stepfather. He was very different from Uncle Edwin, so I learned a new way of viewing life from him. He pointed things out to me and taught me about being a gentleman. We watched TV together, mostly movies and animal and nature shows. We also listened to jazz together, and one day in particular, as we were sitting on the living room couch, I learned from him how nuanced the world was and all the many things I still didn't know about life.

Mr. Morgan turned the television's volume up slightly, calling my attention to it. He moved toward the edge of his seat and was leaning forward confidently, pointing his large but well-groomed hands toward the black-and-white images on the TV screen. He turned to me. "That's Lester Young right there; he's called the Prez, short for the President."

I nodded earnestly.

"Listen to how he plays his saxophone; do you hear the difference from how Dexter Gordon sounds when he plays?"

"No, not really," I admitted.

"Well, then you got to listen more closely," he replied patiently.

I also learned how to maintain my cool from Mr. Morgan, and the importance of thinking before you speak. Mr. Morgan was quite a contrast to Uncle Edwin in this way too. Uncle Edwin was flamboyant and quick-tempered. I never saw Mr. Morgan flare up. But like Uncle Edwin, he was always teaching. He talked about the importance of knowledge, dignity, and serving our community. Standing in front of the mirror putting on his tie in the morning, Mr. Morgan took the opportunity to teach me things. "Knowledge is very important to a man, Wayne. Always remember that."

"Yes, sir," I nodded.

Then I went into my room and looked in the mirror to make sure I looked my best, just like Mr. Morgan. Between Uncle Edwin and Mr. Morgan, I was learning a lot about becoming a man—even though they lived in very different worlds and had very different styles.

Mr. Morgan and my mom were only married three or four years. I had no idea there was trouble in the marriage, even though my mother expressed a little displeasure sometimes. But Mr. Morgan, who was always calm and collected, never let on in his conversations with me. Then one day when I was seven, my grandmother on my mother's side, Lillian Brusard, came to Los Angeles to take me to

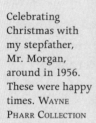

Celebrating Christmas with my stepfather, Mr. Morgan, around in 1956. These were happy times. WAYNE PHARR COLLECTION

Texas to stay with her. I realized later that I went because my mother and Mr. Morgan needed time to sort things out.

My grandmother, called Honey by her friends, was short and matronly but very attractive, with a beautiful brown complexion the shade of toasted honey. She had left Louisiana during the great migration of African Americans from the South to the North, the West, and the urban centers of the United States. But instead of going to California like so many of my relatives, she moved to Port Arthur, Texas. I ended up spending a year with here there, getting to know the ways of the South.

I looked up to Grandmother Honey. I thought she was strong—she wasn't going to let anyone push her around. She was very social, always playing cards with her friends—they played a game called cooncan, similar to gin rummy. She also loved to cook, and I was always the first kid to sit down in front of the red-and-white-checked tablecloth in the kitchen for a plate of her mouthwatering fried chicken, which was served with a tall glass of iced tea.

But my admiration of her strength was ironic, considering that it was my experience with her on our train trip from California that showed me the powerlessness and weak state of black people.

"See this here?" she had asked me, flashing me her pocketknife as we sat on the train pulling out of California.

"Yeah?" I said. My eyes were as wide as saucers. The knife was small and slender, with a smooth yellow handle.

"Anybody mess with us, I'm gon' cut their throat!" she winked at me fiercely.

I thought my grandmother was the toughest woman in the world.

It wasn't my first time on a train, but this particular train trip was one I will never forget. It took us two days to get to Port Arthur. My grandmother and my mother had cooked up a mess of fried chicken and biscuits the night before we left, wrapping them in aluminum foil and putting them in a large brown paper bag. This would have to last us for the duration of our trip, since we never knew which restaurants would serve black people.

As a kid, train rides were something of an adventure. The scenery out the windows was beautiful, and the compartments piqued my interest. I was so excited and full of energy that I spent a large part of my time running up and down the aisle looking through as many windows as I could.

And then the train conductor appeared. Looking up at this white man, I thought he seemed to be a giant, reaching almost to the ceiling of the train, a menacing sight. He wore a black hat and was dressed in all black except for a small gold bar on his uniform. Irritated, his voice boomed. "You can't rip and run all up and down this aisle, *boy*," he said to me with contempt.

I stared up at the Giant, not saying anything, then ran back to my seat and grandmother. The Giant followed, steadying himself with his hand on the seatback.

"Ma'am, you need to keep an eye on this boy; can't have him running all over like this," he said to Honey.

"I will," she said to the Giant, placing her arm around me.

The Giant disappeared down the aisle, and my grandma soon nodded off to sleep. I slipped out of my seat and continued ripping and running, climbing onto seats, and looking through the windows. I headed for the end of the car, racing down to the door and planning to race back to the other end when the Giant made his move from seemingly out of nowhere. He had been hiding just behind the door leading to the next car. He waited until I ran up close and then opened the door fast and hard, *boom!*, busting me over my eye. I howled, equally from the shock as from the pain, and ran to my grandma, my protector, with the conductor quickly following behind.

There was a cut over my eye and it was bleeding. I just knew that my grandma was going to pull that pocketknife she showed me earlier and slay that Giant. My crying woke her up, but before I could even tell my version of what happened, the Giant boomed.

"I told you before to keep an eye on him; I'm not going to tell you again," he growled, looking down his nose at her.

"I'm sorry, sir, really sorry. I'll be sure and keep him close from now on," my grandma apologized. "You sit your little self down right here and don't you move anymore, you hear me?" My grandmother scolded me as she took some tissue and wiped over my eye.

I watched and listened in seven-year-old horror as my grandmother humbled herself before the Giant. I was crushed. The woman I thought was the toughest in the world, the woman who wouldn't hesitate to use her pocketknife to cut someone who messed with us, had bowed down to this mean white man. Yet I was the one who had been busted in the eye and was bleeding! We rode the rest of the way in virtual silence, speaking only when necessary. I guess the truth is my grandmother and I weren't sure what to say to each other. I was glad when we finally reached Port Arthur.

It wasn't long before I began to understand segregation. I noticed that there were black water fountains and black bathrooms and white water fountains and, of course, white bathrooms. The schools were segregated too, as were the parks, beaches, and anywhere else you might want to go. I was confused about the lack of power that black people had, but I didn't ask Honey why. I sensed that she was embarrassed by it, so I played stupid, as if I didn't see it.

One day, I went to the Lincoln Theatre in downtown Port Arthur, the movie theater designated for blacks, with my new friends Donald and Carl. We were watching a cowboy Civil War movie, and at one point I was cheering and hollering for this one group of guys in the film to win.

Suddenly, I felt an elbow in my side. "Nigger, are you crazy?" It was Carl. "Those are the Confederates! They were the ones fighting to keep our people in slavery!"

I didn't know that information at that age, but Carl did. Carl would later educate me on other important issues of race, such as what castration meant and how whites would do it to you if you messed with their women or if you were a bad nigger. "They'll hang you up with some rope 'round a tree, and then they'll take a knife and they'll cut your thing off!" he told me breathlessly, placing his hand over his crotch.

I sucked in my breath, cringing. I recalled the graphic images of Emmett Till.

I witnessed another important event while I was in the South, which demonstrated to me the hatred some whites felt toward black people. Two years after my five-year-old eyes had been opened by the killing of Emmett, I watched white folks on TV engaged in angry mob violence, trying to stop black kids from attending Central High in Little Rock, Arkansas. One of the images was of a little black girl, walking by herself, trying to get through the crowd. They shouted and spit at her, calling her nigger and other horrible names. I could see the white people's hate right there on the TV screen. It was a lot of hate. I began to understand why my grandmother didn't try to stab the white man on our train trip. She probably thought a white mob might get us too, I reasoned.

Food was an interesting issue in the South. We would rarely eat outside the house. It may have been a good way to save money, but it also was a way to avoid facing segregated restaurants. Honey raised chickens and turkeys and made sure that we ate what we raised or grew.

One day, I was playing in the chicken coop and a rooster bit me. "Ouch! *Ouch!* Grandmother Honey!" I wailed.

"What's wrong?" she called out from the house.

"The rooster bit me!"

My grandmother flew into the yard—I don't remember ever seeing her move that fast. She swooped down on that rooster like nobody's business. "Get 'way from him, you old no good . . ." Grandmother Honey grabbed that rooster, held his body with the wings back in one hand, and with the other hand she grabbed his head and twisted it all the way around. "Run, go get me a bag I can put these feathers in," she commanded.

I ran as fast as my little feet could carry me. Over my shoulder, I could hear her still scolding the dead bird. I was horrified.

"We havin' you for dinner tonight!"

In spite of the good food at Honey's, I wished I could buy food at the cafeteria at school in town. I wanted to be like other kids, especially at holiday time. But I was not allowed. "Grandmother," I pleaded, "can I go to the cafeteria to eat Thanksgiving lunch at the school?"

"No," she said firmly. "I don't have enough money to give that school any of my hard-earned savings. What'sa matter with my food, anyway?"

My grandmother made my Thanksgiving lunch, a turkey sandwich and a slice of sweet potato pie, which I took to school. My teacher, who was a kind woman, bought me lunch, which meant I had two lunches that day. The only time I was allowed to eat outside the house was maybe on Fridays, when I could go get a hot dog, and that was it.

In spite of the lessons of racism, my visit to Port Arthur was a great experience. Honey would sometimes take us to Bunkie, Louisiana, to see her other brother, Sugar. He had nine children, and

I thoroughly enjoyed being with them. Another one of my great uncles, Willie, lived in Port Arthur with his wife and seven children. Donald, one of Willie's sons, was my age, so we became running buddies. We would go off into the woods and shipyards. We would also play in Granny's backyard, which was pretty much the Gulf of Mexico. My grandmother made sure I learned to swim because she knew she could not keep an active and rambunctious kid like me from the water. "I know tellin' you not to go to the shipyard won't do any good, so you gon' learn how to swim," she sighed. She took me to the Y for lessons.

In 1957, Hurricane Audrey hit Texas and Louisiana. Port Arthur sits on the east side of Texas, near the Gulf of Mexico, so we were hit pretty hard. Power lines and trees went down, and at least nine people died in our area. I remember because my grandmother made me go to school on the day it hit. There was no discussion about it; a hurricane warning was no excuse for a family that believed strongly in education and upward mobility.

So I got on my bicycle to ride to school. But the winds were so strong, they kept blowing me back; I was fighting to pedal, but I just couldn't pedal against the winds. The wind was pelting me, and it hurt too.

"Come over here!" A voice called out through the shrieks of the wind. It was one of our neighbors, who saw me struggling to ride my bike against the hurricane winds. "Boy, you tryin' to go to school?"

"Yes, ma'am," I said politely, exhausted.

"You done rode past my house three times already. At the rate you going, school will be over by the time you get there! Come on, put your bike in the back of this car. I'll take you."

I did as I was told. Although I didn't know the lady well, I sure was grateful to be in her car! After school, I went back to the lady's house and she drove me home.

After the hurricane passed and the water receded, a lot of my older cousins got jobs from white folks to kill snakes. The hurricane brought many of the water snakes to grasses and drove others from their hiding spots in the woods and weeds. I asked Honey if I could get a job killing snakes too, but she told me I was too young. My cousins were happy to have a chance to earn extra money. I remember thinking that black folks must be OK to white people if they needed us. It didn't occur to me until later that the white folks would rather have blacks kill the snakes because it was dangerous.

3

FIGHTING INTEGRATION

We moved into our new home in the dark of night. I was back in California, and my mother wanted to minimize our presence to avoid the possibility of conflict or even violence; but instead of outright physical brutality, For Sale signs started popping up along our street after neighbors noticed we were there.

My mother had purchased a five-unit building on the Westside. It was on 107th and Normandie, a street that had no black people on it until we arrived. On our lot, there was a three-bedroom front house, two single apartments, and two one-bedroom back houses. We lived in the three-bedroom house in the front. It was a nice investment for a single woman who, two years earlier, had served white folks as a domestic and now worked at the post office. Our new home was painted an understated beige, which helped us maintain our low profile. But still, my mom was finally living her dream; she had renters.

By 1962, segregation in Los Angeles had loosened. The restrictive covenants that required blacks to live only in the South Central

29

portion of the city had been declared illegal. After violent outbreaks resulting from the attempts of black families to move into neighborhoods once considered off-limits, many whites began to accept the reality of desegregation.

After returning from the South, I had reenrolled at South Park Elementary School in the fifth grade. It was off of Avalon and Manchester, about a twenty-block walk from my home. Small, Spanish-style stucco homes lined the streets of my neighborhood, along with every kind of fruit tree one could imagine—orange, peach, plum, apricot, and even kumquat. There was so much fruit, people couldn't even pick all of it. Every summer my friends and I raided the fruit trees and sometimes ate until we got sick. I was a likeable kid, so I had easily reconnected with relatives and friends. But now, we were moving on up to a better neighborhood.

Although I was unsure about this new neighborhood, I liked my new room. It was painted a pale shade of blue, and I had bunk beds for sleepovers. I also had a bookcase, which I treasured because it held my favorite books. My mother placed a lot of emphasis on reading, and so I had a pretty good library. My books transported me to a world beyond the four walls of my bedroom. I visited Mexico in *Captain Cortes Conquers Mexico*; I peeked into the mind of Hitler in *Mein Kampf*; I encountered sheer genius in Italy when I read about Leonardo da Vinci; and I witnessed the Civil War in the American Heritage series on the subject. Through my readings, I learned about the struggles of people all around the world.

Although I was a "city boy," I had become schooled on "gun culture" in the South. I came to know the importance of guns, and in fact, the idea of protection was implanted in me long before I joined the Black Panther Party. My uncles and cousins hunted animals for food. They would go deer hunting and bring the animals back to the meat market to skin, clean, and cut up. They would catch smaller animals like possum or rabbits and prepare them for our meals at home. That's how we ate.

In the South, it was no big thing to give young boys guns as gifts; in Los Angeles, the men in my family continued that tradition. When I was twelve, Bill Pharr, my father's uncle, gave me a .25 automatic.

Uncle Bill had diabetes and was very ill. One day he called me over to his house. "Look in that closet over there," he pointed with his shaky hand. "Get that shoe box at the bottom and bring it to me."

My curiosity was spilling over and trying to come out of my mouth. "Yes, sir." I bit my tongue, trying to hide my eagerness.

He straightened his droopy shoulders and took a long breath. "Take this here." He handed me the gun while looking me square in the eyes. "This ain't no toy, you know that. You keep this, and don't you let nobody mess with you," he said.

"Sure, Uncle Bill," I replied in the most somber tone I could muster. But inside I was ecstatic. I couldn't wait to go admire my new gun.

Uncle Bill was also in the beginning stages of Alzheimer's, and this was his parting gift to me. During the time he had left, I would go and see him, and he would show me how to work the gun and take care of it.

I was fascinated with my new gift, and I saw it as an instrument of survival and self-defense. I would spend hours studying it, taking it apart and putting it back together again. I learned every detail about it, every function. I even managed to get off a few shots in the backyard—while my mother was at work, of course! Eventually, though, my mom found the gun and took it away from me. It had been in the top dresser drawer in my bedroom.

Little did I know that the time I spent learning about my .25 automatic would be extremely useful a few years later, when I decided that I needed another gun. Without having access to a real one, I built my own. Back then, we called them zip guns. Basically, zip guns may or may not look like real guns, but they fire real bullets or projectiles. Some of my partners from junior high school—Little John, Leroy Williams, and others—and I would use iron pipe to make the gun barrel and Mattel cap guns because they had an actual trigger, unlike toy guns, which weren't meant to fire. I would put a real bullet in the chamber or down the barrel; the toy gun already had the trigger, so I would stretch a rubber band from the front point of the barrel all the way to the back end of the barrel, just above the handle. That would be the hammer, or help the hammer hit the bullet or projectile that would then shoot out of the barrel. Sometimes the zip gun actually fired; sometimes it didn't. Even when it didn't fire, the zip gun could still serve its purpose. I could just flash it and guys would leave me alone because I had a zip gun and they didn't.

I started junior high school at Edison, which was in the same neighborhood as South Park. Edison was down on Sixty-Fifth and Hooper, right in the center of what we called Slauson Village. But after we moved to the Westside, I had to change schools. My new school was called Henry Clay, and located on 122nd Street and Western Avenue, miles away from my old neighborhood and school. Moving to the Westside was costly for me. Edison was predominately black at that time, but Henry Clay was primarily white. Clay had modern facilities and equipment, and the campus was really nice and clean. Edison didn't have the same material wealth as Clay, but Edison is where my learning took place. I learned how to type, read, and do math; and I learned about black people.

As national leaders and the adults in my family touted the benefits of integration, "moving on up" only made my daily life difficult. While I was trailblazing for my generation into the outward expression of upper mobility, I was in conflict with white kids almost every day.

On my first day at Henry Clay, this white boy came up to me and stared. "Ain't your mama on the pancake box?" he sneered.

"What?" I asked, stunned.

"You heard me," he snickered.

We were standing at the top of some stairs when he said it. Without even thinking about it, I "helped" him lose his balance—I shoved him and he took a really bad fall. The kids' grapevine carried the news all over the school. Everybody heard what had happened and knew there would be a showdown to exact revenge. I was scared, but I knew I had to stand my ground. I would not betray my uncle Edwin's instruction to not "let anybody mess with me and never back down."

It was around lunchtime when the kid's big brother and cousin showed up to retaliate. But they were in over their heads and didn't even know it. I knew a trick or two from having lived in South Central that those white boys hadn't seen yet. So, when that little white boy's brother and cousin came to fight me for shoving him down the stairs, I was prepared. I was not a bully, but I was a fighter and could handle myself if trouble came my way. I also had heart, which meant I could stand up to a challenge. Like the time when Uncle Edwin had a stroke. My mother and Nanny sent me to Oakland to bring him down to Los Angeles so they could take care of him. That is how I learned how to drive—bringing Uncle Edwin down Interstate 5 by myself from Oakland, over the Grapevine in his green 1956 Buick.

The time I spent in the South, coupled with the images of Emmett Till's mutilated corpse, instilled in me a peculiar fear. The idea that a black man could have his fingers cut off, get castrated, or be burned at the stake haunted me. I could really feel it—and I knew we wouldn't get any mercy. That feeling stayed with me, so being confronted by white boys at school meant that I had to fight for my life. I needed to make these white boys understand that I was not to be messed with, so I had to establish my reputation. But because I was not a physically imposing guy, I had to be crafty and cunning.

By lunchtime, the whole school was eager to see the new nigger get beat down. I positioned myself on an embankment on the field where the boy's brother and cousin would have to run up to get me. I had folded my trench coat over my arm so I could toss it over the head of the first one who tried to run up on me. The guy's brother was red-faced and foaming at the mouth.

I was just about to handle my business when a physical education coach came out and surveyed the scene. "What's going on here?" he demanded.

The kids started running in every direction possible. The coach broke us up before we got started and took me in his office located inside the gym. As I sat in the chair directly across from him, my adrenaline was still pumping and my heart was still racing. The coach pushed back in the swivel chair and looked me square in the eye. I didn't know what was coming.

"Why does a chicken cross the road?" the coach asked.

"Huh?" I answered, a confused look washing over my face.

"Why does a chicken cross the road?" he repeated.

"I don't know," I told him.

"To prove to a possum it can be done!" he said.

He laughed loudly at his own joke and then told me two or three others, laughing at every one. He finished by asking me to please not fuck up any of his students.

"What's your name, kid?" he asked.

"Wayne," I replied.

"Well all right then, Wayne," he said, "Starting today, you are in charge of all those basketballs over there." The coach then put me in charge of the gym and the equipment room. The heat was off me for a while after that.

Still, I had to face the wrath of the Spook Hunters, a racist white gang that made their hatred for black people a badge of honor. Fred Yankey, a blond-haired, freckled-face, racist eighth grader, was the leader of the group. One of our biggest fights occurred after President John Kennedy was killed. The Spook Hunters saw Kennedy as friendly toward black people. During lunchtime one day shortly after Kennedy's death, Yankey walked up to me and a few other black boys who attended the school, taunting us. "The nigger-lover is dead!" he jeered.

I didn't have to say a word. I knew the fight was on. My boys and I knew we would throw down with Yankey and his gang after school.

The bell rang and a large group of students hit the yard. My homeboy Willie Turner threw the first blow: he walked up to Fred, coldcocked him, and he dropped like a sack of wheat. Then about ten of us, five on each side—for and against Kennedy—started throwing punches. The teachers came out and broke it up by separating people and pulling us apart. By the time it was over, a few white boys were bloodied up real good, and one had gotten knocked out during the rumble. Eventually, we all went home. No one was suspended or even punished for the fight; the teachers wrote it off as children being upset about the assassination of the president. The next day at school, things were really quiet.

As integration became more common, the balance of power began to shift at school. I had more help fighting the racist white kids because more black families were enrolling their children at Henry Clay. We also got a few black kids who had been expelled from other schools. I hung with a crew of about five or six people, and we ran the yard. My partners included guys like the Stinson brothers, whose fighting skills were legendary, and the Blackshear brothers, who were athletes and could hold their own in a street fight. Walter Stinson, who had been expelled from another school, was my best friend. People knew not to tease him about his pigeon toes; he was still a couple inches taller than most people and not to be played with. With Walter at my side, I didn't have to worry about backup.

We hung tough and had fun. Talking trash and playing the dozens was part of our bond. I loved playing the dozens. "You so po', I opened up the bread box at your mama's house and the roaches were having a prayer meeting," I would say with a laugh.

Sometimes we rhymed as we were walking down the street. "I was walking through the jungle with a stick in my hand, the baddest little nigga in the jungle land. I looked up in a tree and what did I see? A white muthafucka trying to piss on me. I picked up a rock and hit him in the cock and the stupid motherfucker ran twenty-four blocks!"

Sometimes playing the dozens with other crews would lead to fights. But I was always watchful and ready if it came down to that.

Devil's Dip was one of the spots where we would hang out. This huge open field was located at Imperial Highway and Western Avenue, near our school, where both motorcycle and bicycle riders would tear through the trails. The Dip was also a spot where we would fight away from school property. Sometimes people traveling on Western Avenue would stop and watch us fight. Soon, we stopped having problems with most of the white kids. Some even became friendly and cool.

Though our relationships with the white kids began to cool out, my interaction with some of the white teachers unfortunately did not get better. Some of them openly showed their resentment of integration. Other teachers were not philosophically opposed to integration but tried to keep the peace between the races, often at my expense.

Academically, my grades began to fall at Clay. I was getting Fs on everything although I didn't deserve them. I needed to show my parents that I was being discriminated against, so one day I asked my stepfather, Mr. Morgan, to do my homework with me. The next day, sure enough, the homework I turned in received an F. Even my stepfather, Mr. Morgan, a math teacher, got an F!

And then there was the time I was humiliated in English class. My teacher had given us a writing assignment: a short story on any subject we chose. I wrote a story called "The Attack of the Yetis." It was about an expedition to South America I had read about, where I learned of this band of Yetis. I spent a lot of time researching and putting together my report, and I was proud of my work. Mr. Taylor agreed, giving me an A on it. After receiving our graded papers, he asked us to read our papers in class. Students all around me were called, and I sat there patiently waiting my turn. The clock kept ticking, and as the end of the class period became near, I knew there would be no turn for me.

The bell rang and the class left. It was just Mr. Taylor and me. "Wayne, go ahead and read your paper out loud."

I didn't know what to do; I was embarrassed. I was also very hurt. I had been ready to read my A paper in front of my classmates, but the opportunity had been taken away from me. I read my paper self-consciously, then turned and walked out of the classroom, my ego stung.

Over time, conflicts with other students and teachers began to take their toll on me. After school one day, I went to my mom and told her we needed to talk. She was in the kitchen preparing dinner. "Mom," I said imploringly, "I need to go back to Edison."

"What's your reasoning?" she replied quizzically as she pulled a stack of dinner dishes from the cupboard. I took the dishes from her and helped her set the table as I chose my words. "These white people are so unfair. You've seen how hard I work and the grades that I get, and you saw how even the homework that Mr. Morgan did with me got an F."

She turned around from the counter and studied me, considering what I'd said.

I put the rest of the dishes down and looked at her squarely. "They blame all of the fighting on me, even though everybody knows about the Spook Hunters."

She sighed, a long, sad sigh. "You'll go back to Edison in the fall."

4

LEGITIMATE GRIEVANCES

Suitcases in hand, I knocked on Mr. Morgan's door. He opened it and shook my hand. "Welcome, son. Come on in and let me show you around."

"Thank you, sir," I said, trying not to show my excitement. My mom was all right, but she couldn't understand what it was like to become a man.

"I heard you had some trouble," he finished as he led me down the hallway to my new room.

"Yeah, but I handled it," I said with pride. I wanted Mr. Morgan to know that I had held my own.

He ignored my bravado. "Well, you won't have to worry about that at Edison."

It was one week before school was to start and my mom had agreed to let me stay with Mr. Morgan in order to be closer to Edison. And he wasn't just closer, he also taught there. Though he and my mother had separated, they had made the decision to raise me together, which I thought was a great move.

I was glad to be going back to my predominately black school. I felt comfortable and more relaxed now that I wouldn't have to feel like a target of white racism all the time. If I got into trouble, at least I could explain how and why.

That Saturday I went to the park to see some friends. I made sure I was dressed well so that my boys from the neighborhood would know I hadn't changed. Nana had always told me to "look the best you can look," so over the years I had honed my sense of fashion. I guess my style was a combination of Mr. Morgan and Uncle Edwin. Sometimes I wore suits, and other times I would sport my black leather jacket.

Harold Taylor was at the park, and he walked up to me with a grin. "Woo-ooo, check this brother out!"

Then Tyrone saw us both. He walked over. "Wayne, what are you doing with a suit on in Watts?"

I laughed. "Do you know how tough you have to be to wear a suit every day in Watts?"

We laughed again and then walked over to the corner store, which gave me an opportunity to show my homeboys the benefits of being well dressed. We checked out the girls along the way, and they checked us out too. I was back in my old neighborhood. I was feeling good and ready for anything that came my way.

On the first day of school, I met a guy named Leroy and we got to be tight. He came up to me, smiling. "Check me out!" he said. Leroy had been to New York for the summer and his hair was rounded and fluffed out. He patted his head with both hands. "It's called a natural." Up to this point, brothers were wearing conks, processes, fronts, or pompadours, with plenty of grease and hair pomade—Murray's or Royal Crown. Leroy explained to me, "All the brothers on the East Coast are wearin' it."

I thought the natural was cool. I was wearing my hair front and pompadour style. Soon though, I started growing it out into a natural too because it showed race pride and it was natural to black people.

Leroy was also into boxing, one of my favorite sports because it kept me in shape and prepared in case I needed to win a fight. I thought Leroy was a cool cat, so we began to hang out on the weekends, going to the skating rink and practicing boxing.

We also spent a lot of time talking about politics. It was 1964 and the Civil Rights Act had just passed, which black folks were real glad about. But Leroy was more into Malcolm X. I was already familiar with Malcolm since the local Nation of Islam would occasionally come on the radio, but Leroy had actually seen Malcolm speak live when he was in New York. He even attended some of the classes the Nation of Islam taught at their mosque in New York and in Los Angeles after he returned.

Leroy and I would listen to some of Malcolm's recordings. "Do you want to integrate with a cracker?" Malcolm X asked.

When I heard that I thought, *Right on!*

"With an old white cracker so you and this cracker can sit on a toilet together? This is what you want to integrate for, right? For you and this cracker to sit on the same toilet? This old white cracker?" Malcolm asked.

My experiences integrating at Henry Clay came rushing back.

I began to make my own analysis of the civil rights movement, Martin Luther King Jr., and Malcolm X. I saw King as part of the "old guard," a southern black preacher who advocated integration and nonviolence. I thought King had a good message and was the type of leader the older generation could relate to. But Malcolm X was from Detroit, and he spoke more to the urban, young people. He talked about nationhood and Black Nationalism. He said that black people should control the businesses, jobs, schools, and police in our neighborhoods. As far as I could see, Malcolm X was right, because integration wasn't really working for us anyway. I mean, look what I had just been through in middle school.

One of the most memorable conversations I had with Leroy occurred when we were walking one day, talking about self-defense. "Wayne, I just can't understand King's position that black people should lie down and let themselves be brutalized to make America better," he argued.

"I think King is really about protecting us," I agreed, "but I believe that all people should have the right to defend themselves. If my uncle Edwin and uncle Bill Pharr saw me walking away from a white boy who tried to jump me, they would both kick my ass."

Later that night, I lay in bed thinking about that conversation. I decided I agreed with Malcolm X when he said we should not be nonviolent with people who were violent with us. Under my breath I said amen.

I was at home alone, watching TV, when I heard that Malcolm X had been assassinated. It was February 21, 1965. I was devastated that we had lost such a strong leader. But I was even more pissed off that black people had shot him—seven bullets at point-blank range—when he was speaking and trying to maintain peace. My first thought was that whoever did it was stupid as hell and really didn't give a damn about our people. This only made me more determined to promote Malcolm X's ideas and teachings. And his influence in my life would never die.

That same year I graduated from Edison. In June, I started summer school at Washington High, where I became friends with Mark and Tony, whom I met in auto-shop class. Both guys were in the eleventh grade, so they were older than I was. I was impressed with them. Not only did they have cars, but they were into low-riding. Soon, we were hanging out regularly. But I was still reading Malcolm X, so my race consciousness was being elevated at a rapid pace.

Interestingly enough, it was my low-riding friends who informed me that Watts was on fire. It was August 11, the first day of the rebellion, when Mark excitedly ran into the class. "The shit's on!"

I asked, "What's on?"

"Didn't you hear? They fightin' the police in Watts!"

"No shit?"

Mark went over to the window, pointing. "Look east," he said.

We got up and went to the window and saw black smoke rising into the sky, coming out of Watts. As we were standing at the window, an announcement came on the intercom system that school would be ending early that day.

"Man! Let's go check it out!" Tony said. So we jumped into Mark's car and drove three miles, going down side streets into Watts, avoiding police along the way.

The word out on the streets was that in the afternoon a twenty-one-year-old black male named Marquette Frye had been pulled over by a white California Highway Patrolman. The cop radioed for Frye's car to be impounded, claiming that Frye had been drinking. Frye, who lived not far from where he was stopped, was riding with his brother Ronald, who went home to get their mother. When she came back, the story goes, she was angry that Marquette had been placed under arrest and went off. That caused the cops to manhandle her; seeing their mom being treated like that, Marquette and Ronald went off too. At this point, Marquette was handcuffed, so the cops claimed he was resisting arrest. It was a mess. The folks in the neighborhood saw this whole family getting jacked by the police and decided that they had had enough. They were yelling at the cops; then somebody—or some bodies—started throwing bottles and rocks, attacking the police and trying to drive them out. People had gotten fed up with police harassment, which is why many of us adopted an outlaw mentality—because the law was not intended to work for us. The crowd got bigger, more police came, more stuff was thrown.

Once we got to Avalon and Imperial, streets on the outskirts of the uprising, it was complete madness. We couldn't believe our eyes. *"Man, look!"* I said. A guy was running down Central Avenue carrying a TV set.

"Hey, look at that guy throwing a firebomb at the cops!" yelled Tony in disbelief.

"Where'd all the other cops go?" Mark asked.

"Man, I bet they ain't going over there," I hollered. "Right on! *Right on!*"

The police had pulled back and the crowd was enraged, going crazy, breaking windows, throwing bricks, and starting fires. It was as if all the anger and the pent-up frustrations of African Americans from four hundred years of oppression and the civil rights struggle all came to a head in one big explosion of violence and fury. It seemed like the whole community was in support of the riots. We went farther into Watts, and I realized that the people were in control of the streets.

We stayed out there for about an hour. Mark and Tony had to leave, so they dropped me off near my house; I'd moved back with my mom for high school. She was living in a new home that she had purchased on Eighty-Seventh and Broadway, a two-bedroom with a wooden frame. She was renting our old house on Normandie. There was a little shopping center near our new home with a cleaners, a liquor store, and a Thrifty's that was vandalized during the riots. The glass windows were busted out of the storefronts and there was glass everywhere.

As far as I could see, the police protected the power structure. I had no illusions about their role in society. Even though the national headlines were filled with the sadistic actions of policemen in the South like Bull Connor of Alabama, Los Angeles police chief Bill Parker was no better. Parker believed that his job was to keep black people in their places. He had specifically recruited white racist bullies from the South to serve on his police force. One of the popular sayings in the streets was that "the LAPD killed a nigga every day," and we waited to hear about who it would be that day.

As for me, I didn't have any real contact with the police. I avoided situations that might lead to any police confrontations. Once I got caught by a teacher smoking cigarettes at school and the police were notified. I didn't get arrested; they just tried to scare me. However, I knew several people who had suffered under the blunt ends of their racist batons. My cousin Al Prescott was a case in point. Al was a Vietnam War vet who was wounded during the war. He lost an eye and had to have an iron plate put in his head because of his injuries. Despite his disabilities, he secured a job at Lockheed after he was discharged. One day I ran into Al at my great aunt's house. He was swollen, beat up, puffed up, and bruised up. I didn't even recognize him at first. According to Al, the police had pulled him over the night before. They yanked him out of his car for no reason, jumped him, and beat him almost to death. He begged them not to hit him in the one good eye he had left. What kind of assholes would beat a disabled man?

The violence in Watts continued for days. My mother could not get off of work during the riots, and since she didn't want me staying at home alone, she sent me to my aunt's house, which was farther west, around Manchester and Normandie. There were still some whites living in that particular neighborhood, and they were traveling in packs. As I was walking down the street to my aunt's house, a carload of white boys pulled up. "There goes one of them right there!" I heard, as the car screeched toward the curb. Before they had a chance to come after me, I pulled out my zip gun. It had a .22 caliber bullet in it, and though I didn't know if it would even fire, I pulled it out anyway. I was lucky I had it with me. When the white boys saw my gun they jumped back in their car and drove away.

For the most part, my family stayed out of the uprising. They weren't out in the streets protesting, nor did they attend any of the community meetings. They were happy to have the little jobs, businesses, and homes that they had, so they kept out of the fray. But they understood that as black people we were still oppressed. They remembered having to work under white folks in the South, so it wasn't hard for them to understand anger at the oppressor. It was the topic of the hour in my family.

"Nanny," I asked, "what do you think?"

Instead of giving me her opinion, she told me a story. When she was a maid, she worked for this one white man who owned a farm. "Lawd, he sure did treat us black folks bad," she told me. "But the good Lord was watchin' out for us. One day he took his family up in the airplane, and the whole thing came crashing down. We never saw any of them again."

5

BLACK
IS BEAUTIFUL

After the city quieted down, Tony and I decided to survey the scene. It was surreal. There was blood splattered in the streets, shattered glass, broken furniture, and trash everywhere. Some people were milling around seemingly in a daze; others were sitting out on their front porches.

"Damn!" Tony said, with a look of disbelief on his face. "Is this for real?"

I just looked at him and shook my head. I was so overwhelmed. "Will Watts ever be the same?" I asked.

The collective exhaustion was so heavy it hung in the air. And then there was the charred debris from the fires. We could smell the smoke and destruction. Thirty-four people had lost their lives during the six days of anger and protest—how many of them to police brutality we would never really know.

By the end of the uprising more than fourteen thousand guardsmen, sheriffs, and police had descended on Watts. It was obvious the government, from the local to the federal levels, felt a pressing need to respond. The response locally was to bring in more law enforcement; nationally, the response was to conduct a study on the causes of the uprising. In the end, the studies stated that people were angry about police brutality and the lack of jobs. Unbelievable! They spent all that money to tell us what we already knew.

Another government solution was to establish programs designed to address the economic and social problems in South Central Los Angeles. The Teen Post was one such program. It was set up to keep the angry, urban youth off the streets. One of my aunts, Caffie Greene, a longtime activist, was a director. She called my house to tell me about the program. "Wayne," she began, "I want you to come down and see me in my office."

"What's up, Auntie?" I asked.

"There is a new program called the Teen Post that I am running. It's set up to give teenagers work experience, and I think it would be great for you."

"What about school?" I asked.

"It's an after-school program," she replied. "It won't pay much, but it will put some money in your pocket."

That got me interested. "OK," I agreed. "I'll come by on Monday."

The Teen Post locations were set up in various neighborhoods, and most of us did menial work like cleaning lots. I worked out of the Eighty-Fourth and Broadway office. Even though I made minimum wage, I was working. The first paycheck I ever got was from my job at the Teen Post.

Each Teen Post became a hangout spot, but a lot of consciousness-raising occurred there too. The most passionate political conversations I'd ever had in my young life took place at the Teen Post—conversations about why blacks suffered as we did and why we seemed to have so little compared to whites.

One day, Tyrone Hutchinson and Paul Redd were standing in a corner, going back and forth in a heated discussion about Bill Cosby's role in *I Spy*. "It's about time we got a black man starring on an evening show," Paul said.

"But Bill Cosby is not playing the lead. You know they ain't gonna let a black man be the star of the show," Tyrone argued back.

I was sweeping when I overheard the conversation. I walked over and interjected, "Yeah, Bill Cosby is still not in charge. He is just like Tonto was to the Lone Ranger. But still, it is cool to see a black man on TV."

"Yeah, man, at least he's not playing a clown," said Paul.

Conversations like that could go on for hours until we had to get back to work.

Teen Post offered some benefits to our community, but the program was not without its issues. One of the problems with government programs like Teen Post was that they were based on an assumption that all black youth were involved in criminal activity or gang violence, not that we needed more industry and business opportunities. That couldn't have been further from the truth.

One year after the rebellion, the first Watts Summer Festival showcased the emergence of black pride. It was a beautiful experience. The weeklong celebration was a great coming together of people. All of Watts had come alive. It was rather amazing to see the community spring back with such resiliency when just a year ago it had looked like a war zone. The center of the festival was at Will Rogers Park, which was abuzz with music, talent shows, parades, giveaways, and lots of vendors selling food, T-shirts, and other items expressing black pride. We partied in the streets to James Brown and recited the lyrics to songs like "Papa's Got a Brand New Bag," as it blasted through the speakers:

> He's doing the jerk, he's doing the fly
> Don't play him cheap 'cause you know he ain't shy
> He's doing the monkey, the mashed potatoes,
> Jump back Jack, see you later alligator.

The mantra of the day was "black is beautiful!" Just saying those words was empowering. The brothers and sisters were young and strong, wearing their hair natural. It was the time of creative expression. We wore bell-bottoms and platform shoes. The girls wore hot pants and halter tops. We smiled and greeted one another with "Brother!" "Sister!" "Right on!" and "Black power!" It was the beginning of the Watts Writers Workshop and the Watts Happening Coffee House. We had entered the age of the Black Arts movement on the West Coast.

At the same time, gangs did exist. However, they weren't like the gangs of today: the drug phenomenon hadn't come into play yet, nor were the gangs as money-driven and intense. Most of them had originally started off as self-defense groups to fight off white gangs like the Spook Hunters. Others began as social clubs and then became territorial. Ironically, after the Watts Rebellion, gang activity was on the decline.

Some of the gangs back then were the Business Men, Gladiators, Rebel Rousers, Swamp Boys, Orientals, Huns, and of course the Slausons, which was the largest gang. The Slausons' territory covered a five-mile radius, from Manchester Boulevard north to Slauson Avenue and from Figueroa Avenue to Compton Boulevard east. They had many subsets or smaller groups with names like the Flips, Saints, Warlords, Baby Slausons, and Renegade Slausons. My set was Broadway, but we were all Slausons. At first, to officially join the gang, a person had to be jumped, which meant the initiates had to go through the gauntlet and fight their way through it. But things changed, and people started to become identified with the gang in their neighborhood. I wasn't jumped into the Slausons, but I lived in the neighborhood, so I eventually took on the persona of a Slauson and identified with the organization.

For the most part, harmful gang activity involved fighting, with rank attached to skill. Being able to box and to fight with your hands was considered an asset. If a brother could handle himself in a fight, he could go just about anywhere in the city and be respected. I had a reputation as a good fighter because one of my hobbies was boxing. But I also knew how to run if necessary.

I had a strategy for handling a bunch of guys who wanted to jump me. "Look up," I would say. They would look up and then I would run.

"You got to be fast; you can't be no dummy," I told Tyrone one day. "If a gang is chasing you, stop running, turn around, and toss up the guy closest to you and then run some more."

Tyrone chuckled, but he was also taking note.

It was rare for gang members to use guns in this era. Treetop, an original Slauson, was the first person I knew who got shot and killed, in the early 1960s. We called him Treetop because he was so tall and thin. He was about ten years older than me. Treetop's murder was the talk of the neighborhood for years to come. Little did we know that Treetop's murder would foreshadow the volatility of gang warfare.

Although my mom and I moved a lot, I remained a Broadway Slauson. My closest homeboys in the set were Tyrone and his brother, Dwight. Tyrone was tall, chiseled, and a good street fighter. Dwight was the older of the two but slightly smaller and more intelligent than both of us. Their mother, Mrs. Hutchinson, was a very attractive brown-skinned, curvy woman who looked like she had been a party girl in her younger days. She was also down-to-earth and let us hang out at her house. She made sure we always had food to eat and were comfortable when we were there. "Boys, I am getting ready to go out. Don't bring any girls in here and don't tear up my house," she would jokingly say. Even though she was smiling, we also knew she was serious about her instructions.

One day, Tyrone met this cat at the park and invited him to hang out with us at the house. But when he got there, he tried to bully Tyrone *in his own crib*.

We were shooting craps with him and he started losing. All of a sudden he became belligerent. "You niggas are cheating!" he screamed. "I want my money back!" He had a wild look in his eyes and started grabbing for Tyrone.

I jumped in between them and then Tyrone grabbed a lamp and hit him over the head with it. He staggered and grabbed his head. Together we tried to shove him out of the door, but one of his legs got caught in the doorjamb as I pushed the door against him. "Let go of my leg!" he screamed. But I held the door steady. Meanwhile,

Tyrone ran into the kitchen and grabbed a turkey prong out of one of the drawers. Next thing I knew, Tyrone was poking him in the leg with it. The guy started screaming so loudly that we finally opened the door. Immediately, he scrambled and ran down the street.

For weeks, Tyrone and I were constantly looking over our shoulders, expecting that guy to appear out of nowhere. Amazingly, we never saw any sign of him again.

A few hours later, Mrs. Hutchinson came home. We told her what happened, expecting the worst, but she surprised us both. After looking back and forth at us in a serious manner, she finally said that she wasn't worried about the lamp but was just glad we got him out of the house. This is why we all liked Mrs. Hutchinson so much.

The baddest guy in the Broadway Slauson set after Treetop was Ealy Bias, an OG (original gangster) Slauson. I went to school with his brother Alex, and we became close friends. He was staying with my mom and me, because his mother had kicked him out of the house. Alex lived in Ealy's shadow. He was dark-skinned, had a gap between his two front teeth, and stuttered. Instead of pursuing the gangs, Alex was preparing himself for a different kind of future. He was a gymnast, a good student, and a hard worker. His work ethic got him promoted to checker at ABC Market on Manchester and San Pedro, and so he helped me get his old job as a box boy.

Alex was a positive influence on my life in so many ways. I stopped hanging out as much as before and decided that I wanted to become involved in sports.

"What are you doing with that shit?" Alex said to me one day, as I was lighting a joint.

"Cool out, man," I replied. But that got me to thinking.

"You should come to work out with me," Alex suggested.

"But I am not really sure I like gymnastics," I replied. "I really want to sign up for football or basketball."

"Well, you need to stop smoking either way, and besides, it's too late for basketball or football."

Eventually, I quit my brief experimentation with cigarettes and weed so I could focus on getting my body ready. I lightened up on smoking and drinking and signed up for gymnastics. I hadn't been a heavy drinker or smoker anyway, so it was easy to let go of those vices. Off and on, I would steal a drink around the house or have someone buy me a Country Club or Colt 45 beer. But I didn't like the feeling of being out of control, and I certainly did not want to be high in the streets.

I was good at gymnastics and eventually became the number-two guy on the parallel bars at Washington High. Alex had been on the gymnastics team in high school, so he was able to give me some pointers on the sport. He performed on the rings and was an expert at the iron cross. Alex and I hung pretty tight. We were always working out, working, or sometimes going out to parties and school dances. Alex stayed with my mom and me for about a year and a half, until he graduated from high school and went off to college.

As a result of holding down the job at ABC Market, I earned and saved enough money to buy my first car, a 1958 Chevrolet Impala. Overnight, I became a low-rider. My righteous homeboy Louis Wise, who I had met in church, was low-riding a 1963 Catalina at the same time. Louis's father was an assistant reverend at the Freewill Baptist Church, which was in the neighborhood and where I would sometimes go with my mother.

One day I ran into Louis on the way out of Fellowship Hall. "Man, I just got a new ride," I said to him. "You should come by and check it out."

Louis looked excited. "Sure, and I'll bring tools."

When I purchased my car it was black, but I had it painted sky blue. I was running six-and-a-half-inch rims, which was something else back then! We put bucket seats in the front, and in the back we had tuck-and-roll rear seats. I had an AM/FM radio with a cassette tape player and a "doughnut" steering wheel. The windows were tinted black, and the springs made the car lift in the front and drop in the back. This car had a great effect on my life. It was more than something cosmetic or just a toy. Even though it was what young folks today called tricked out, that car got me out of the neighborhood and gang mentality. It was my escape.

I really understood the need for having my own transportation one night as I was leaving my grandmother's house. I saw several brothers from Broadway—Tyrone Hutchinson, Snake, and Arthur Huey—riding in three or four cars. "Hey Wayne, we going up to the park," Tyrone called out. "And then, we gon' fight these Manchester fools, the Park Boys. Get in the car. Come on!"

"Sure. I'll follow you right over there," I said. They drove off, and I went the other way.

The wheels not only got me out of the neighborhood but also gave me access to others. My car gave me another type of access too—as my friend Louis would say—to girls and more parties. Instead of hanging in the neighborhood and getting into fights, we could now travel to catch some girls. We partied at the Kappa House, the Omega House, and other places all over the city. We even traveled to other cities, like Long Beach. We were on a roll.

Eventually, I quit my job at ABC Market. My aunt helped me get a job at Trans World Airlines (TWA) in fleet services, cleaning planes. The planes would land at the Los Angeles airport, refuel, and then head on to their next destination. Our job was to run in and clean them quickly so they could be on their way. I was feeling quite high by then—I had a job, money in my pocket, and a low-riding car. I couldn't wait until the upcoming Watts Summer Festival so that I should show off my car. But by the time the summer festival rolled around, I had contracted ptomaine poisoning from eating those dinners on the plane, so I couldn't go.

While I was sick in bed, Louis came by my house one day during the festival. "The police just shot up Will Rogers Park." Louis was talking so fast, I could hardly understand him.

I shook my head. "Why, what happened?"

"The police rolled up like the military, shot a few people, and then closed down the festival."

I was stunned. "But why?"

"Man, they're retaliating against us," he said. "It's because of the Watts Riots and black pride."

I recognized the names of the people injured that day, but I didn't know any of them personally. Still, I was infuriated by the police action. I realized that it could have been me at the park that day. The shootings conjured up flashbacks of the murder of Leonard Deadwyler, a twenty-five-year-old who had been shot and killed by the police while taking his pregnant wife to the hospital two years earlier. Images of his bloodied body slumped over his wife, while his little girl looked on from the backseat, pissed me off. It was the case that made Johnnie Cochran famous when he sued the city for wrongful death.

I sat up in my bed, still feeling queasy, and gave Louis a hard look. "I think it's time we talk about serious protection."

"What do you have in mind?" Louis asked.

"These pigs are trying to exterminate us. We have to arm ourselves."

"I'm down with that," he nodded.

"I can talk to Joe and Rudy—my barbers," I said. "I know they can tell us where to go."

After talking things over with some people at the barbershop, I began my senior year at Washington High armed and, if necessary, ready. I had a .45, a .38, and a shotgun too. I paid $100 a pop for each one.

Our house had a large backyard and a basement; it was the perfect space to work on survival skills. I had my guns hidden where I knew my mom wouldn't find them. I invited my homeboys over to lift weights in the backyard. We'd put on our boxing gloves to perfect our fighting skills.

At school, I excelled in my business and political education classes. Those classes became the foundation for my entrepreneurial endeavors and my political activities later in life. Mr. Whyte, my political education teacher, issued a challenge to the class, which was basically, if you do not support what is happening in society, especially with government, then you owe it to yourself and community to get involved.

"How many of you heard about what happened at Will Rogers Park during the summer?" Mr. Whyte said at the opening of class on Monday.

I looked around and saw a sea of hands—everybody in class had their hand up.

"How many of you knew at least one of the six individuals who were shot?"

I left my hand up and so did several other kids.

"What happened?" Mr. Whyte pushed. "Explain to me what you think occurred that day."

The whole class erupted.

"It's because the cops hate black people!" one girl exclaimed.

"Yeah, and they know they can get away with it!" another kid added.

"Most of them are KKK anyway," someone else finished.

The more I sat there, the angrier I got.

Mr. Whyte left his desk and walked solemnly to the middle of the room, forcing us to really pay attention. "So, here is your challenge," he said. "The police and the government are organized forces, so that means you need to be organized too."

"What do you mean?" I asked, really interested now.

"It's impossible for an individual to effectively challenge an organization, especially a strong one," he replied.

Similar messages were coming from other adults as well. My English teacher motivated us to read more, become informed, and act on our ideas. And of course, I was still in touch with my stepfather, Mr. Morgan, who continued to instill in me the importance of community service. It was because of the information and encouragement from these mentors that I began to work with other students to establish the first Black Student Union at Washington High School.

We were part of a trend. Students throughout California were working to establish BSUs on high school and college campuses, and we had a lot of support among our peers. Our new BSU held weekly meetings of about forty people. Shortly after we were established, we organized a strike in support of having a black studies class included in the curriculum. Most of the students walked out of school to force the school administrators to negotiate with us. I was a part of the negotiating team, and we succeeded. The school agreed to teach a black studies class, but it wouldn't begin until the next year. That would mean that the students coming after me would benefit from the class, but I would not, because I was graduating. Still, I was glad that we were helping them gain some knowledge about their history and culture.

In the midst of the political turmoil, there was some beauty in my life. During my senior year, I met Sharon Alford, who became my girlfriend and lifelong friend. Sharon was beautiful, a chocolate girl. She was sprinkled with freckles and quick to laugh, with a pleasant disposition.

I met her at the ABC store while I was at work, boxing groceries. She saw me talking to her brother Marzel. She stood there watching us for a while, and then she turned to Marzel. "You should introduce us," she smiled.

Marzel stood there and looked back and forth at us. Hesitantly, he finally said, "Wayne, this is Sharon."

I took the pen out of my pocket and ripped a piece of paper from a grocery bag. I asked her for her phone number.

Our first date was a Clint Eastwood movie, *The Good, the Bad and the Ugly*. I took her to the Century Drive-In, the perfect venue for a first date. Sharon and I were a good couple. Not only was she fine and smart, but she also accepted my politics.

The month of April started out full of optimism and bustle. We were still riding high from the success of the BSU and our upcoming black studies class. I had Sharon in my life now, and I was busy planning for my graduation.

But then on April 4 I learned that Martin Luther King Jr. had been murdered. I was at school when I heard the news. It was a sobering moment. But I wasn't surprised at all. I actually couldn't believe he lived as long as he did, especially considering the violence and racism in the United States.

Louis and some of the other guys, however, sat around on the lunch benches in a fatalistic mood. Biting his lip, with his jaw clenched and tears streaming down his face, Louis slammed his hand down on the table and stood up. "Man, I can't believe he's dead!"

"But I can," I replied glumly. "It only proves to me that nonviolence is a dead-end theory."

They all turned and looked at me with gloomy faces.

"Here was a man," I continued, "who had said to the white racists in the country, just give us some basic equality and we will not be a threat to this unfair system. Despite the hundreds of years of slavery and discrimination, we can start over. But instead of receiving support, he was shot and killed on a balcony of a motel."

"Right on, right on," they all exclaimed in unison.

King's murder had resulted in the opposite of what he had preached. Cities throughout the country blew up, and uprisings occurred everywhere. A lot of people died. But there was also a growing militancy in the streets. The antiwar movement picked up steam, and Stokely Carmichael began calling for black power. Malcolm X's message of Black Nationalism was being embraced from coast to coast by various organizations: Robert Williams and the Republic of New Afrika, the Student Nonviolent Coordinating Committee (SNCC), the Us Organization, the Community Alert Patrol, the Deacons for Defense, the Black Panther Party for Self-Defense, and the United Front. These were the organizations on the opposite end of the political spectrum, as opposed to more mainstream organizations like the National Association for the Advancement of Colored People, the Southern Christian Leadership Conference, the Urban League, and the Congress of Racial Equality.

I knew at some point I would hook up with one of the Black Nationalist organizations. In my view, if Martin Luther King Jr. could be assassinated in broad daylight, then nobody was safe.

6

A NECESSARY STEP TOWARD JUSTICE

Militancy in the streets was growing. Almost everywhere I turned, my homeboys were joining organizations set up to fight for black people. And many of the guys who became activists had previously belonged to gangs. Ron "Crook" Wilkins, a former member of the Slausons, became a leader of the local SNCC branch and of the Community Alert Patrol, an organization that monitored the cops. Kumasi, who was the leader of the Baby Slausons, eventually joined the Black Panther Party and became a leader in the California prison movement. I was still trying to make up my mind about which organization to join, but I knew that I wanted to play some sort of meaningful role in the fight for black liberation.

I was no believer in fate, but the events of my life seemed to orient me toward the Black Panther Party. The pivotal year was 1968. That year I graduated from Washington High School, and my mother and Nanny proudly attended the ceremony. I then immediately made plans to take the Greyhound bus up north to visit the family my mom and I left behind when we moved to Los Angeles.

My cousin Donald Pharr took me to a house party in Oakland to hang out and possibly meet some young ladies. The party was nice. There was some good music and dancing, and the DJ played one of my favorite songs, "Stay in My Corner" by the Dells. I was having a good time. At one point, I noticed these real serious-looking brothers in slacks and leather coats, holding down intense conversations in the corner. I realized that they were members of the Black Panther Party and that they were recruiting. These were not the leaders I had heard of, like Huey Newton or Bobby Seale, but rank-and-file members. I listened to some of their dialogue but decided not to engage them at the party. However, it was that night that I really began to check them out.

The very next day, Donald and I were getting something to eat. "You know I'm sort of digging the Panthers, because they seem to understand how power goes down for real," I said to him. "It makes all the sense in the world to me that if your oppressor, the state, the police, or whoever, is going to be strapped with gun power, then you better have some too. Otherwise, how can you ever hope to stop them from running all over you or respecting even your most basic rights?"

"That's right," chimed Donald. "We see every day what they're capable of. Hell, it could even get crazier than this. What's stopping them? Thank goodness that enough of them colonial crackers peeped this same thing and were intelligent enough to write that Second Amendment."

I agreed. "Yeah, that is some deep shit. By really looking out for their own asses, they built a door for us to walk through as well."

Donald couldn't help but bellow out a loud laugh. "Yeah, what goes around comes around."

He then talked about how the Black Panther Party had opened up an office in Oakland. He respected the Panthers, but with all his other responsibilities, including working and school, he couldn't even think about joining.

During my bus ride back to South Central, I wrestled with my level of commitment to black people and my willingness to sacrifice to attain black power. Talking with Donald had helped, but I wanted to get some input from someone closer to me. I immediately thought of Sharon. I called her from the Oakland bus station.

"Are you OK? Is everything all right? You're not in any danger, are you?" I must have scared her a bit, because she had grave concern in her voice.

"No, I'm fine. I'm fine," I reassured her. "I've just got a lot on my mind. It's time for me to make some changes in my life. I need to be more engaged in the solution to the problems facing black people."

"What are you talking about?" she responded.

"Solutions to how black people can bring about a better life for ourselves, for our families, for our communities. I can't lay it all out now, but as soon as I get back I want to talk this through with you."

"All right, that's fine by me. Call me when you're back. Be safe."

"I will," I finished, as I hung up the pay phone.

My mother, of course, had other ideas, which only added to my frustration. It seemed like she didn't even understand what it was like out there. "This is about your life, Wayne. Your life!" she scolded.

I just looked at her.

But she wasn't done. "Don't you understand how important education is for giving you the skills you need to make sure you have a decent future? You have had opportunities that most black kids can only dream of. Don't squander it on low-riding in the streets. This is not at all a game."

It was important to my mom that I go to college, but I hadn't prepared for that path in any great detail, so going to a four-year university would not be an option for me, at least at that time. I could tell that she was getting emotional, so I said to her calmly, like Mr. Morgan had taught me, "Mom, I understand what you're saying and I do hear you. But nothing has clicked for me yet. I'm not sure what I want to do with my life."

"Son, the reason why you can't see the future is because you are too comfortable with the present. Working that scrubber's job at the airport is certainly not helping. I knew I should've never let you take that job," she complained.

"That's not true. That job gives me a sense of freedom, a feeling of being my own man." It was like I was getting stifled from both sides: first, there was hardly any place a black man could go in the streets and feel safe, and now my freedom was getting squashed at home, too.

"A man free to do what?" she yelled back at me. "Sentence himself to the life of a janitor, getting sick from stolen, bad food?"

She was hitting hard, real hard. I knew school was important to her. It wasn't as if I didn't want more for myself. It was just that no fire was burning in me as far as school was concerned. I was much more interested in what was happening to black people and our fight against racism. That was something with a greater purpose! Couldn't she see that? However, my mother did have a point about preparing for what might come my way. As a compromise, I decided that I would at least attend a community college. But I was feeling restless.

Harbor Junior College sat wedged right next to the Harbor Freeway in the South Bay area, nestled in lots of wide-open regional park space and farmland. It was a clear contrast to Los Angeles City College (LACC), which was located in the heart of South Central on Vermont Avenue. I ultimately selected Harbor because several people from my neighborhood were going to LACC. I knew that being around them at school would interfere with my ability to focus, and since I had made the decision to attend, I didn't want to flunk out the first semester.

While I waited for school to begin in the fall, I worked on my car and continued to low-ride with friends. Then on a balmy August day I ran into this fine sister named Marcia, who was what we called a fox, because she was so good looking. I stepped back to admire her smooth brown skin, straight black hair, and pleasing face. I even loved her bowlegs. But what she said that day changed everything. "Have you heard about Tommy?" she frowned. "He got killed last night."

I replied coolly. "That's not unexpected news. What happened?"

"Well, he got in a shoot-out with the police. The police killed him," she said angrily.

"Tommy was in the Black Panthers, is that right?" Now I was interested.

"Yeah, he was," she nodded.

Marcia was talking about Tommy Lewis, nicknamed "Monkey Man," who had joined the Black Panther Party. I had known Tommy for years, and even though we weren't the best of friends, we weren't enemies either. We both went to Edison Junior High; he was a pretty cool cat, but we bumped heads from time to time. A lot of it related to turf and personalities. I grew up near Broadway and Avalon on Manchester, and he grew up at Compton Avenue and Florence. We were both in Slauson territory but at different ends. I was affiliated with Broadway, and Tommy was with the Flips. Tommy tried to jack one of my cousins at the skating rink, and we got into it over that. And one day when I was at Edison, he sent one of his friends to try to jack me and take my money—but I tossed his friend up before the rest of his gang could come help him. So they didn't like me too much.

Later that day I investigated what happened, and I found out that Tommy, Steve Bartholomew, and Robert Lawrence were blown away by the LAPD at Adams Boulevard and Montclair near Crenshaw. It was August 25, 1968, and four guys from the Party had stopped at the gas station and were approached by several policemen. At some point during the questioning, Steve Bartholomew and Robert Lawrence had been shot in the back of the head and killed. Tommy, who was only eighteen at the time, was also killed. At least before he died Tommy got off some shots and wounded two of the pigs. Steve's brother, Anthony, ran and got away but was eventually caught and charged with assault with a deadly weapon.

These murders affected me greatly. The police had gunned down those brothers at the gas station for no apparent reason. Even though we had had our differences, I was sorry to see that Tommy had gotten killed that way. I knew Robert and Steve, but not as well as I knew Tommy. Nonetheless, I was impressed with the brothers. They didn't die like hogs, "hunted and penned," as Claude McKay wrote; they went out in a hail of gunfire, fighting back.

After that day, the tension in the air became so thick you could scoop it with a spoon. I knew it was time for me to do more.

I started taking classes in September and joined the Black Student Union right away. I developed some great relationships at Harbor. I met Melvin X, Brother Shabazz, and Dedon, all leaders in the Black Student Alliance. My affiliation with them led to my involvement with other BSUs throughout Southern California. The BSA's purpose was to help establish BSUs and black studies programs. They also encouraged students to actually complete their college education. I would say that the difference between the BSA and other organizations set up to establish BSUs was that they advocated an Afrocentric and socialist political perspective.

Because there was a scarcity of black students at Harbor, it was easy for us to get to know one another. In fact, it probably forced us to rely on each other, the very same way that many black communities did before the era of integration. We carved out an area in the student center where we gathered to play cards and dominoes. It was here that I first noticed Joe Thompson, who later became a close friend. Joe had gapped teeth and wore a big Afro. I quietly watched him as he effortlessly wooed the ladies.

One day as I was rolling off campus, I saw him waiting at the bus stop. I honked and waved him over toward me. "What's up, man?" I asked.

"Nothing," he replied. "Just getting ready to head to the crib."

"Hop in," I offered. "I'll help you get there a bit faster."

He looked at me. "You sure?"

"Ain't no problem," I said with a nod, not even asking where he was going. He seemed cool enough to me, and I wasn't in any big hurry that day.

When we arrived at Joe's house, he invited me in.

"Sure," I said with a shrug. "Why not?"

As we walked through the door, I looked up and saw a suited-down, dark-skinned guy with big bugged eyes standing in the entrance, looking like he was just preparing to leave. His presence startled me a bit, so I stood ready to fight; but Joe immediately reached out to embrace him. Then Joe turned, pointing toward me. "This here is my man Wayne, one of my boys from campus. Wayne, this is my cousin Freddie, Freddie Hale."

Freddie and I both extended our hands at the same time, clasping in a firm and energetic grip, a kind of universal thing among black men then. It was one way that brothers exhibited our respect for each other, as well as our excitement about the possibilities that seemed to hang in the air everywhere. "Well, Mr. Scholars," Freddie said with a grin, "this here suit is about to go get his loot."

"Well, go on do that there, Mr. Suave, Mr. Flair," grinned Joe. We all laughed.

Freddie really was a mack man and a supreme hustler. But he was also a generous brother who would later come to have a major influence on me. One of his lucrative hustles was to chase accidents for an attorney. He would also stage accidents, if they weren't happening on their own frequently enough. Freddie would have a driver hit a car, get a police report, then take it to the insurance company. The passengers in the car would go to the chiropractor and get a neck brace or have some other kind of treatment. After three months or so, everybody involved would get about $2,500.

One day Joe rode with me to pick up Sharon at Washington High. As we were cruising on our way home, some fool ran a stop sign and hit my damn car, right on the front passenger side, where Sharon was sitting! One minute I was just smoothly gliding through the intersection and the very next minute I heard the sound of screeching tires, then crunching metal, followed by that "into the middle of next week" jolt. Of course I was initially stunned, responding by instinct with a "What the hell?" I looked to my right and saw what had happened. It took a minute for me to clearly take it all in. My mind raced.

Was everyone all right? How bad was the damage? Was the idiot in the other car hurt? Did he have insurance? An image of my mother even flitted through my thoughts. Eventually, Joe, Sharon, and I got out of the car slowly. After we discovered that none of us was hurt badly, Joe told me not to worry about the damages. He would notify Freddie, who would get us paid. Knowing that my car would be fixed and I might also get some extra money quieted the anger I would have been ready to fire at that other driver. Sho 'nuff, about three months later Freddie's hustling got us paid.

Joe eventually started hanging with Louis and me, and Joe, like Louis, was heavy into chasing girls. I was down with that, but I also had the struggle for black liberation on my mind. By this time, I had become aware of another of Joe's passions: red devils, a drug we called stumblers because they made you stupid.

Joe coaxed me into trying them one time. That one time let me know I wasn't interested in that kind of high. "Look, man, we're all grown and to each his own, but them devils don't do nothing for me. I didn't like the way they made me feel, as though I'm not in control of myself."

"That interesting, because they definitely relax me," explained Joe. "I feel real chilled."

"To each his own," I said again.

That was that. We never broached the topic again.

Ramon Mann was my guidance counselor at Harbor. He was a tall Hispanic man with a hawk noise and black hair sprinkled with gray. He was a very progressive teacher who had previously helped to get black studies started at Jordan High School. During my visits to his office, he and I discussed various issues: the school board, racist cops, and of course how I could excel as both student and organizer. He wanted to know what area of study I was interested in. I told him that drafting piqued my interest, but I was much more interested in activism.

"OK, Wayne, but remember, to succeed you must have goals and you must be organized. Students must be organized. Organizers must be organized."

"Organizers must be organized," I chuckled. "Well, you don't say."

Mr. Mann kept a straight face, totally ignoring my humor. "You're obviously smart and well read, but it takes more to become successful at whatever your goals are," he said. "It takes the discipline of continued execution. You can know it and not be it. And that's where most people fall off the wagon. Don't become one of them, Wayne."

I allowed what he was saying to roll around in my brain and then answered back, with my best effort at a reassuring tone, "I won't be."

By that point in my life, Mr. Mann's advice was not foreign to me. He was talking about success, my future goals, and becoming better organized. My high school teachers, Mr. Morgan, and my mom had repeated those ideas to me throughout the years. I took their statements seriously and was ready to put some of those pearls of wisdom into action. But not toward school as much. I was seriously considering joining the Black Panther Party for Self-Defense.

There was a branch of the Party in Los Angeles. Bunchy Carter, a leader of the Renegade Slausons, the largest and perhaps fiercest gang, had organized it in late 1967. Bunchy had spent time in Soledad State Prison with Eldridge Cleaver. After they were released, Eldridge joined the Party in Oakland. He recruited Bunchy, who started the Southern California chapter.

I was familiar with Bunchy and thought he was the right person to lead a revolutionary organization. In addition to his loyal following of tough young men, he had charisma, intelligence, and fighting skills. Everybody knew of Bunchy's power. He was not to be messed with.

My first contact with Bunchy, in fact, had occurred back when I was about twelve years old. My crew and I were walking to the skating rink and some older guys starting calling out gangs: "Watts!" one yelled; "Farmers!" the other side hollered. My crowd started yelling, "Watts!" But I hollered "Slauson!" the gang based in my neighborhood. Plus, I had realized that our challengers were from the Slausons, led by Bunchy. In their eyes, I was the only one ready to defend my set. So they jacked my buddies for not having the heart to stand up for their set, but they let me go. My boys weren't hurt, but it taught them to stay true to who you are and where you come from.

Over the years, I saw Bunchy hanging with Ernest Bird, Skillet, and Treetop. Those four were the main players in South Central; they wore a uniform of Levi's and white shirts or T-shirts and Stacy Adams "biscuits" or Spanish boots.

I got to know how Bunchy operated a little better after he began working at the Teen Post on Central Avenue. Like me, my aunt Caffie Greene hired him. She was having trouble controlling some of the young men at the Teen Post, but after she hired Bunchy her troubles lightened because Bunchy immediately began to organize them as soldiers in the army for black liberation. Bunchy used the Teen Post to recruit for the Party. He required the young men enrolled in the program to learn the Party's ideology, he trained them in self-defense tactics, and he taught them how to properly shoot guns. Aunt Caffie used to tell me about how Bunchy would line up the young brothers and bark orders at them, which, to her surprise, they would obey.

While sitting on a bench in the park one Saturday, I decided to engage Louis about his views on black revolutionary groups in Los Angeles. "Man, what do you think about the Nation of Islam?"

"I guess they're all right, but they seem like a bunch of robots to me, man," he said. I laughed. "They all dress alike, talk alike, and eat alike. You know, they don't even eat pork," he laughed. "And, I loves me some bacon and pork chops. Why do you ask?"

"No particular reason," I replied. "I respect what they do and even some of their beliefs about white folks, but their rules are too damn strict."

Another group that had become popular in the black community was the Us Organization, founded by Ron Karenga. Us was built on the idea that black people needed to claim their lost heritage and culture in order to rebuild a strong community. I respected their organizational structure but thought that their definition of black culture required its members to be against other groups. I was not anti-white or anti- any other group, and I didn't believe that all white people were enemies either. I had the ability to make a distinction between pigs in the power structure and white people in general.

I knew some of the guys who had joined Us, like George and Larry Steiner, brothers who had once been in the Gladiator gang. It wasn't surprising that many of the Us members were former Gladiators. Ron Karenga's boys recruited from the Gladiators' neighborhood, around Fifty-Fourth and Vermont, near Manual Arts High School. On the other side, the Black Panther Party recruited from the territories run by Slausons.

"About Us," I said to Louis, "I just can't understand why they spend so much time trying to get people to learn an African language, when most black people haven't even learned basic English, because the education system is so fucked up."

"Right on, man. I wouldn't learn an African language right now, even if they paid me."

"Plus, them Us niggas want us to wear a dashiki every day, wear a ten-foot Afro, and put five earrings in our ears and a bone through our noses."

Then we both fell on the ground laughing.

Finally, it was Sharon's turn to weigh in on the conversation, so I got together with her as planned. We grabbed some food to go and rode out to a quiet place. I wasn't looking at it as a picnic, but I did want to keep out distractions: gawking brothers, hunger, seeing people she or I might know. When we finally sat down, she jumped in immediately.

"So, what on earth is going on?" She searched my eyes for a clue as to what I was thinking. "You sounded pretty serious when you were up in Oakland."

"I was," I replied. "In fact, 'serious' is pretty much on point; things are serious all around us. Brothers getting shot up left and right by these racist police. It's like black people are getting bulldozed every day. We've got to stand up to this shit."

"I hear you," she responded with a knowing nod of the head.

"I feel like we are at war," I continued. "It's time that I do more in response to this war."

Sharon sat quietly for a long while, chewing her food and looking up into the sky. Finally, she said quietly, "War is real. People die in war, and real undertakers pick up real dead bodies. This ain't no Hollywood movie. Everybody ain't going home in the end, to eat some good-ass chicken and greens like we doing right now."

We both chuckled at the last part of her point, but it was real talk. I knew that. No one knew that better than me. I guess somewhere along the line, maybe when I purchased the second or third gun, I had already come to grips with that. Sitting there then, realizing that, I was amazed at how we could make such big decisions inside ourselves without even noticing.

■ ■ ■

The Black Panther Party of Los Angeles had several offices. The branch closest to me was on Eighty-Second and Broadway. Most of the brothers from the 'hood worked out of this office. Since I knew so many of the Panthers there, that's where I ended up going to check out their program.

I went up to the door, and a tall, lanky dude by the name of Ronald Freeman answered. He invited me in.

"I know you guys have been fighting with the police, and I'm down with that," I announced as I walked through the door.

I noticed a few other people in the office, including Ronald's younger brother Roland. We talked for what seemed like a long time. They told me about the reasons the Black Panther Party existed, the programs of the organization, and their focus on recruiting more young people. In fact, they were on their way to UCLA, they told me, to organize students there and talk to them about the Party. Roland said they were waiting on a ride.

I made an instant decision and asked them if they wanted me to take them to UCLA. I didn't want to boast, but I was proud of my ride, and I felt they would know what kind of cat I was by the way

I took care of my low-rider. We all hopped in the car and drove the forty-five minutes to UCLA. I had some guns in my glove compartment; I thought it was important I let these dudes know I was packing. "By the way," I said casually, "I've got some guns."

Roland studied me. "What you got?"

"A .38 and a .45." I showed them my weapons.

For a long moment, no one said anything, and I wondered if I'd made a mistake by saying what I did. Then Roland laughed. "Right on," he said.

We drove on up to UCLA and parked. I realized that I was hanging out with some outlaws when Roland took the parking ticket off of somebody else's car and put it on ours.

We walked up to the room where the meeting was being held, and I saw a boatload of students and Bunchy leading the meeting.

"Hey, man, you're on guard duty since you're packing," Roland nodded at me.

"Good," I replied.

The meeting lasted about an hour, and then we left. On the way back to the office we got into another discussion about guns. I really wanted to check out what they had, but they didn't produce any. I wanted to brag as well as let them know that I could make a major contribution to the party. So I went home and got a few more.

I came back with a couple of my pistols. "If you going to throw down with the police you need some real heat," I told Roland and the rest of them.

That was my introduction to the Black Panther Party, taking me one step closer.

7

COMMITTED TO WATTS

There were five Party offices in Los Angeles, but I wanted to operate out of Watts. The office was located in Charcoal Alley, so named because of the large number of buildings in the area that had burned to the ground during the Watts Rebellion of '65. It was the smallest of our offices in L.A., located near the railroad tracks on 103rd Street, east of Wilmington. Some people considered the area a wasteland, but I didn't mind at all. I picked the Watts office precisely because there weren't a lot of people I knew in that part of Los Angeles. In fact, the Broadway office was in the middle of my neighborhood, which meant I was either friends with or associated with most of the guys there. But I didn't join the Party to hang out with my friends; I came to put in some serious work for my people.

Tyrone Hutchinson had joined the Party a few months before me. He was based out of the Broadway office and couldn't understand why I was considering working out of Watts. "Man, what the hell will you do over there at the Watts office?" he asked me one day when I stopped by Broadway. "It's in the boondocks and ain't hardly anybody there!"

I looked at him and smiled. "That's why I want to be there. Seriously, Watts needs a lot of work. Recruiting needs to be done. The community there needs our presence."

"Well, good luck to you, then, brother," he shrugged.

I looked at him and smiled.

Tyrone was right, though. The Watts office suffered from a manpower shortage, with only six or seven of us operating from there on the regular. It was hard to get cats to volunteer to work in Watts. Vacant lots were everywhere. The big shopping stores, like Kress, were gone or gutted out. The closest market was a few miles away from the center of the city, so people shopped at mom-and-pop stores or went to Compton. Even the satellite police station on 103rd Street was being phased out. No matter what reasons local officials and the police claimed, we knew the truth was that the station couldn't defend itself against the wrath of local residents.

"Broadway is popping, Central is popping, even Adams," Tyrone added. "You should come join us at Broadway or at least work where you can see how things are really being done and get yourself groomed for taking on a leadership role."

I joked, "In Watts, I'm developing the Party's model for 'Food and Finance Management: How to keep your belly full when your pocket is empty.'" I explained to him that between the twenty-cent hot dogs at the Chinese spot and Pappy's twenty-cent hamburgers, a brother could win the war on hunger hands down.

"Right on, brother," he said with a laugh as I turned to head for the door.

"Right on," I replied with a nod. "All power to the people." I left Tyrone and went straight to the Watts office, my mind made up.

The building was an unassuming one-story storefront with an ugly iron gate surrounding its perimeter, and it had a bad paint job to match the gate. Party offices were always open to the people, so I just walked in. James Wilson greeted me. Originally from Watts, James was a dark-skinned brother, muscular, and about a year younger than me. He was sitting at the desk in a black leather coat, reading the Ten Point Platform. He looked up at me and immediately started talking. "Power to the people. Come on in, brother," he said invitingly, standing up to greet me.

"Absolute power to the people," I shot back, not missing a beat as I stepped inside.

"When the people have power, then we can make this earth civil and humane," James nodded.

"I agree," I retorted. "So every day that the people are out of power brings just another day of the madness."

"Right on, right on," James said, clenching his fist and raising his arm toward me in the black power salute. "So, what can I do for you today, brother?" he asked.

"I'm here to learn more," I replied. "And maybe join."

As I engaged him in dialogue, I simultaneously checked out the layout of the office. I noticed three desks, but other than that, it was relatively empty. The room was divided by a partition separating the area with the desks from a large open area that I learned was where the political education classes were held. There were two windows— one on the door and a larger one in the front area covered with a collage of the Party's leaders, Huey Newton and Bobby Seale. Included in the collection was the famous picture of Huey sitting in a wicker chair and a picture of Bobby Seale holding a shotgun with a string of bullets across his chest. Besides the posters covering the window, the revolutionary artwork of Emory Douglas, the Party's minister of culture, was taped to the walls. Of all Douglas's images, I identified most with the iconic one of a pig, going "oink, oink."

"I see you're reading the Ten Point Platform," I said to James inquiringly, as I nodded my head toward the papers on his desk.

"Yes, brother," he replied. "The Ten Point Platform is as important as the Ten Commandments. It gives the people the blueprint needed to build and sustain our community. If one understands the Ten Point Platform, then he will know the kind of foundation necessary for political education, awareness, and revolutionary action. Can you dig?"

"That's exactly why I am here, because I *can* dig it," I said decisively.

He smiled. I thought he was probably glad to have some potential new recruits.

"I was just over at the Broadway office and was saying how I really preferred to come here with the Watts crew. I'm in this area a lot already, from hanging out with my boy from Harbor College, Joe Thompson."

"That's good, man," James responded, "because we can use all the help we can get."

"So what's the state of affairs?" I asked. "What needs to be tackled first?" I was ready.

James cleared space for me by his desk and motioned for me to sit. "Well, first," he said as I settled in, "let me tell you who's working here out of the Watts office. There's Larry Scales, who's the captain here. Larry's originally from Watts, right up the street. He doesn't take no shit. He's for real about the business."

"Right on," I nodded. A stick-to-business man. Sounded good so far. "Who else?"

"Al Armour is the section leader in charge of our office. His job is to run the office, recruit, hold political education classes, and make sure papers get sold. Al is from the Westside and so is Luxey Irving, who is in charge when Al is not here. Al and Lux are both book crushers over at UCLA."

I laughed. "I'm a student, too, at Harbor."

I later learned from James about other comrades stationed in Watts, such as Nathaniel Clark and Craig Williams. Nathaniel was light-skinned and thin. He had a thing for red devils, but he was always ready to defend the office; he had guns and wasn't afraid to use them. Craig was from Compton and served diligently, selling papers and recruiting. Nathaniel and Craig didn't show up every day, but everyone knew their work.

I met Al and Luxey at the Watts office later that week. Al was serious and dedicated. He was another light-skinned brother and stood a solid six feet. He stood out because he had such bad feet, which gave him a funny hop to his walk. One of his quirks was that he played with his mustache, and when you were talking to him it could be distracting. He was from the Westside, and his family lived in the Venice/Buckingham area of Los Angeles, which was a mixed working-class neighborhood of houses and apartments. I liked Al.

Luxey, who preferred that we call him Lux, came from middle-class parents. His father was an entrepreneur who owned a barber-shop in Watts on Central Avenue. Lux wore glasses with thin wire frames like Malcolm wore; they gave him a studious, deep-thinker look. He, too, was dedicated, friendly, very calm, and controlled. No matter what we were up against, I never saw him fly off the handle. I learned that Al and Luxey were recruited by Bunchy, who then sent them both to the Watts office. I guess Bunchy wanted these Westsiders to get their hands a little dirty.

The more time I spent there, the more I liked working out of the Watts office. It was off the radar and kept me away from the intrigue at the headquarters on Central Avenue and away from the jackanapes and clowns who joined the Party to get girls or some other kind of attention. I soon developed a close working relationship with James and Craig. We worked well together as a team, building support for the Party and our office. Our practice was to hang out in the 'hood and persuade people to drop by. Al and Lux didn't have the same street credibility as us, but they took care of their responsibilities well—making a lot of runs to Central, handling Party business, and recruiting at UCLA.

Although we recruited throughout Watts, we focused on those who lived in the housing projects of Imperial Courts, Jordan Downs, and Nickerson Gardens. The projects were established and funded by the state and federal government to provide affordable housing for poor people during World War II. Initially, a diverse group of people lived there, including whites. But after years of neglect and inadequate funds for maintaining the buildings, the projects became slums: a wretched sight, with rats and roaches running amuck, and children running around hungry. The public image of the projects was dilapidated centers of poverty and crime.

But the Black Panther Party considered the project residents our people, part of the lumpenproletariat, people who might see the usefulness of the Party. The lumpenproletariat, as opposed to the proletariat, who formed the basis of Marxist theory, had been excluded: Marx thought they had no revolutionary potential. According to Marxist theory, the proletariat was made up of the working class, who would overthrow the upper classes and the oppressive forces of government to create a new and just society. But when we applied Marxist theory to our situation, we realized that our blackness and minority status in the United States made us different from the general working class. Our folks lived at the lowest basic level, even lower than the working class. These were the people who took the most menial jobs, those even the "working class" didn't want to do. Some of them had given up on work altogether, were hooked on drugs, or just couldn't make enough money no matter how many jobs they worked. They were the people who might snatch a woman's purse, rob a liquor store, engage in prostitution, or sell illegal goods to get by. These were the people who had given up on the system altogether. They were the ones who could really understand the need for revolution, once they were educated about their position in society and the nature of capitalism.

Each project in Watts had a section called the parking lots, where most of the outside activity on the grounds took place. People hung out in the parking lots, engaging in daily craps games or selling and buying drugs. The police would always go there first if they were looking for someone. But now we were there too, to get to know the residents and, we hoped, recruit them into the Party. As they got to know us, we began to earn their respect. Soon, they were coming to our political education classes. And at the office, we began to take calls and settle disputes between people who didn't want to call the police.

One day, a woman named Anne, whom I had met a few times in the Jordan Downs, called during a fight with her husband.

I happened to answer the phone. "Hello. Black Panther Party, Watts office," I said into the receiver.

An agitated voice yelled at me from the other side. "Can I get some help with this crazy motherfucker over here?" It was a woman's voice, but I had no idea who she was.

"Whoa, sister, slow down. What's going on? Relax. Take your time and tell me what's going on. Where are you?" I said coolly and calmly.

"This punk-ass nigga actually slapped me. Can you believe that? After all I do for his no-good ass, he gonna actually put his hands on me!"

"Where are you? Who is this that you're talking about?"

By now, she was screaming. "I'm in the Downs! Apartment 3-G. Y'all betta come get this motherfucker—I don't wanna call the police up here. They might be haulin' off a lotta folks around here—you know how that goes. They just need to come get this half of a man, this no-good-ass S.O.B.!"

I could hear the man she was referring to in the background, speaking with an angry tone. "How the hell you gonna be calling somebody on me?" he was raving. "Who the hell you callin', Super-Damn-Man or somebody? Tell whoever it is to fly they ass over here, so I can give them some of what I just gave you," he growled.

We took down her address and left right away, headed straight to the apartment.

When we arrived, we knocked on the door and the woman who made the phone call immediately opened it. I saw that it was Anne and said hello.

"I'm glad y'all came," she said excitedly. "Thank you, because this motherfucker done lost his mind. I don't want my family from Mississippi to have to come all the way up here and deal with his ass."

About that time, a burly brother, standing about six foot two and weighing about 250 pounds, appeared in the doorway. He had a daunting presence and hovered angrily over the front door. "Who the fuck are y'all?" he snarled. "Are y'all the Superman squad her ass calling on me?"

"We're members of the Black Panther Party," I said, firmly but politely. I could see an immediate change in the brother's demeanor. "There's no need to continue fighting. Why don't you step outside and just talk to us? Perhaps that can help calm things down a bit."

After some back-and-forth, eventually her husband agreed. He grabbed a shirt and stepped outside with us, slamming the door behind him as Anne tried to position herself to watch what was going down.

"What's your name, brother?" Craig asked.

"Jerome," the man replied, and then immediately began trying to justify his actions.

"Look, Jerome, we're men too," Craig began. "We understand how things can easily get out of hand, but hitting on sisters just ain't cool, no way we slice it. These are the queens of our community. They bear the children for the nation, so we need to find another way to solve our conflicts."

With that, Jerome had no comeback. He scowled in thought, not really knowing what to say, but I could tell he was considering the wisdom of Craig's words.

We went on talking, trying to reason with him in a nonthreatening way. We pointed out that, besides the importance of taking care of our women, Jerome wouldn't want to run the risk of going to jail. He was somewhat agreeable, finally calming down. It took us about half an hour, but by the end of our little chat, he was smiling and happy, assuring us he would go back inside and take care of his queen.

These kinds of interventions were not uncommon for us, and that first one with Jerome was a good experience for me. It was incidents like this that taught me how to talk to people respectfully and sincerely listen to what they had to say.

Many times these encounters left such a positive impression on the neighborhood that we became more effective in recruiting and mobilizing. In fact, the Watts office became one of the most productive offices in Los Angeles. Al Armour was so impressed with my work that he soon began letting me run the office. To this day, I am thankful to Al for that opportunity, because I carried those experiences with me throughout the rest of my life. Everything I know about managing an office I learned while I was in the Black Panther Party.

Most party members sold the *Black Panther* newspaper to raise money. For me, selling the newspaper was one of the best parts of my work because it required me to leave the office and go into the community and interact with people. I also sold papers at Harbor College, which helped me to maintain my connection with the students. Other times, I would drop them off with a BSU member and come back later to pick up the proceeds.

Russell Washington was in charge of distributing the papers. We connected immediately the first time he came by the office to pick up the leftover papers and collect the money from our sales. I was in the office with my head deep in some paperwork when Russell walked in. "Is this the place where they're selling them revolutionary papers?" he queried boisterously. "I heard it was."

"Sho 'nuff," I replied. "You ain't never lied. How many bundles you want to buy, good brother? That'll be the best thing you ever did for the community," I finished with a hearty laugh.

Russell broke out in a wide grin, then strode over and gave me a vigorous black power handshake: two strong moves where we first clasped our hands together with thumbs on top, then pulled each other's fingers as we drew our hands apart. From that day on, the two of us just found it easy to flow with one another. We just clicked like that.

Sometimes I'd even roll with Russell on his collection runs. Afterward, we liked to sit down over a drink and share political analyses, including our ideas about how the Party could continue to move forward. Russell liked to drink what we called Bitter Dog, sometimes referred to as Panther Piss, a combination of white port wine and lemon juice. It was popular with a lot of the brothers. It was an old-school ghetto drink that would get us high and didn't require us to dig too deep into our pockets to get there. Personally, I was more into beer, particularly Country Club Malt Liquor, but in its absence I wouldn't turn down some Piss. Before we took a swig, we'd always pour a little for the brothers who weren't there—dead or locked up. I admired Russell. He knew the streets of Los Angeles very well, including all the shortcuts for getting around town.

For me, the work for the Party didn't seem like work; it was a commitment, my raison d'être. At times, though, I had a lot of fun with my comrades just blowing off steam. For instance, Nathaniel, Lux, and I would sometimes hang out at Al's graveyard-shift security job in the twenty-four-hour funeral home located on Forty-Eighth and Avalon. The place stayed open 'round the clock to serve people who wanted to visit their deceased loved ones at any time of the day or night. Nathaniel's fool behind would actually play with the corpses, which scared the daylights out of me. The first time I saw him do it, I thought it was just plain creepy. I said to him, "Man, what is wrong with your crazy ass, playing with dead people?"

"Yeah, man," Lux chimed in, "somebody's relative is gonna come in here one night and find your ass playing with their mother, then whup your fool behind."

"Aw, man, chill out," Nathaniel said as he tickled one of the bodies. "We just having a little fun. Besides, the dead, they don't mind at all." With that, he busted out in laughter, thinking he was witty.

Staring at us, shaking his head with an *I-don't-believe-I'm-watching-this* grimace, would be Al, nursing his Piss, looking from one of us to the next, as if he were sitting in a comedy theater.

Even though I loved those nights we hung out at Al's gig, I was a little nervous about being around dead people. I could swear I heard noises in the coffins sometimes, even when I knew it wasn't Nathaniel joking around.

In addition to the work we did at our offices, all comrades were required to go to the Panther headquarters once a week for office meetings. The headquarters was located on Central Avenue, one of the most popular and famous streets in Los Angeles. During the 1940s and '50s, jazz clubs populated the area, along with black businesses such as insurance companies, hotels, and the offices of African American physicians. It was also the place where jazz artists from all over the country would play, including greats like Louis Armstrong, Charlie Mingus, and Lionel Hampton.

The Black Panther Party headquarters at 4115 South Central was the hub of all Panther activity around the city. The office was a two-story brick building that at one time had served as a store. On the side and up a flight of stairs was 4115½, where we had more offices. In order to enter that part of headquarters, we had to go outside and walk up the stairs along the outside of the building. Altogether headquarters had plenty of space, about two thousand square feet. In the downstairs area were the general office, the gun room, and a large room with a back door. Located upstairs were the meeting rooms and areas for communications and printing. In addition to Central Headquarters, Party leaders operated out of apartment buildings and other houses to throw off police.

James hipped me to the chain of command that governed the Party. "It's rather simple to follow," he explained. "There's an order of leadership at the national level, and this same order is replicated in each of the Party's local branches. There are ministers, as you already know, at the national level, and all local chapters have ministers as well. The ministers at the national level are organized into a Central Committee that governs the organization. All local ministers, of course, are subordinate to the Central Committee."

Having already done extensive research on the Party before I joined, I knew a lot of what he told me. I didn't want to offend him, though, so I nodded attentively to everything he said.

He continued, "For example, in the L.A. branch of the Southern California chapter, Bunchy Carter is the deputy minister of defense, which corresponds to Huey's position as minister of defense on the Central Committee."

"Who appoints those lower in command at each office?" I asked.

"It's the minister of defense's responsibility to give members their rank," James explained. "So Huey gives rank on the national level, and consequently Bunchy gives out rank at our local level. Does that make sense? You see the parallel?"

"Yeah, I see it clearly. Bobby Seale is chairman of the Central Committee and Shermont Banks is deputy chairman here. Eldridge Cleaver is the minister of information nationally, and John Huggins is the deputy minister of information locally."

"Yep, you got it down cold," James said with a look of approval. "Also remember," he added, "that political awareness and dedication to the cause would get someone appointed section leader by Bunchy."

I nodded my head, wondering if that was what James was aiming for.

I had already had a brief encounter with Deputy Minister John Huggins before I joined the party, the day I had gone with the brothers up to UCLA. To me, John didn't really look like your average Panther. He wore the kind of clothes you would expect to see on a white hippie, thrift-store stuff, sort of mismatched clothes. He was a light-skinned dude with a big curly Afro. He had come to Los Angeles from Pennsylvania with his wife, Ericka, to join the Black Panther Party. That day at UCLA, he welcomed me to the meeting with the words, "Glad to have you, comrade." I had smiled and clasped his hand. I could tell that Huggins was easygoing and had a friendly personality, and I immediately liked him.

Elaine Brown, a beautiful sister with deep, soulful eyes and a smile that could light up a room, was the secretary of the Southern California chapter. Elaine was always busy, and I could see that she was deeply committed to our work. Ronald Freeman and Long John Washington were field secretaries. Their job was to travel throughout the Southern California region to check on the offices and the work of all Panthers. Whenever they showed up, they were in charge.

There were also several captains operating out of Central Headquarters. I was already familiar with two of them before I joined the Party: Frank Diggs, who was nicknamed "Captain Franco," and

Roger Lewis, whom everyone called Blue. I knew Captain Roger "Blue" Lewis from the neighborhood, going back to when I was a kid, but I didn't know him well. He was a clerk at a shoe store, and I used to run into him regularly. He was a dark-skinned brother who had a disarming smile and a real charismatic personality, real easygoing. I respected him.

I had met Franco in the neighborhood when he tried to recruit me into the Party. He wasn't a big guy, about five foot nine with kind of a medium build, but what he lacked in size he made up for in intensity. Tyrone introduced us to each other. We were just leaving a party one night when Frank strolled on up.

"Captain Franco, what's up? I want you to meet my homeboy Wayne," Tyrone said, slapping me on the back. "He's a Broadway Slauson and also a student out at Harbor College. But he's not letting all that book knowledge blind him to the reality of our struggle for the people."

I nodded at Franco coolly.

"Sounds good," Franco said forcefully. "We always need brothers with their heads on straight. So have you joined the Black Panther Party for Self-Defense?" he pressed.

"Thinkin' about it, brother," I replied.

"And I do put emphasis on the self-defense part, Brother Wayne," Franco finished, in an official sounding tone.

"I'm seriously checking it out," I calmly replied.

"Well, don't wait too long, because whitey ain't waiting at all to put his foot down harder on the necks of our people. Study long, study wrong."

I looked at Franco without saying a word, deciding to back off. I realized then that he had what seemed to me a crazed look about him, and I didn't want to push any buttons. Who knew what might have resulted from that.

Right on cue, Tyrone said, "All right, Captain Franco, we gonna push on. We'll catch you later."

"All right then, brothers," Franco answered. "But remember, the black man will never be free until he can look the white man in the eye and kill him. Especially them fuckin' pigs, who think they can't die or something."

As we walked away, I stole a long look at Franco and made a note to myself to always be alert when he was around.

Elmer "Geronimo" Pratt was another captain who operated out of Central Headquarters. G, as we called him, was a commanding presence, and I could tell immediately that he had military training by his stance and demeanor. He was medium brown, short, and bowlegged, with an air of physicality about him, always in motion. Word was that he fought in Vietnam but returned to challenge racism because he had seen so much discrimination by his fellow US troops. Bunchy had given him the name Geronimo ji-Jaga, indicating that he saw Geronimo as part of a tribe of strong and feared African warriors.

G and I met after a political education class at Central Headquarters one day. The meeting had already broken up and most people were gone. I noticed him, Long John, and Blue competing against each other in a knife-throwing contest that stabbed several holes in the office door. I sat quietly, watching them, entertained by their competitiveness.

After the contest, G walked over to me and said, "Right on, brother. Thanks for joining the organization." Apparently, someone told him that I was a new member.

"All right, man, power to the people," I replied. I was pleased that he took the time to acknowledge me, because I knew he was a major player in the organization.

Later, back at Watts, I asked James about him. He explained, "Blue, G, and Frank are all captains under Bunchy."

After listening to other comrades rap about the three captains, I got the sense that they also did some of Bunchy's dirty work—or rather, if Bunchy had a problem and didn't want to handle it himself, he could rely on one of them to handle it for him.

After two months in the Party, I had met so many new people I thought my head might spin off trying to remember them all, and my life had changed drastically. *What was I thinking?* I wondered when I thought about all I was trying to do. I was serving as the elected president of the BSU at Harbor and working heavily with the Black Student Alliance on other college campuses and training students to become activists. And then I was a Panther.

In my student life, I was closest to Jerry Moore. I thought he was one of the most politically astute of the student activists. He was a few years older than me and a former Baby Flip from Slauson Village. I knew Jerry and his sister from Edison Junior High, and now he was a student at Pepperdine University, studying law. Jerry and the BSA supported the Black Panther Party and often supported our members who were underground. Aboveground, Jerry had a job at the Ascot library on Broadway and Seventy-Eighth, and he allowed the Black Panther Party to use its facilities to hold meetings.

Jerry was affiliated with the United Front and various organizations designed to uplift people suffering from race and class oppression. It was through Jerry that I developed a relationship with Diana, a Hispanic activist whose family owned a restaurant on Alvera Street. She introduced us to the Brown Berets and other Hispanic radicals. Meeting activists of other races and nationalities was good for me, because it just reinforced the idea that black people weren't the only ones suffering and that working with other groups was essential.

Baba and Yusuf were BSA members who went to Southwest College; they were also strong figures in our activist crew. Both had done time before, but instead of going back to street life they enrolled in school. Baba, Yusuf, and others, including Wendell and Jackie, used to stop at Jerry's house for political conversations. We were always debating, and we had great discussions. I really looked forward to those discussions because they were so stimulating. In fact, I began to hang out at Jerry's place so much that eventually I moved in.

As a member of the Black Panther Party and a student activist, I would speak at campuses about the Party. It got to be something I was pretty good at, standing and rapping as a crowd would begin to gather.

"Listen up . . . I need to rap to y'all for a minute. Need to put something on your mind. Something that can help you find clarity about all the craziness you see around you. Things like why black and brown people are always down and whitey and his pigs are on the top. What's that all about, huh? Somebody tell me. What's that all about? Well, the Black Panther Party can tell you what's it's about and what you can do to fight it."

I would talk about the Black Panther Party's Ten Point Platform, telling my audience that it made a lot of sense. I would explain the nature of racism in the United States and then discuss the need for black people to have the ability to determine our destiny.

"Some have accused the Party of being racist. The Party is not a racist organization; we believe in Black Nationalism and self-defense as laid down by Malcolm X, but we also believe in power to all people! The Black Panther Party works in solidarity with all people for the common good."

In some of my speeches, I emphasized the injustice and racist nature of the war in Vietnam. "What does power really mean? It means the ability to say no to war, especially no with our precious lives: the lives of our brothers, uncles, friends, and neighbors. Why the hell should we travel to the other side of the world to kill and be killed? What's in it for us? Not a damn thing. You know that. I know that. The Black Panther Party knows that. If somebody just rolled up in your living room, shooting up your house, destroying your hard-earned stuff, you would deal with them, wouldn't you? You'd have to, or be offed. That's exactly what the yellow peoples of Vietnam are doing. They are dealing with invaders, attackers, thieves, destroyers, and robbers, strangers who have come to take their stuff—their land, their wealth, their self-governance. We black people can't be caught up in the middle of

Recruiting for the Black Panther Party in 1969 during a May Day Rally at Will Rogers Park in Watts on 103rd Street and Central Avenue. Craig Williams, a Party member who worked with me out of the Watts Office, is also pictured. COURTESY OF ROZ PAYNE

whitey's craziness, especially when it means our well-being and our lives. Get the hell out of 'Nam, whitey. Power to the people."

Nanny and my mother were fully aware of my decision to join the Black Panther Party. When I joined, I didn't make a grand announcement of it, because I wasn't the type of person who would talk a lot about my personal thoughts, nor would I bring my outside issues into my family. But I think my disposition must have changed shortly after I joined and began to incorporate the Black Panther Party into my life. I know they noticed. I became more intolerant of mainstream stuff, like entertainment on TV. Shows that I might have stopped to take in or accepted as just killing time before, I now had total disdain for. This attitude left me out of some conversations with my family. I didn't want to be antagonistic or anything, but who gave a damn about Jackie Gleason, Lawrence Welk, or any other tired-ass aspect of cracker culture? Surprisingly, this extended all the way to sports and athletes too. I wasn't able to just jump in and jive about the latest matchups like I did in the past. My always-on analysis kept me keen on the exploitation involved.

My mother had serious concerns about my involvement with the Party. She would catch me when no one else was around. "Wayne, think about what direction you are heading with your life. Think about your future."

"Yeah, Mom, I hear you. But somebody has to stop those in power, who are destroying our communities and our people."

She would shake her head and walk away. Then she would come back with more ammunition. "There are a lot of different characters up in there," she'd scold. "All of them are not the same, and all of them don't have the same intentions in mind. You don't want to have to suffer because of somebody else's mess."

As for Nanny, she wouldn't say much while others were around. But when we were alone she'd make sure to give me her words of wisdom, too. "Listen, Wayne, good people always start off doing right, or wanting to do right, but somewhere along the way they sometimes get turned around. Before you know it, they're crossing lines they had no intention of ever crossing. They'll bring other people down when they fall."

"I know, Nanny," I'd insist reassuringly. "I can tell the difference."

"*Good people*," she'd emphasize, peering at me with a hinting expression in her eyes.

Nanny was always on my side, though. She had faith and confidence in me and never directly questioned my decisions.

I told my mother and Nanny not to worry. I knew what I was doing.

8

LEADING PANTHERS

"Free Huey Newton!"

It was the battle cry of the Black Panther Party. In September 1968, about a month before I joined, minister of defense and Party cofounder Huey P. Newton began serving a two-to-fifteen-year sentence for allegedly killing a police officer. He pleaded not guilty to the charge of murder and told his side of the story in court. From what I understood, two Oakland officers had stopped Huey without cause as he and a friend, Gene McKinney, were driving to a Party fund-raiser. Recognizing that he was a Black Panther, they called him a bunch of racist names, pulled out their weapons, and began shooting. Huey defended himself, and when the battle ended, one of the officers was dead, the other seriously wounded, and Huey had been shot in the stomach. Based on some of the stuff that had already gone down with the pigs throughout the United States, I had no trouble believing Huey's version of events. Now he was in jail—a political prisoner, convicted for defending himself and his political beliefs. As comrades, it was our job to set him free.

Raising money for Huey's appeal and legal defense had been an important part of Party work. As a matter of fact, soon after his indictment, comrades from the national office such as Chairman Bobby Seale and Chief of Staff David Hilliard had traveled throughout the country organizing with local chapters and speaking at Free Huey events. A rally and fund-raiser had been scheduled at the Los Angeles Sports Arena on February 18, 1968, just one day after an Oakland celebration of Huey's twenty-sixth birthday.

I remember being excited about going; I believed I would learn a lot more about the Party and its philosophy, helping me to decide whether it really was an organization I should join. There was a lot of buzz about it in the community. I made arrangements with Louis, my BSU partner, to ride with me. I got up that morning full of anticipation. When it was time to go, I pulled on my Levi's and a dark blue T-shirt, grabbed my ski jacket, and was out the door. I stopped and picked up Louis, and we cruised in my low-rider over to the Los Angeles Sports Arena.

Walking into the Sports Arena that day, I was not disappointed: we witnessed an inspiring demonstration of black unity, and the energy was palpable. I remember what a dazzling sight it was: thousands of beautiful black people, a sea of Afros and bright colors. Members of the Black Panther Party were conspicuous, standing proud and dressed in black leather coats, light blue shirts, and berets. Pictures of Huey Newton were everywhere. Posters, buttons, and T-shirts were being sold, and Panthers were collecting donations. Right in the mix was a heavy presence of guns, signifying the Party's open commitment to self-defense. It was a definitive day for me, pushing me another step closer toward becoming a Panther.

During the event, an exceptional group of black power leaders spoke to the importance of Huey Newton and the Black Panther Party. Even from far away, Eldridge Cleaver was an imposing sight, standing about six foot five and broad-shouldered. He electrified the crowd as he discussed the system that oppressed all of us and then called on us to defend ourselves. SNCC activists H. Rap Brown and

Stokely Carmichael had recently joined the Black Panther Party, and they spoke to the issue of solidarity among movement activists. The crowd was pulsating, as people were taking everything in and cheering on the speakers. Other speakers included Ron Karenga and James Forman, both of whom had helped to organize the event, along with members of the Black Congress. It was a great coming together of revolutionary organizations, and I was glad to be in the room with all of them. It was a moving day, and I left the rally believing we were ready for freedom!

The Free Huey Newton Rally that day also signified the "coming-out" of the Southern California chapter. Now the local group could move from being underground to being a recognizable organization, in full operation and ready to challenge the power structure. It was officially live and would be the first fully organized chapter of the Party outside of Northern California.

The great success of the rally also led to substantially increased membership in the chapter. Soon college students, former gang members, and all levels of the working classes—people who were fed up with police brutality and oppression—became members. The Southern California chapter consisted first of Los Angeles and then spread all the way south to San Diego, north to Fresno, west to Riverside, and beyond. Several of my friends from the Slausons even joined; they were already rooted in the neighborhood and ready to be recruited. At that point, however, I had been impressed but not ready to make the commitment. I was going to school and leading the BSU at Harbor. And I was still trying to hit every party I could in the Los Angeles basin.

About a week after the rally, Baba and I were hanging out at Jerry's house after school. The establishment of the Southern California chapter had created a lot of excitement in the community, and we were still talking about the rally and the energy and the possibilities that we had seen from that experience.

Jerry lit a joint, took a big toke, and passed it to Baba.

Leaning back in my chair, I pondered out loud, "All of us know that the community desperately needs a force to take it forward."

"Mm—yeah?" Baba squeaked out as he inhaled.

"We need someone who can educate but also inspire people to get involved," I continued. "There's not a single person on the scene right now who does that better than Huey Newton, and his ass is in jail. That's a bad mother right there," I finished, taking the joint from Baba.

Jerry had gotten up and gone into the kitchen, where he was busy pulling food from the fridge so we could make some sandwiches. "Yeah, I hear what you're saying," he hollered out. "Anybody who rolls around with law books in his car, pulling them out to school some damn pig, is definitely on another level."

I handed the joint back to Baba.

"That's all well and good," Baba countered, "but how is that different from what the Community Alert Patrol has been doing here for years? That ain't nothing new."

"CAP is doing good work," I answered. "But nobody outside of L.A. knows they exist. Huey is a national and even international symbol of defiance against the entire system. Did you see all those people at the rally? Multiply that by some more, because that same excitement is bubbling up in other places right now as our black asses speak."

Jerry walked back into the room with all the fixings for sandwiches: bread, bologna, salami, mustard, mayo, and sliced cheese. "Huey seems to be the right man for the right time," he said, "but I don't want us to turn this into some kind of hero-worshipping cult. We've been down that fucked-up road before." He put the plate down. Baba and I both dove in. "This is about organization," Jerry continued thoughtfully. "This is about the blueprint for revolution that must be accepted by all the people, not just a few."

"I think the pattern of this being bigger than one person is already in place," I observed. "You've got Chairman Bobby Seale giving a good balance to Huey. He speaks to the issues on a grassroots level where people can understand it. Seale also got some guts too. Seale led the move against Ronald Reagan and the Mulford Act [a 1967 law prohibiting the public carrying of firearms] by walking into the capitol in Sacramento armed to the teeth. Somebody needed to

94

confront those lawmakers, or let me change that to law *breakers*, who were trying to stop us from being able to defend ourselves against the pigs."

"How did those two meet anyway, Bobby and Huey?" asked Baba with a mouthful of food.

"They met at school," I answered, "on the campus of Merritt College in Oakland. They were both student organizers."

"People are getting fixated on Bobby and Huey, but it's actually Eldridge who's the baddest of 'em all," Jerry offered. "He's an elder in a way and has lived through a lot more than the other two. He knows, firsthand, what it is to live at the bottom. A decade spent in Folsom ain't no joke. I imagine one learns some serious shit from doing that kind of time. Probably more than you two jokers are learning at Harbor and Southwest," he chuckled sarcastically.

Baba and I both laughed.

"He ain't the minister of information for no reason," Jerry continued. "He's the real deal. Let's not forget that Eldridge is from L.A., and he's the one who schooled Bunchy on the Party."

Jerry went on to explain that Bunchy and Eldridge met when they were both doing time at Soledad State Prison, when Bunchy was in for bank robbery. At first Bunchy had rejected the Party. But after visiting Eldridge in Oakland and learning more about the Party's program, Bunchy changed his mind.

Baba looked at Jerry. "I don't know what kind of 'good' balance Eldridge is," he argued. "The word on the vine is that fool be actually raping sisters. What kind of example is that for a revolutionary?"

"No shit?" I said, surprised.

Baba frowned. "That's the stuff we're trying to stop in our community, committing crimes against our own people. How is anyone going to call himself a revolutionary but then commit rape? What kind of shit is that?" he asked incredulously.

The three of us fell silent, not knowing what on earth to say or think about the charge that Baba had just leveled against the minister of information.

Finally, Jerry broke the silence. "Well, maybe he's a wiser man now. Perhaps all that time in prison changed him. I know we can't justify his shit, but hell, life is tough. We all carry some demons, and at some point hopefully we get the upper hand on them."

Inside the Party, Eldridge was known as Papa because of his age. When I joined at the age of nineteen, Eldridge was thirty-three, almost twice my age. We considered him an elder who had more experience than almost everybody in the Party when dealing with "the man." As a member of the rank and file, I never got the chance to sit down and talk with Eldridge, but I admired him nonetheless. He could speak well, write well, hold it down with the ladies, and he didn't take no shit off of whitey and the pigs.

After I joined, one of my roles as a Panther was to work with the security and advance team at our rallies, festivals, and fund-raisers. Long John Washington trained me on the art of security, which meant I had to check out the locations before the rally, make note of where the lights and exits were, and determine if doors anywhere were locked. I also had to be primed for the possibility of violence. Long John or Ronald Freeman would check my weapons sometimes, making sure they worked. Working so closely with them, I found they became my mentors, and they tried to make sure us new cats weren't put in dangerous situations. Long John also told me to watch myself, and that I could voice my concerns to him. If I had a beef with other Panthers or outside organizations, I could share that with Long John or Ronald and they would deal with it.

Because I came into the Party with knowledge of guns, I didn't receive a lot of weapons training. But we new guys all had to spend time learning about self-defense tactics, which I was always happy to do. At each office, comrades had to take time to break down guns, clean them, and make sure they were in good working order.

At the Watts office, I mainly worked with Al and Lux on guns. One day while we were cleaning some of our guns, I shared my philosophy on the topic. "You see this piece of iron right here?" I announced to Al, Lux, and James. "This is the real passport to freedom and respect. People got it twisted by thinking that it's money. Nah, man, nah. It's actually this steel right here."

"I agree," said Al. "But freedom comes with responsibility," he continued solemnly. "This freedom right here ain't no plaything at all. One squeeze means life or death—to one or to many. But I know I'm preaching to the choir. Wayne, I'm glad you're here to help us build up our strength in this area. It's critical that we are able to show people how they can stand up."

"Wouldn't have it no other way," I said.

Most Panther rallies were on college campuses or at parks, with lots of speakers. We saw rallies as recruiting tools for the party. A lot of white kids came to our rallies too. We saw that as a good thing, because we needed to educate white folks on how and why they needed to engage in revolutionary activity along with us. The police, of course, were always around as well—on foot, in cars, or in helicopters flying over us. They took a lot of pictures. It was at these events that we would likely wear black leather coats and berets. Otherwise, we rarely wore those uniforms, because it almost guaranteed harassment from the police.

It was because of my role in security and as part of the advance team that I was able to get a glimpse of Eldridge Cleaver up close. One time in particular I got to see a lot of him: when he campaigned for the presidency in late 1968 on the platform of the Peace and Freedom Party. He came to Los Angeles to speak—some white activists whom we partnered with to fight against the Vietnam War led the Peace and Freedom Party—and they kept me busy in my security role as we traveled from location to location campaigning. It was during that campaign that I really understood how effective Eldridge was at articulating the position of the Party. He could masterfully curse in a way that wouldn't turn people off—now that's an art form.

I remember one day when I was on his security detail he took the podium and let loose. There he stood before the packed house of a majority-white audience in his black leather coat. Minister Cleaver didn't flinch or try to be someone he was not. He just said it as he saw

Deputy Minister of Information John Huggins (far right) leads Los Angeles Black Panthers in a military style drill at a Free Huey Rally at Bobby Hutton Park in Oakland. The shirts were designed by Deputy Minister of Defense Bunchy Carter. COURTESY OF IT'S ABOUT TIME ARCHIVES

it. "We see the world as being divided into two types," he exhorted; "there's the people, and then there's the pigs. People tell me that Ronald Reagan says the Black Panther Party for Self-Defense is racist." The crowd literally roared at the notion of Ronald Reagan having the gall to call someone else racist. "The Black Panther Party is not racist," he continued. "We want *all* people to be free. It's just that either we're going to be free or nobody's going to be free. Wanting to be free from pigs having their damn foot on your neck is not being racist. It's being rational. It's having common sense. It's wanting the full life that you were put here to live."

The entire audience stood up and cheered. It was a great speech, and I was lucky enough to be right there. The man knew how to engage a crowd!

Some of the naysayers in the community couldn't understand why Eldridge would waste his time running for an office he couldn't win. In our political education classes, Al Armour addressed that issue directly. "What's important for you all to understand, and understand clearly, is that this is one of the most racist elections of recent times," Al explained. "On one hand, you got this Tricky Dick character running on law and order, scaring white folks into voting for him. On the other hand, you have the door-blocker George Wallace, who actually tried to prevent black students from attending the University of Alabama, a school their families' tax dollars help to run."

"Hubert Humphrey, even though he's not for the war, don't stand a chance against them racists," somebody declared.

"One of the reasons he doesn't is because he don't have enough fire in his torch," I responded forcefully. "What's needed in the mix is a voice that's sharp, powerful, and yet eloquent, like the minister of information for the Black Panther Party, Eldridge Cleaver."

"That's all well and good, but Cleaver definitely don't stand a chance in a presidential election either," said a sister as she stood up in the back of the room. "Especially if even a white man who's been vice president don't stand a chance." The conversation was escalating.

"To win, for our purposes, is to raise the level of consciousness of the people," I replied, feeling my own adrenaline kicking in.

A number of people around the room murmured in agreement of my point.

I was standing now too. "It's to broaden awareness of issues and highlight glaring contradictions in this whole Wizard of Oz fairy tale called United Capitalist of America," I declared. "Minister Cleaver is running for that very reason."

It was very important to us Panthers that everyday people understood the importance of analysis and dialogue, which leads to a deeper grasp of issues. While not everyone left the classroom that day in agreement, they did have their eyes opened a little more, had more food for thought.

I was thankful I had that chance to provide security for Eldridge, because he disappeared shortly thereafter. In late November, a few days before he was required to turn himself in to the authorities to serve time for a parole violation, Eldridge went underground. The next time we heard from Eldridge, he was in Cuba.

Although Eldridge played a major role in the Party, we didn't suffer because of his absence or that of any individual Party leader. Huey was in jail, and Bobby had done time around the Sacramento incident, but we kept moving. It was understood that at any time, any one of us could be jailed or killed for challenging the system. We were now too busy with the important work of the Party to appropriately mourn the loss of a comrade. Selling newspapers, attending political education classes, weapons training, and meeting and training the hundreds of new recruits joining the Party was a twenty-four-hour, seven-day-a-week commitment.

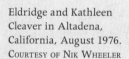

Eldridge and Kathleen
Cleaver in Altadena,
California, August 1976.
COURTESY OF NIK WHEELER

9

DIVIDE AND CONQUER

I was a comrade in a national revolutionary organization but still naive about the dangers that might come about because of our willingness to confront the system. One thing I knew for sure was that whatever came my way, I could count on my comrades to have my back. But on New Year's Day 1969, my confidence was shaken, and suddenly I found myself questioning the bond that held the Black Panther Party together.

It was bright and sunny that day, so Tyrone and I decided to hang out at the All Nations Pool Hall on Broadway. We agreed to meet there, and when I arrived, I saw him standing outside waiting for me.

I immediately knew something was up with Tyrone. The first thing I noticed was his gloomy demeanor. I thought to myself, *Maybe he has some bad news.*

"Captain Franco is dead," Tyrone said as I walked up.

Dumbfounded, I just stared at him, trying to wrap my head around the news.

"They found him in an alley in Long Beach, with three bullets in his head."

"What the fuck! Who did it?" I said angrily at Tyrone.

"Nobody seems to know. It could have been the pigs, but I don't know. Some say it was agents."

"Do you know why?" This seemed senseless, and even though I knew it had nothing to do with Tyrone, his response made me angrier.

Tyrone shrugged his shoulders, signaling that he had no answers. I waited for more dialogue on Franco, but it wasn't coming. I calmed myself down, and we walked into the pool hall.

Captain Franco had been the leader of a small squad of three to four people. Actually, Long John worked under him. He was older than most of us, by about ten years. He had served more than a decade in Sing Sing, a notorious prison in New York, for armed robbery and attempted murder. Sing Sing was well known for its high number of executions, including that of Ethel and Julius Rosenberg, who had been convicted of espionage—a conviction that helped fuel Joseph McCarthy's campaign against "anti-American activities" in the 1950s. Captain Franco had experience and knowledge that were very valuable to the organization, and he used those skills to train Party members on how to avoid getting killed. He was also the leader of the Party's local underground apparatus in Southern California, teaching Panthers how to rob and steal to liberate resources on behalf of the community. Sometimes Franco could be inappropriate, but you couldn't deny that he was committed.

Tyrone's news threw me into deep thought. I hadn't had much contact with the Captain after I joined, because I was mainly in Watts and working with the BSU. Franco operated out of Broadway and spent a lot of time at headquarters with G and Bunchy. However, in that moment of realization that he was gone, my mind flashed back to the times I had listened to Franco's diatribes, mostly revolving around how he wanted to kill as many white people as possible, before they killed us. "I'm finishing up what Nat Turner started," he liked to boast. Franco truly understood the enemy.

How the hell did they get him, of all people? I wondered to myself. It was unnerving.

Over the next few days, stories about Franco's death started flying around from everywhere. Some thought he was an agent provocateur because of his advocacy of killing white people. Franco's open hatred for white folks, it was said, was bringing heat to the Party.

Eventually, more facts surfaced: apparently FBI agents had put him in a no-win situation that was bound to get him killed, while at the same time creating more confusion and dissension within the Party. It was the age-old war tactic of divide and conquer. Shortly before his death, Captain Franco had been arrested for armed robbery after leading the police on a high-speed chase. Shortly after the arrest, he was mysteriously released without charges being filed, which led some Panthers to say that he had snitched. How else could he have just walked away from that kind of situation with no consequences? It was hard for comrades to accept.

Franco, for his part, had begun to feel like he had been set up. In fact, on the night before he died, he told Roland Freeman, a Panther out of Broadway and the brother of Ronald Freeman, that he was feeling like some of the leadership no longer trusted him. Roland had pressed Franco on the matter. "That's some deep shit you're saying there. Maybe you're just paranoid," Roland told him that night.

I thought to myself that there should be an effort to avenge Franco's murder. But it never happened. Neither was there any real investigation; at least that was the rumor. I heard that G had been questioned by the police about Captain Franco's murder, but that was it. No witnesses ever came forward. I decided not to go to the funeral, because I didn't want to be viewed as going outside of what appeared to be the conventional view that Franco had turned snitch. But the matter of Franco's murder weighed on me for days.

Eventually, though, the discussion around Franco's death subsided, the needs of day-to-day business demanded our attention, and we went back to work. Ironically, a year after Captain Franco's death, the bullets found in his body were supposedly matched with a 9-millimeter automatic pistol that was seized in a raid of one of the Party's headquarters. Some of my comrades were stunned, while others believed that the police had planted the bullets or just lied. But for me, it wasn't a head-twister at all. I had already concluded that the police had not murdered Captain Franco. It was an inside job, and I felt it was a dirty deed. I wasn't sure who had given the order, nor did I know how high up the chain of command the matter had gone. Was it a directive from the leadership of the Southern California chapter, or was the Central Committee in Oakland involved? One thing I knew for sure: my grandmother's words of caution were echoing more stridently in my ears. It was like a prophet foretelling that which was to come: "Wayne, watch your back." I wasn't paranoid, but I began to seriously watch those around me. It was no time to sleep.

Although I thought the Party had taken out Captain Franco, I felt relatively secure in my relationships with comrades in Watts and on Broadway. I rationalized Captain Franco's death by concluding that he might have died soon anyway. He wanted to kill white people so badly at times that he would have always been a risk to himself and the Party. Captain Franco was not destined to live a long life. The primary threat to the security of the Black Panther Party and the black community came in the form of blue uniforms and tailored suits. At the time, I didn't think that a real life-and-death threat would come from other black liberation organizations. But I was wrong.

The Us Organization, a group that also saw itself as the vanguard in the struggle for black liberation, was willing to fight and kill for that title. Ronald Everett, a migrant from Maryland who had come to Los Angeles in 1958, led Us. He was short and stocky with light nut-brown skin and was known for his ability to articulate important ideas. But he did so with a high-pitched voice that I found irritating. He attended Los Angeles Community College (LACC) and University of California, Los Angeles (UCLA). People knew him as Ron Everett, a student activist, until he changed his last name to Karenga. As he became more confident in his gifts and talents, he changed his first

name to Maulana, which means "master teacher" in Swahili. Maulana Karenga founded Us in 1965 in Los Angeles with several known
movement leaders including Hakim Jamal, a cousin of Malcolm X,
and Tommy Jacquette, an activist who helped to establish the Watts
Summer Festival. The founders of the group named it the Us Organization, as opposed to *them*—white people. Their early meetings were
held at a black-owned bookstore called Aquarius, but they eventually moved into their own building in 1967. Infighting and ideological disagreements caused the group to fragment; when it was over,
Maulana Karenga was its leader.

My own encounters with Us were minimal prior to joining the
Party. They promoted Afrocentric ideas, wore dashikis, and advo-
cated Swahili as an alternative language for black people. The men
wore shaved heads, and the women sported their hair in large Afros.
One major component of their program was changing Christmas to
Kwanzaa.

The group was organized in paramilitary fashion like the Fruit
of Islam (FOI), the security wing of the Nation of Islam. Us's soldiers
were known as Simba Wachangas, which meant "young lions." I was
impressed with their martial arts program and weapons training, but
I didn't like how they tried to come off as too hard, too angry, and
too uniform in their stoic looks. Hell, they were less friendly than the
FOI, and that's really saying something.

I wasn't afraid of them Us niggas, but I never felt comfortable
around them, either, because they were overimposing and worked
hard at putting out the vibe that a fight could jump off at any time. In
early 1968, I had attended a rally organized by Us at Green Meadows
Park on Eighty-Eighth and Avalon. As I walked through the park, I
took note of the Simbas, looking mean as usual, wearing sunglasses
and dashikis. I listened to their ideas, which were cool, but I wasn't
down with their robotic feel. Like the Nation of Islam, they all looked
and dressed the same and all parroted the words of their spokesperson. I decided then that I didn't need to get any closer to Us, because
it seemed to me like they were scripted, blind, and brainwashed.

After I became a Panther, I didn't even think about Us unless someone brought them up.

In activist circles, criticisms of Us were becoming common. The first person who complained to me directly, and with great emotion, was Mrs. Ventress, the mother of Shay-vee, a beautiful young lady I met at Harbor College. Shay-vee and I had started hanging out together. We became so close that she invited me to her home to meet her mother, who she told me was a community activist. Mrs. Ventress was a member of the local chapter of the Congress of Racial Equality, CORE for short. She was a smart lady who wore her hair in an Afro and spoke a lot about black consciousness. I liked Mrs. Ventress because she reached out to young people and tried to build up our self-esteem.

One day while I was visiting Shay-vee, Mrs. Ventress called me into the kitchen, where she was sewing. I came in and sat down at the table, careful to keep my good manners.

"Let me tell you something, Wayne," she began. "The older folks in the community don't like the way that Karenga and the Us people act."

I sat and watched her, nodding my head as she talked and sewed.

She continued, as I took note of the serious look on her face. "They feel uncomfortable with all the arrogance, scowling, and cold looks coming from them."

I nodded attentively, letting her know I understood.

"And then they try to dictate and impose their ways on us elders and the nonviolent groups, like the NAACP and SCLC. Ain't nobody gonna trust them if they act like we're a bunch of sheep!"

"Yes, ma'am," I responded.

Mrs. Ventress continued to sew and talk. "Maulana Karenga is trying to force all of the Black Congress to accept his teachings, but we don't even understand his name."

"Really?" I chuckled.

"Yes!" she exclaimed, her arms waving vigorously in the air. "Karenga is a bully with an oversized ego who is trying to control all the activism in Los Angeles."

I nodded as my eyes widened, taking her message in.

"You Panthers need to step in and stop them from intimidating people and dictating to our groups." She was adamant.

Mrs. Ventress was referring to all the groups that belonged to the Black Congress, an umbrella organization for civil rights and black power groups such as the NAACP, SCLC, CORE and CAP, the L.A. Black Panthers, the Watts Happening Coffee House, and the Freedom Draft Movement. The Black Congress also included socialist organizations like the United Front and organizations that emphasized black liberation like the Republic of New Afrika (RNA), Nation of Islam, and the Us Organization. Some organizations combined many of those ideologies but also pushed self-defense, like we did. Individual activists like Caffee Green would also attend the Black Congress meetings.

The Black Congress was an organization of groups, but it was also a building known by the same name. It was a medium-sized two-story stucco affair with a brick foundation, located at Broadway and Florence. Small rooms used as offices for each group divided the bottom floor, and there was a larger room where classes and meetings were held.

I was aware of the Black Congress years before I became a Black Panther, because it was in our neighborhood. For me, the Black Congress was similar to the Aquarius Bookstore, a place where we would go to buy a book or hear a speech. I had visited the Congress a few times to pick up flyers and hear presentations. I liked what I perceived as camaraderie within the Congress organizations: there was always a vibe of black consciousness when I visited.

The Black Panther Party of Southern California used space at the Black Congress building as its headquarters when it was first established. The location was beneficial to the new organization because people interested in the Party could pick up some up-to-date information or stay to listen to one of Bunchy's speeches. Being affiliated with the Black Congress also meant that the Party had relationships with other activist groups, and could coordinate work and support each other—except for Us and the Panthers, who did not get along.

The animosity between the Black Panther Party and Us began during the time when they both held offices at the Black Congress. In February 1967, the same month of the rally at the Sports Arena, Bunchy located space at 4115 Central Avenue and moved the Party from the Black Congress to its new Central Headquarters. Because the organization was growing so quickly, Bunchy soon opened up a second office in my neighborhood, on Eighty-Fourth and Broadway. But that didn't do anything to abate the feud between the two organizations.

I was still new to the organization and had a lot of questions about the enmity between the two. One day, I was hanging out with Russell Washington, helping him distribute newspapers, still trying to figure out why the Panthers and Us didn't get along. I decided to query Russell flat-out. As a lady was walking away with a paper I had just sold her, I turned and looked at him.

"Comrade Russell," I said bluntly, "why is there so much friction between Us and the Panthers?"

He considered me for a moment. "Because *we* are revolutionaries who understand political struggle and practice dialectic materialism," he replied matter-of-factly.

"Of course," I said with a shrug.

"Karenga and Us are pork-chop cultural nationalists," he continued, "who look down on the masses because they don't wear African clothes or speak Swahili. But we embrace the masses, even if they're wearing their hair conked and don't speak anything but street slang."

I nodded my head. "Right on," I smiled.

Russell began to laugh. "Karenga got pissed off when Bunchy used some of the money we got from the Sports Arena to open up headquarters," he snickered.

I was surprised when he said that, but I decided to avoid asking questions about the issue of money. Also, I knew it wasn't my territory, but I was still curious about the differences between Us and the Panthers on the question of working with white people. At Harbor, some of the students who supported the BSU were white. They weren't members, but they would contribute and help us organize events on campus. I knew that Us refused to work with whites, while the Black Panther Party saw whites and other races as important to the struggle.

I went ahead and asked Russell about the issue.

"Those fools got the wrong idea about what we should all be doing," he responded sharply. "They're so caught up in racism that they can't see the wisdom of people like Mao Tse-Tung and Karl Marx, because they aren't black. They don't understand that capitalism is a big problem for all people."

"OK, comrade, I can dig that," I replied. We studied the teachings of both Mao and Marx extensively in PE classes. Russell filled in a lot of the blanks for me that day.

The Panthers and Us also engaged in different recruitment methods and ways of motivating people to work to free black people. The Us Organization came off like gangsters, attempting to force people and entire organizations to accept their philosophy. But our approach was much smoother, using conversation to show people the righteousness of our program. We also demonstrated our philosophy through political activism and met people wherever they were in their political growth. We didn't take the position that *everybody* had to be in the Panther Party; we wanted to give people free will.

Despite its differences with Us, the Black Panther Party put up a united front within the black community. But our disagreements were getting more intense daily, especially when student groups would ask us to intercede because the Simbas were showing up at their meetings trying to strong-arm them into accepting leadership from Us.

As Russell and I came to the end of our day selling papers, he stopped and looked at me squarely. "We know that Us has been trying to run the show on some campuses. Are you having to deal with them Us niggas at Harbor?"

"At Harbor? Nah, we don't have any trouble with Us," I assured him. "They know we accept Malcolm's philosophy of working with all people who are against capitalism and imperialism. Plus, I don't think Us wants to spend the gas money to come all the way out there and try to influence us."

Russell laughed at that. "OK, let me know if you start having trouble," he said.

"Right on, brother," I said, acknowledging his concern.

While they did at least try, the Panthers' and Us Organization's attempts at peace were always short-lived. I had heard that Ronald Freeman became involved in some serious conflicts with Us, so when I saw him, I asked him what had happened in that incident.

"Well," Ronald answered with a frown, "Comrade Sherwin, who was hanging with us from Oakland, had come to L.A. to check us out when we were at the Congress. He needed to go to the bathroom at some point, but the only way he could get there was to walk through a room where some of the Us members were practicing martial arts. The Simbas wouldn't allow the brother to walk through a room to get to the bathroom!"

I shook my head. "So what happened?" I asked.

Ronald continued. "He called me. So I met him there, and we walked on through the room to the bathroom, which the Simbas saw as a challenge." He shook his head. "They were heated!"

I could see where this was going. "Then what?" I said.

"One of the Simbas pulled a gun on me, so Sherwin pulled a gun on them. No one in the room showed fear, but I know some hearts were beating faster, and there was cold sweat flowing. In the midst of the stalemate, one of the Us members walked out and made a phone call. He came back, and they put away their guns.

"Was that it?" I asked, surprised.

"Hell no!" he said quickly. "Later that evening, one of them Us niggas came to my house and knocked on the door. When I answered they started shooting, and bullets came flying through the door! We defended ourselves and had a damn shoot-out at my house! Our only casualty was our Oakland comrade, who got shot in the hand. Even to this day, we don't know if we hit any of the Karangatangs. And dig this: even though the Karangatangs came to *my* house to shoot it up, the pigs arrested *me*. Then, when Roland came home after everything was over, they arrested him too! And he wasn't even there!"

"Damn, that's fucked up," I frowned. "How are we going to deal with this kind of bullshit?"

As members of the Party, we were obligated to defend ourselves against violent attacks by any means necessary. And I intended to defend the Party, my comrades, and myself to the fullest.

This matter between the Panthers and Us was tricky, for sure. Ronald told me that at the leadership level, Karenga and Bunchy had several conversations about how to keep the peace between the two organizations. Bunchy didn't want disagreements with Us to look like gang fights or war between two black liberation groups. And to stress the point, during one of our meetings at Central Headquarters, Bunchy told us to keep our eyes on the real enemy, the pigs and the power structure. He told us to not let ourselves get sucked into petty conflicts with other activist organizations. He then issued an executive order mandating that we should avoid physical altercations with other black organizations, to ensure that we understood the importance of working through problems rather than drawing blood.

Bunchy's mandate, however, did not end the violent altercations. It couldn't, because Us didn't adhere to a similar mandate. So, while Panthers attempted to avoid confrontations with Us and other black groups, others didn't share the commitment to a nonviolent relationship with the Black Panther Party.

The Panther-Us conflict reached its highest level of violence in January 1969, when the Black Student Union at UCLA objected to Ron Karenga's efforts to dictate who would head a new black studies program at their university. The Black Panther Party had strong ties to the students there because a number of our members, including Al, Lux, Bunchy, John Huggins, G, and Elaine Brown, were all registered students in UCLA's High Potential Program. High Potential was set up to open the admissions process to disadvantaged youth. After UCLA administrators proposed a black studies program, the

Karenga-backed candidate to head black studies drew opposition from students in the BSU. They organized to fight for their voices to be heard, calling several meetings to discuss their concerns and determine how to proceed with administration. Some of the students asked Panthers who were attending UCLA to be present at the meetings because of their fear of retaliation from Us.

This brought together a volatile combination of interests, resulting in one of the most devastating encounters in Black Panther history. It was this conflict—among Us, the BSU, and the Black Panther Party—around black studies at UCLA that changed the trajectory of black power politics in Los Angeles forever. At a BSU meeting in Campbell Hall at UCLA on January 17, Bunchy Carter and John Huggins were shot and killed by members of Us.

On that infamous day, I began my day in the usual manner. I headed off to Harbor and went to class. After I left school, I went to Jerry's to hang out. We were eating when Baba walked into the house. He looked dazed. "Bunchy and John are dead," he said numbly.

There was a pause for a few seconds, and none of us said anything. Yes, I heard him, but it didn't register in my brain. So I just stared at him.

"What do you mean, Bunchy is dead?" Jerry blurted.

"There was some kind of meeting at UCLA, and there was a shootout. Bunchy and John got killed," Baba replied sadly, still looking like he was in a state of shock. We were all in a state of shock.

Even though I trusted Baba, I still didn't believe him. Bunchy was our symbol of strength and power, so maybe he got shot and wounded, but he wasn't dead! No way. Not Bunchy!

Jerry turned on the TV and then turned the channel until he found the news. We all sat down on the couch, glued to the set, listening to the breaking news report in disbelief. It was being reported, just as Baba said, on CBS. *Three members of Us, after a BSU meeting, around 2:40 this afternoon, shot Alprentice Carter and John Huggins.* It was unbelievable!

I decided to make a few phone calls to find out what happened. The first person I reached was Larry Scales at the office in Watts. "What's happening?"

Larry responded gloomily, "Tomorrow you need to definitely be here, so we can deal with this. The word from G and Long John is that we don't need to say anything individually. They are in touch with Bobby and David in Oakland. They want us to respond with one voice."

"Understood," I said. "I know we need to stay focused. But does anybody know the next move that might come from Us?"

Larry paused a moment and then cleared his throat. "Well, you know that all the comrades who were at UCLA, plus a few others, have already been arrested."

"What?" I said, surprised.

"The pigs claim that they're just trying to prevent anyone from retaliating and causing more bloodshed."

I asked Larry if any of Karenga's boys were arrested, and he said he didn't know. I decided to lay low.

Baba, Jerry, and I spent that evening talking about Bunchy and John. Bunchy's brother Arthur Glenn Morris had already been killed, on March 13, 1968, in a friend's backyard. Nobody really knows what happened because the other two men involved in the murder died in the shooting too. Morris was a Panther and served as Bunchy's bodyguard. Damn, we felt really bad for Bunchy's mother.

No one could sleep. We talked and talked. How in the hell could Bunchy and John get killed with all of the other Party members in the room we asked each other. G, Nathaniel Clark, Al Armour, Joe Brown, Joan Kelly, and a few others had been up there that day. I was sure everybody was armed. How could this have happened?

The next morning, I went straight to the Watts office, where I met up with James, Larry, and Lux. We sat around the office and went over what had just happened, at first expressing our emotions, which ranged from anger to sadness to a desire for revenge. I was ready to put my foot, plus a .48 caliber pistol, in the ass of Karenga and all of them Us niggas. We began to strategize the many ways we could blast them motherfuckas. As we were going over the possible plans, Long John came by the office. He quietly listened in for a few minutes. Then, with a wretched but stern look on his face, he admonished us not to engage in any independent action against Us. Comrades at the top would handle the matter.

The next day, we found out the background on what happened at UCLA: Long John came by the office again and reported what he knew. Apparently, a member of Us, Harold "Tuwala" Jones, was accosting Elaine Brown, and in her defense, word was that John Huggins pulled his gun. But some Us nigga by the name of Claude "Chuchessa" Hubert shot John in the back. Hubert also shot Bunchy in the chest.

Bunchy and John died two feet from each other in a blaze of bullets not from the pigs or the power structure but from a conflict with another activist organization. We knew there was much more to the story.

Alprentice "Bunchy" Carter, deputy minister of defense, Southern California Chapter, BPP, martyred January 17, 1969. COURTESY OF IT'S ABOUT TIME ARCHIVES

10

ALPHA AND OMEGA

I had only been in the Party for three months when Bunchy and John were murdered and Captain Franco was killed. Just a few months earlier, the police had murdered Tommie, Steve, and Robert in broad daylight. I knew it was time to check in with my family to let them know I was OK.

I walked into my mother's house and found her in the family room watching TV. It seemed eerily quiet. I walked over to her and kissed her on the cheek. "Mom, how are you?"

She didn't answer my question but asked me wearily, "Are you all right? I've been watching the news."

"I'm cool, Mom. I just wanted to let you know that everything is fine with me. You don't need to worry."

"Where were you when those boys were killed?"

"I was at school."

"Good. That's where you need to be. You know I really want you to leave the Panthers alone. At least for now, while there's so much violence."

I didn't say anything. I just looked at her and then got up and headed for the kitchen to get something to eat. She followed me in there, and we sat for a while and made small talk about the family. By the time I left, she seemed to be OK, although I knew she was still concerned.

Later that day, I called Nanny and got the same response from her that I received from my mom. The next conversation I needed to have was with Sharon, the other important woman in my life. So I called her up and asked her if I could stop by. As it turned out, I ended up liking Sharon even more after our conversation. She knew that my involvement with the Party could put me in danger, but she also understood my commitment. She didn't need to be educated about why I remained in the Party, because she was active in the BSU at Washington High. Unlike other women who would have immediately asked me to withdraw, Sharon told me that we would stand together.

On the day of Bunchy's funeral, we all rode to the church caravan style, stopping traffic along the way. The funeral was held at Trinity Baptist Church on Jefferson Boulevard. James and I rode together in my car, mostly in silence. It rained that day, but the sun was shining too. Chairman Bobby Seale did the eulogy, and Chief of Staff David Hilliard spoke as well. Although the service was sad, it still contained the revolutionary fervor of the Party—even bolstered it. After the funeral, we went to Woodlawn Cemetery in Compton to bury our comrade. I felt sorry for Evon Carter, Bunchy's wife, who I learned later was pregnant at the time. As for John Huggins, his body was shipped back to New Haven, Connecticut. Ericka and their baby went with him. Bunchy and John were so young when they were murdered: Bunchy was twenty-six and John was twenty-three.

After the funeral, a large contingent of us went to the Panther apartment on Main Street to get a grip on the gaping emptiness we were suddenly left with and to pay homage to our fallen comrades.

A heavy sense of grief and melancholy gripped the air. We drank Panther Piss; we told stories. I wished that I had spent more time at Central Headquarters so that I could have worked more closely with Bunchy and John.

David Hilliard and Bobby Seale visited Los Angeles to keep us encouraged, and they helped us to reorganize. There was no question that Bunchy and John would have wanted us to get back to work immediately. To help close the gaps left by the loss of our leaders, other comrades were moved into new positions. G became the deputy minister of defense, which had been Bunchy's position. He would now lead the Southern California chapter. Elaine Brown was appointed to the position of deputy chairman, while Paul Moffett became the deputy minister of information, taking the place of John. Others maintained their positions, like Blue, Long John, and Ronald Freeman, who remained field secretaries.

Some animosities developed because some of the members thought that they should have been given the chance to play a much larger role after the reorganization. Julius "Julio" Butler, a section leader who ran the West Adams office, was one of those disgruntled. He had hoped to move up to one of the minister positions. Long John called him an "old-man hairdresser" and said I should stay away from Julio because he was strange as hell.

"What makes him so strange?" I asked, amused at his description.

"He had a few younger comrades kill some cats and dogs to prove that they could kill. You ever heard of such bullshit?" Long John said with disgust.

"No, not really," I answered, a little disgusted myself. Then I asked, "So, then why is he in the Party?"

"I can't really answer that, but a lot of people say he might be an agent provocateur. I don't know. Bunchy had the ability to keep him in a cage where he could only do minimal damage."

I shrugged and nodded, thinking to myself that Long John was right. Stay away from that fool.

Long John continued, "But with Bunchy gone, we need to watch him closely."

I nodded in agreement.

In addition to the leadership changes, our membership base began to change. Some of our people just stopped coming around. That didn't bother me, because I thought we had too many "dress-up Panthers" and "black leather coat suckers" in the Party. These were the fake revolutionaries who would show up for rallies and try to look like a Panther but never put in any measurable work. After the Us killings, those niggas understood that being a Black Panther was not about playing games; it wasn't the BSU; and it definitely wasn't styling and profiling: it was black liberation.

Some people actually got expelled too. Shermont was spokesperson for the L.A. branch, so he had been appointed to make public statements on behalf of Bunchy and the Party. Bunchy didn't want the press and the public to fixate on his criminal past, which could throw shade onto the Party, and Shermont came off sounding like a bourgeois college student, so his presence made the Party look better in the press. After Bunchy passed, though, Shermont faded away into oblivion. The last thing I heard about him was that he had been expelled.

Then there were those who disappeared who weren't asked to leave but whose commitment was shaky because of outside influences. People like Larry Scales, a Watts native and captain in the Party, just kind of drifted away; in Larry's case, many of us believed he left because he had gotten hooked on dope. It's hard to handle the commitment the Party required and to chase drugs at the same time.

The Central Committee was giving us more attention. In April, Chairman Bobby Seale again traveled to Los Angeles to meet with us and to reiterate the Central Committee's position that we should not engage in war with Us. We were reminded of Bunchy's mandate that we were not at war with other black people. Our fight was against the system of oppression, so we needed to honor Bunchy by not going to war with Us. While he was in town, Chairman Seale also spoke at

Los Angeles Trade Technical College to recruit and to inform people about the community service work of the Party, such as the Free Breakfast Program. I provided security for him during his visit.

Interestingly, as we attempted to put things back in order, people started demonstrating their love and support for Bunchy, John, and the Black Panther Party. Posters of Bunchy were showing up everywhere—on the walls at community centers, even in liquor stores—and his poems were being recited at major events. We hoped that this public attention would remind people of the ideas Bunchy stood for and to support the work he and John sacrificed their lives for.

However, I still wasn't satisfied with the explanations about what really went down at UCLA. I kept wondering how some suckers could just kill Bunchy Carter like that. Hell, Bunchy was the leader of the Renegade Slausons, the most dangerous gang in Los Angeles. No one could lead the Renegade Slausons without a serious edge, and Bunchy had that edge. He knew how to engage in warfare. Why wasn't there real muscle in the room with Bunchy and John when everything went down? Where were G, Al, and Nathaniel, the people who would have put some bullet holes into those Simbas and protected Bunchy and John? I needed some answers. I didn't want to find myself in a similar situation with some Simbas and no defense coming from my comrades.

In fact, Al was at UCLA the day Bunchy and John were killed. I asked Al, "Where was G when the shooting went down?"

Al told me that Bunchy had asked G to go and visit a friend at UCLA's Medical Center.

"But Al, that doesn't make sense to me. Why the hell would Bunchy do that, knowing how dangerous those Karangatangs were?

Al looked at me. "I can't get into Bunchy's head. The whole day was a little off to me."

What I believe happened played out like this: Bunchy and John are at a meeting. Elaine gets into an altercation with this Tuwala fool. Bunchy pulls her to the side, but John is trying to defend Elaine.

And of course John would do that, because he and Elaine were in a sexual relationship. John pulls a gun out, and Bunchy tries to defuse the situation, as always. But Bunchy didn't even have a gun because he didn't want to be intimating. Now, if G, Blue, Roland or Ronald Freeman, or Long John had been in the room with Bunchy, things wouldn't have gone down like that.

11

SERVING THE PEOPLE

I walked into the Watts office and found Lux sitting at the desk, listening to Sly and the Family Stone. "Hey Lux," I hollered over the tune. "Turn down the music, man. Time to talk business. We got to do something about this violence; Us and the pigs are vamping on us."

"I know; this shit is tripping me out," he answered as he reached for the stereo knob. "It's like they got nothing else to do but chase us. I wonder what they got up their sleeve."

"Man," I shook my head, "I'm thinking that we need to spend more time at Central, to find out what the pigs got planned. I feel like we getting the news secondhand."

He nodded in full agreement. "Yeah, brother, we need to know what's coming next. I know we can find out if we go to the PE classes at Central."

My commitment to Watts was still in full force, but I believed that attending more meetings and PE classes at Central Headquarters would give us a better intelligence on our enemies.

It turned out to be a good decision, because the conversation at headquarters was at a higher level, and it involved more discussion of outside forces against the Party. The closer I got to the Party leaders, the more useful information came my way. When I'd arrive at headquarters, the leaders would nod my way or salute me with the black power fist, which let me know I was recognized as a respected comrade. As I went more frequently, I developed closer relationships. I had crossed paths with those in leadership before, but Lux made it a point to make solid introductions.

Geronimo Pratt and I began to develop a friendship. We'd first met at the Watts office when he was just passing through; he periodically stopped by all the offices to make sure everything was going well. During those brief stops, though, he mainly talked with Al or Lux. Then we spoke at Central when he was throwing knives with Long John and Blue. The rumor about G was that he had a bad temper, but he struck me as a friendly guy.

When I saw him at Central Headquarters after Bunchy and John were murdered, he immediately embraced me. "Comrade Wayne," he said with a stern look that belied his words, "Bunchy talked to me about your work with the BSU and the students. He felt that those connections could benefit the Party."

Damn, I thought to myself. *G and Bunchy were talking about me.* I didn't realize that Bunchy felt what I was doing was important to the Party. "Oh, really?" I replied, showing my surprise.

G continued, "Bunchy didn't want you broadcasting that you are full time with the Party. He didn't want you on the muscle end either."

"What did he want me to do?" I inquired.

He studied me for a minute before replying. "We've been thinking about establishing a separate organization of students, specifically to monitor Us on campuses."

I smiled at G. "Right on. Let me know when you want me to start."

Although we never got around to starting that student wing of the Party, my conversation with G that day was the beginning of a lifelong friendship. I developed a lot of respect for him because he was direct, and I always knew where we stood in our relationship.

The PE classes at Central were democratic, and people were encouraged to speak up. We openly discussed the state of the Party, membership, self-defense, and current events. We still engaged in the study of the Red Book, Marxist-Leninism, the Ten Point Platform, and the US laws and Constitution, but as state repression and other attacks increased, we devoted more time to safety and protection. Generally there were about forty people in a class, unless there was a major event; then, more people would come. Paul Moffett, Elaine Brown, or Long John would lead the political education classes.

Elaine Brown impressed me as a great speaker and an intellectual. It didn't hurt that she was easy on the eyes too. I also met Melvin "Cotton" Smith and Masai Hewitt at Central Headquarters. These were the people who began to play important roles in my life, and it was because of them that I began to look forward to going to Central.

One day, I was talking to Long John after a PE meeting, and Cotton walked past us. Long John stopped him and said, "Comrade Cotton, I want you to meet Comrade Wayne; Wayne works out of Watts."

Cotton was about forty years old. To my nineteen-year-old eyes, he was an old man. But he was fit. He was thin, some might say kind of wiry, and he always wore handyman-type worker's clothes, especially the classic Pendleton plaid shirts and painter's pants.

"Wayne," Long John continued, turning to me, "Cotton is really important to the work we do. He supervises our buildings and handles repairs. Bunchy recruited Cotton into the Party."

"It's good to meet you," I said to Cotton. "We might need your skills at Watts."

I realized later that Cotton was a great asset to the Party because he was a jack-of-all-trades. He appeared to be a contractor or someone who worked in construction, but either way, he was highly skilled. Cotton was an easy person to talk to, also, because he had an even temper. Cotton didn't fly off the handle or try to show off, like some of the guys did. He was a good dude, and we got along well.

Masai Hewitt, on the other hand, was recruited into the Party in 1968 because of his intellect and understanding of Marxist theory. He came out of an organization called the United Front, a politically left-wing group; he was one of the teachers there. It was a revolutionary socialist organization whose members were also into karate and self-defense. Masai, whose former name was Raymond, had been an OG Slauson with Bunchy. His street name was Bright Eyes. He was tall, dark, and handsome, and he had a booming bass voice. The women loved Masai, and Masai loved the women. Masai was also disciplined. Every morning he did fifty push-ups. These weren't fifty regular old push-ups, though; what made them so difficult was that he would do ten and then raise one finger on each hand and do ten more. He'd keep going until he was just on his thumb and pinky.

I always thought that Masai was a good counterbalance to G. Masai was an educator, and I could listen to him spouting off about world politics for hours. G was very intelligent too, but he lacked the discipline of Masai; G was a street fighter. Together, they created a

Party leader Ray "Masai" Hewitt on the telephone at Central Headquarters in 1970. COURTESY OF IT'S ABOUT TIME ARCHIVES

great team. When I was around people like Elaine, Masai, G, and Cotton, I felt that I was a part of something great.

The more we went to Central, the more the political education classes proved valuable. During one particular class, Elaine explained to us the reason why the character and actions of the LAPD had recently changed. "Listen up, comrades," she said, standing before us and rapping her hand on the desk to get our full attention. "It is very important that you realize the vice squad as we knew it no longer exists. It has been transformed into what is being called the 'Metro Squad,' which is really the LAPD's Panther unit."

Someone in back of me shouted, "I knew something was up!"

Elaine continued. "Their focus is counterterrorism and responding to high-risk barricade situations. But you all know that means they are focusing on us. There are about two hundred officers in the unit, and they operate out of LAPD's headquarters. Everybody should be on high alert. These pigs are even more vicious than most."

There was a lot of nodding and agreement in the group and a new buzz of energy. The conversation then moved on to the FBI's Counterintelligence Program, called COINTELPRO for short. G explained, "This is a federal program designed to destroy revolutionary organizations like ours."

"So we've got to watch our asses from all sides," somebody commented.

"Exactly," G nodded. "We've got to fight Metro on the local level and COINTELPRO on the national level."

G further explained that the FBI was doing shit like planting agent provocateurs in black power organizations to create conflict, fights, and even murder. This is what I believed happened in the murders of Bunchy and John. The Us Organization, or actually a plant from the FBI, was creating tension between the Black Panther Party and Us, because we were viewed as a threat to the system. That would certainly explain why Us was so quick to pull the trigger on the Panthers. It also explains why, after Bunchy and John were killed, the police came down on the Panthers but not on Us.

Three Us members were arrested and convicted for the murders; two were former members of the Gladiator street gang, George and Larry Steiner. A guy named Donald Hawkins was also arrested, but the main shooter, Claude Hubert, was never caught. For me, that was another indication that Us was working with the man. I'm sure it was quite easy for provocateurs to operate freely within Us because of Karenga's egomania. A person who refuses to accept critique or challenges to his authority is more likely to allow goons to use violence to maintain his status.

We had lost a few members after the shoot-out at UCLA, so we knew at this point that those who stayed and those who joined understood that being in the Party was serious business. We discussed the need to beef up recruitment, expecting it to be difficult. But we were wrong. Bunchy and John's murders had received international attention, which drew people to the Party. Others came because they had heard about police repression and they wanted to stand up and fight right beside us.

We made a conscious decision not to hide from the pigs while we worked. We escalated our educational programs, fund-raisers, and demonstrations at the downtown state and federal buildings. Elaine, Masai, and sometimes our white radical and Chicano allies would speak. We also increased our services to the community. We added a free breakfast program and gave away used clothes and shoes.

The John Huggins Free Breakfast for Children Program became our signature program. We knew that black kids living all over the country were going to school hungry, so the Central Committee requested that each local office establish a breakfast program if it was capable of doing so. We already had built support from the mom-and-pop stores, who voluntarily gave food to the program. Some of the other comrades would request donations from grocery stores.

One of the first detailed conversations I had with Elaine was related to fund-raising for the program. I approached her at Central

Headquarters. "Elaine, you know I'm still head of the BSU at Harbor, and we could raise even more money for the breakfast program from the students there," I told her.

"Well, what's your strategy?" she asked.

"The BSU would be in charge of placing containers at junior colleges to collect money," I told her.

"I think that's a good idea, comrade," she said. "You should move forward with that. I will let the rest of the officers know that you're spearheading that program."

The money we received from the junior colleges provided extra cash. It was a successful project. The BSU would leave jars or cans in student centers so that people could donate. Later, we would go back and pick up the contributions.

We rented a house in Watts, on Anzac Street, where we could cook for and feed the children. Word spread quickly; soon, grateful parents from all over the area were dropping their kids off for the free breakfast. The pigs, however, hated the breakfast program, because they saw it as a way for us to generate even more community support. Sometimes they would raid the house for no reason, throwing milk and eggs on the floor, even while the children were there. I thought, *How petty is that?* They would come in under the guise of looking to arrest someone, but they really wanted to scare the community so that they wouldn't participate in our programs.

Renee Moore was put in charge of the breakfast program. We called her Peaches; she was a pretty, brown-skinned sister with a sharp nose who wore a short Afro hairstyle. Originally from South Central, Peaches grew up near Florence and Western, which was closer to the Westside. She was also in the revolutionary singing group Elaine led. They sang hippie style, and she was an alto. Peaches hung with several women in the Party including Brenda Frank and Glenda Josephs. Like G and so many other comrades, Peaches came to the Party after dealing with racism in the military. She worked out of Central Headquarters, but sometimes she would come and hang out

Renee "Peaches" Moore and other dedicated Party members serve children at the Free Breakfast for Children Program. COURTESY OF SOUTHERN CALIFORNIA CHAPTER, BLACK PANTHER PARTY

with us at the Watts office. When she became head of the breakfast program, we started seeing her more. Although Peaches was in a relationship with Paul Redd, she and I became close friends.

Peaches called the Watts office one morning, and I picked up the phone. "Comrade Wayne!" she said breathlessly. "The pigs vamped on the breakfast program!"

My stomach clenched up. *Damn them*, I thought. "Are you OK?" I asked her. "Tell me what happened."

"They came up in here and tore up the breakfast," she replied. "They threw food everywhere."

"I'm on my way," I said, grabbing my coat before I even hung up the phone.

When I arrived, I checked out the place and made note of their destruction and the mess that was left. I asked Peaches, "Did they take anything or arrest anybody?"

She shook her head. "No, but they said they were looking for somebody I didn't even know. I told them that, and that's when they started throwing stuff around and scaring the kids."

Looking at the ruin made my blood boil, but there wasn't much we could do. We were at the mercy of the pigs. "Well, let's start cleaning," I said. We had to make sure the kids could eat the next day.

■ ■ ■

We were at war, fighting several levels of onslaught against us, and we needed weapons. But for some unknown reason, it was harder than usual to purchase guns from my usual sources.

One windy morning, Jerry, Wendell, Baba, and I were hunkered down inside discussing this problem. I said to them, "It seems like guns are drying up in the streets."

In response, Jerry said, "Well, you know one place where there are plenty of guns—the armed forces."

We all laughed.

But then Baba, with a serious look on his face, said, "Yeah, well, everybody has a cousin in the military."

Baba was right: one of my relatives had even left a gun at the base for me to pick up. Other comrades had similar connections with

Children raise their fists in a "power to the people" salute. WAYNE PHARR COLLECTION

people sympathetic to our struggle who would help us get access to guns and ammunition.

"Fort Ord is one of the best places around," observed Wendell.

I knew what they were referring to. Fort Ord was a military base in Northern California, near Monterey Bay. Several of us had relatives or someone we knew there.

We decided to drive to Fort Ord to pick up the package. Troy Ferguson of the Black Student Alliance took the lead in this mission. Because one of my roles in the Party was to make sure we had weapons, I went with them. Like a hunter searching for his prey, Troy targeted a soldier who was patrolling the base. He sized him up to determine the best way to approach him. Troy had a sap, a common weapon used by sheriffs. They're about the same length as a billy club but flat in a kind of beaver-tail shape, made of thick leather on the outside, with powdered lead sewn inside at the round end and sometimes metal springs in the arm. Troy walked toward him with the sap and busted him upside his head. He beat his ass some more and then took his gun. It was vicious, but I understood the move. He had to move fast and draw blood to create the element of shock, so that the victim wouldn't have the nerve or the heart to fight back. That was the technique: come in hard and fast so the soldier wouldn't fight back; it was a way to replenish our weapons, and no one had to die.

During the summer of 1969, Jerry used one of the M-14s we had received to shoot at a police helicopter in the neighborhood that was chasing somebody. The ground police eventually zeroed in on his gunfire and arrested *him* instead. They also searched his house and retrieved two more guns. I had just left his place—what luck. I was so grateful to have missed that run-in with the cops. Jerry did a little time behind bars for that one, but considering the crime, he got off easy.

Many of us thought that after the murders of our deputy ministers of defense and information, the Us Organization would stay away from the Black Panther Party. But we were wrong; instead, it became clear to us that they were hell-bent on destroying the Party, even if they had to do so by murdering us one by one. Two months after the UCLA shoot-out, bad blood between Us members and Ronald Freeman resurfaced. The conflict revolved around the attempt of college and high school BSUs to work with Carver Junior High School students, who were advocating for a black studies curriculum. One evening, several college and high school students made a presentation to students at Carver Junior High about the importance of BSUs and the need for a black curriculum. During the presentation, one of the junior high school administrators saw what was happening and called the police. The pigs showed up to close down the meeting. But the students resisted, which led to altercations and confrontations with the police.

In protest, the Carver students boycotted the school system and walked out of classes the next day. Following that student strike, they decided to hold a meeting at Victory Baptist Church to continue organizing. The meeting was held on March 14, 1969. Black Panther Party and Us members also attended the meeting.

I was with Lux and Al at the funeral home when Al got a call from one of the junior high school students. The student was so keyed up, I could hear him from where I was sitting. "Captain Ronald has been shot!" he yelled. "You guys need to come right away!"

"OK, stay cool, brother," Al tried to reassure him. "We're on our way. Where are you?"

"Victory Baptist Church," he said excitedly.

We all got in the car, and Lux drove to the church, but by the time we got there everybody was gone—even the student who had called. The only ones still there were the police, patrolling the area. From there, we headed to Jerry's, because we were pretty sure Baba would be up there and he could fill us in on what happened since he had been at the meeting.

We walked in the door, and Baba was there, as we had guessed. "Do you know what happened at the church?" Baba asked, not even waiting for us to get all the way inside.

"Not really," Al answered.

"Those pork chop nationalists shot Ronald," Baba said angrily, before any of us could even ask.

I got upset. "Where did he get hit? Is he alive?"

"They got him in the chest and I think in his groin," he replied as he paced the floor.

"How did the shooting start?" asked Al.

"Us didn't want Ronald taking pictures at the event, so they confronted him. The next thing I know, loud popping noises are coming from outside, from the parking lot. I run outside, and I see Ronald lying on the asphalt in a pool of blood and Us driving away."

"Damn," I said.

"And check this out," Baba finished. "The police are out there, watching the whole thing."

Jerry looked surprised. "And they didn't intervene?"

"Hell no!" Baba answered emphatically.

The anger was thick in the room. We knew it would be difficult to retaliate because we were under intense police scrutiny.

I looked at the group. "We need to bust a cap on these niggas. Move on them once and for all to get this shit over with."

Lux spoke up, trying to be our voice of reason. "But remember, we can't forget Bunchy's mandate."

"But Us is on the warpath, and Bunchy ain't here—because of those suckas," countered Al.

"I know we want to take the high road and not go to war with a black organization," I added in agreement, "but we need to let Us know they're not dealing with punks. And we are not going to let them continue to shoot Panthers down like dogs in the street."

Everyone in the room nodded in agreement.

We continued to discuss our options, acknowledging the role of COINTELPRO. We'd learned that the FBI was sending inflammatory letters in our name to Us and vice versa. They even drew cartoon books that they disseminated, depicting conflicts between the two organizations in order to provoke more violence. When I saw the cartoons, I thought the FBI must really be afraid of us, since they were trying to find a way for the two organizations to kill each other off. But the more we understood the FBI's tactics, the easier it was for us to avoid falling into their traps.

The leadership of the Southern California chapter decided to send Us a warning after Ronald Freeman was shot. But this kind of warning wasn't in the form of a letter: bullets sprayed the homes of Us members as an initial notice. That punk James Doss, who went by Tayari, cried to the press about it. He was vice president of the Us Organization, so we knew that he was involved in Us hits on Panthers. He needed to be warned too, so his home was hit with at least thirty-five to forty rounds.

Obviously, that warning was not enough. Us had a strong presence in San Diego and was known for harassing Panthers when they were out recruiting or selling papers. On May 23, 1969, a Karangatang named Tambozi confronted comrades John Savage and Jeffrey Jennings. That fool just walked up to them and started an argument. Then he drew a gun and shot John in the back of his neck. I heard that the Panthers drew guns, but they were late on the draw because they didn't know the Us niggas would take it that far. That situation reminded me so much of what happened at UCLA. Us was out for blood, and we were treating them as if they were reasonable human beings.

A few months later, three members of Us accosted comrade Sylvester Bell while he was selling papers in San Diego. They asked him if Us was being talked about in the Party newspaper. One thing led to another, and them Us niggas shot Sylvester. What was so cold was that he had fallen while trying to get away from those fools. They shot him while he was on the ground. That was some cold shit. At that point, Sylvester Bell became the fourth Black Panther Party member to be murdered by Us.

The killing had to stop. But retaliation wouldn't be easy, because we believed Us was working with the police, which meant that they were monitoring our moves. Putting a hit out on them niggas was going to be difficult. Still, we had to let anyone who worked with Us know that we would not be sitting ducks.

G finally let us know when it was time to take action. He had been in a Special Forces unit while in the military, so he didn't move on people with a lot of fanfare. He wouldn't shoot people in broad daylight or at a school, like Us did with Bunchy and John. The Los Angeles branch of the Black Panther Party was more methodical and always made sure we had access to an escape route. G sent the muscle from Los Angeles to San Diego, they put in some work, and the killing stopped.

12

NEW BLOOD

The Southern California chapter had suffered heavy losses. Within a year, the cops had assassinated three of our comrades, and the Us Organization had murdered four. And then there was Captain Franco, who got three bullets in the head because of an internal Party riff. Sure, I was aware of casualties in other chapters: the cops killed Bobby Hutton in April 1968 in Oakland, and Alex Rackley from the New York chapter was found dead in Middlefield, Connecticut, in May 1969. But our chapter seemed especially hard-hit. Despite the blitz of dirty tricks, espionage, and bloody murder, I understood that such danger was the consequence of our no-compromise position on self-defense, and our stance would lead to even more casualties—maybe including me one day. I chose to live with that reality and take it one day at a time.

During one of those stressful days, while I was working at the Watts office, this fine, sassy, brown-skinned girl walked in. She had a beautiful laugh and sparkling eyes. I welcomed her and introduced myself. Her name was Pam, she said, and she had dropped by the office with her friends on the way home from Jordan High School. I was playing a speech by Eldridge Cleaver—we made sure the community could hear speeches by putting the speakers outside. Pam and her friends stopped to hear the speech, so I engaged them in conversation. At some point in the exchange, I asked for her phone number, and to my delight, she gave it to me. I called her a few days later. We set up a date for Friday night and planned to meet at her home in the Imperial Courts project.

I took Tyrone with me to Pam's because one never knew who might turn up in the projects. When we got there, we were surprised to find out that her father was Big Ed, or, as some called him, the Golden Arm. "Hey, don't I know you?" he asked, looking straight at me.

"Yes, sir!" I exclaimed. "Big Ed, good to see you. What a surprise! How's that golden arm of yours?" I stuck my hand out to shake his. I hoped he wasn't going to give me a hard time for taking his daughter out.

Big Ed nodded. He grabbed my hand and held it firmly. "You kids have a nice time tonight," he said to me. "Stay out of trouble, you hear?"

"Absolutely," I replied, "we will."

Big Ed was a pool hustler who hung out at the All Nations Pool Hall and at Sportsman's Billiards on Broadway. We hung out in the area a lot; there was a movie theater, a bowling alley, a hair salon, a chicken shack, and a Thrifty's right around there. The red bus came through Watts and Compton; it stopped at Manchester and Broadway. What a small world! Big Ed used to teach us how to play pool.

During our evening together, Pam let me know that she was in a relationship. Of course, I was too. Earlier that year, in January, Sharon informed me that she was pregnant. We knew that having a baby would change our lives, but we were committed to each other. Even though Sharon was my woman, I was having a good time that evening with Pam. So, I decided to put in the full-court press anyway and got her into bed. We made passionate love and then kissed good-bye. She was a fine lady, and it was a wonderful interlude; it helped calm me from the intensity of the Party work and police pressure.

A few months after meeting Pam, Sharon had our baby. I was now a father with family responsibilities. Sharon was in Pasadena when the baby was born, and I immediately went to see her and my new daughter, Tammy. I was glad to have a baby, and I knew Tammy would be my legacy. Nanny and my mother enjoyed having a new child in the family to fuss over too.

I wanted to be there for this new family I had created, but there was no way I could just end my commitment to the struggle. I found myself living in two worlds: one where I was Dad, just a regular guy with Sharon and our baby, and one where I was a revolutionary, head of the BSU and member of the Black Panther Party, focused on community service and self-defense. I felt it was important for me to continue my service to the people. I wanted so badly for my daughter to grow up in a world different from ours: a world where social justice was a value our society embraced and where black people could walk the streets freely, without being harassed or killed because of our skin color.

But the pigs were not about to accept a group of black men who weren't afraid to fight back. And they identified me as one of those men: my work with the Panthers in Watts had begun to increase my visibility. When I was at the office, from time to time, the police would circle our building. And when they were driving by, sometimes they'd pause and look me dead in my face to purposely let me know they recognized me.

How much they recognized me, though, didn't become clear to me until one particular day, when I was standing in front of the office talking to some children who were passing by. Inside were about four or five students listening to tapes and reading some literature. We had a lot of activity going on that day. It was sunny outside, and I was feeling good about our status in the community and especially pleased with the good work we were doing for them. In the course of my conversation with the kids outside, I noticed a blue Plymouth drive by a few times. I could tell that these were special agents in plain clothes, riding in an unmarked car.

They eventually stopped the car right in front, where I was standing. The pig on the side closest to me rolled down his window and looked me straight in the eye, with unveiled hatred behind his squinting glare.

"Hey, we just left Sacramento, where we raided the office and took some of you niggers down," he sneered. "So, before we have to bust all of you, let us come in so we can check out what's going on in there."

"Do you have a search warrant?" I said defiantly, before turning and walking back into the office. The kids I was talking to had already scattered.

"No, and we don't need one," the cop said with a smirk.

"Then you can't come in," I replied, and closed the door.

Once inside, I didn't want to alarm the students, who were studying intently. I turned to James calmly and said to him quietly, "Undercover cops are outside and they want to come in."

James immediately went to get his shotgun so he could stand guard behind the door, just in case they went crazy. I glanced out the window and saw both policemen get out of their car and approach our building. A hush fell over the students, who were now listening closely. The police didn't bother to knock; one of them just grabbed the door and rattled the doorknob, trying to open it. "Let us in," he barked.

"No, you can't come in," I yelled back.

Silence.

They stood outside for a while, looking over the premises and trying to peer through the window. As they got ready to leave, one of them said to me, "We will see you again, Wayne."

A chill went down my spine. I knew they had come to disrupt our operations. But what I hadn't known until that moment was that the cops knew my name.

Now that I knew I had become a target, I began to take extra pre-cautionary steps, especially when I was by myself, to avoid a run-in with the police. I walked on the opposite side of the street so I could see the cars coming. That way I could bank to the left if I saw a pig. I also avoided riding in cars, so I wouldn't get jacked up at a stop.

In the early summer of 1969, the Watts office got a much-needed injection of fresh energy. Walter Touré Pope, Bruce Richards, Kibo, Hasawa, Chris Means, and Romaine "Chip" Fitzgerald all walked into the Watts office to join the Party. They had done time together at Tracy and had made a pact to connect with us upon their release. The day they came by, I was officer of the day; my job was to make sure the office was staffed at all times, the phones were covered, and we were ready to handle any situation that might require our atten-tion. I was reading the newspaper in the early afternoon when all six of them walked in. I noticed right away that they were all yoked-up from lifting weights. Based on that alone, I figured they had all done some time. Their ages ranged from about eighteen to twenty-three, which was similar to most of us in the Los Angeles branch of the Party at that time. They wore a combination of army coats, bush jackets, leather jackets, and Levi's, which let me know they were interested in putting in some work for the people.

As I checked out their faces, I immediately recognized Hasawa, who had gone to school with me at Edison Junior High School. Back then he went by Lemelle James, but he changed his name as he had become more conscious of the black struggle. Hasawa was friends with Leroy Williams, my main dog back then. Hasawa had gotten kicked out of Markham Junior High in Watts, so he was transfered to Edison. But some of the Edison boys, like Big Munson, wanted to jump Hasawa because he was from Watts. Munson would later become a leader of the Avenues, one of the baddest gangs in Los Angeles during the 1980s and 1990s. But Leroy and I kept Munson and his boys off of Hasawa by letting it be known that he was our homeboy and that we were willing to go down with him. Munson knew us, so he let it go.

Right away, Hasawa and I acknowledged each other with the black power salute. "Right on," we said in unison.

"It's good to see you again," I said.

"What's happening, Wayne?" he grinned. "I didn't know you had joined the Party."

"Man, I've been here for a while now, trying to give power to the people. I hope you're here to join. I know you could add strength to what we do."

"That's why we're here," Hasawa replied with a nod. Hasawa's strength and street cred would bring people in that he knew from the streets. I'd be glad to have him on board. "I haven't seen you in a long time; where have you been?" I asked.

"Been hanging with this crew up at Tracy," he said as he pointed to the other men he had walked in with.

Hasawa told me they had all been there for typical ghetto crimes, like car theft and robbery. But while they were in prison they educated themselves by reading revolutionary books by Frantz Fanon and Malcolm X, as well as Mao's Red Book. They were also getting information about the Black Panther Party for Self-Defense and realized they wanted to join to help end the brutal systems of capitalism and racism.

Kibo, whose real name was Virgil Smith, was also from Watts. He was wearing a leather coat and sported a Fu Manchu mustache, which I thought was stylish. He was a cool brother who was more considerate than a lot of us soldiers. Next was Bruce Richards, who hailed from Compton. He was a tall brother, about six foot two, and had a very intelligent demeanor. Bruce would become a recognized player in the Party. He brought mental toughness and a fighting spirit and worked every day and everywhere. He might be at the breakfast program in the morning, the Watts office in the afternoon, and then later at a rally to provide security. Bruce wore a lot of hats and could be counted on to be available.

The fourth brother was Chris Means, also from Watts. He was a serious foot soldier, which meant that he wasn't coming into the

Party looking for glory. Chris was down for doing mundane work, hard work, all the work; it didn't matter to him, he'd do what was needed. Although Chris liked getting high—especially drinking Bitter Dog and taking pills—he could come down long enough to work for the Party. Every now and then I had a drink with Chris to discuss his time at Tracy and talk about Party work.

Romaine Fitzgerald, whom we called Chip, was a short brother, strong and muscular. He spoke at a fast pace and had a lot of ideas and plans he wanted to implement. Like the others, Chip was dedicated and participated in a number of Party programs, such as tutoring kids, selling papers, and building the Free Breakfast Program.

Of the group that came in that day, it was obvious that Walter "Touré" Pope was the driving force. A striking image in his dark leather coat, he reached out to shake my hand. "They call me Touré, after Sekou Touré, the first African president of Guinea," he said with a firm grip on my hand.

"I like that, man," I nodded in welcome, returning his firm handshake. "Where you from?"

"These parts." He waved his hand in a broad stroke. "We've been looking forward to becoming a part of the organized struggle for a while. What do we need to do to get started?"

"First, you got to start coming to our political education classes on a regular basis. Then you'll receive training on how to work with the people, sell papers, and work our community service programs. If you're ready, we can start now," I suggested.

All the brothers turned to me, in a booming chorus of "Yeah, brother!" and "Right on!" I respected their enthusiasm; I was glad to have them on board.

Touré became a fund-raiser for the breakfast program and sold and distributed the *Black Panther* newspaper with zeal. Early on, the leadership recognized his ability to lead and take initiative. It wasn't long, in fact, before Long John and G tried to recruit him away from the Watts office by assigning him duties at Central—after he had only been in the Party for a few weeks. Despite their efforts, Touré and I continued to work together, even if it wasn't full time. He loved the Watts office, so he came in from time to time to help out. We worked together well and established a strong bond.

Added to the members we had already, these new recruits put the Watts office off the charts. The energy flow was high, and our adrenaline was pumping day and night. Around the time the new crew joined, Al had given me the charge of sprucing up the office. I decided to use the new recruits to help liberate some wood, paintbrushes, and other equipment. I chose Chip and Touré, who were definitely up for the task. We found what we needed at a construction site operating in Watts. We staked the place out for a few days to determine the best way and time to enter and gain access to what we needed.

One quiet evening, we broke the locks on the fence, walked onto the site, and took the equipment. Touré served as our lookout to make sure the police didn't catch us. It took about thirty minutes to get what we needed. Back at the office, within just a few days, we fortified the windows and doors with the material we had lifted. We also painted the office and gave it the newer, fresher look it deserved. The office building had been white, and the new paint was also white, so we weren't concerned that the upgrade would create any unwanted attention from the cops.

Over time, I realized the sound of my name was ringing though the streets, even though I had no police record and I wasn't part of the Bunchy-Geronimo goon squads. It was because of my organizing skills and the relationship I had built with the community on behalf of the Panthers. I was sure of that.

The cops finally decided to vamp on me that August. On the day it came down, I had been assigned to security at a Panther rally for Huey Newton at South Park. After the rally was over, I hopped in the car with Lux, who was playing taxi in Al's blue Volkswagen, driving people home. Also with us were Touré, Rachel, and Robert Williams. Rachel was a Panther based in Watts with us. She had joined before I did and worked closely with James and Larry Scales. Her involvement was sporadic, but this was one of the times she came through. We called Robert Williams "Caveman," because he was a really big brother who wore a wild, curly Afro. He also looked like he had a lot of Indian in him. I met Caveman at the Teen Post when we were in high school; we hung out at his house sometimes, smoking weed, drinking, and getting into fights on Main Street. When Caveman became a Panther he worked out of the Broadway office, then later switched to Watts.

Lux was driving Rachel home first, because she was closest. She asked him to stop by the office on the way because she had left her notebook there. "OK, no problem. That's a quick stop," Lux said agreeably. We were all in a pretty good mood after the success of the day's rally, so nobody minded.

We pulled up to the big, black iron gate in front of the office that we kept closed by using a big rock. Caveman got out and opened it so we could go in. At the same time, I noticed that an old, overweight street cop who went by the name of Cigar had pulled up. Cigar was the kind of cop who tried to know everybody, and he acted like he was the sheriff of Watts. The word on the street was that he was called Cigar because he used to walk around with an old chewed-up cigar in his mouth. We all saw him but stayed cool and went about our business, although everyone was watching him closely out of the corner of their eye.

"Hey," Cigar snarled at us gruffly, stepping out of the shadows. "Let me see your driver's licenses."

Still cool, we all acquiesced to his demands without saying a word, handing over our IDs. While he was pawing our licenses, I noticed that he had a partner with him who'd stayed in the squad car. Then I noticed Metro watching from a distance. Cigar returned our IDs and started to walk away.

As he walked, he turned around and looked back. "You're never going to make twenty-one," he said directly to me.

I laughed at him, while thinking to myself, *That's what you think, greasy-ass pig. If I die, we're going down together.*

After Cigar and his partner left, we got back in the car and Lux headed down 103rd Street toward Rachel's, and then he made a right on Wilmington. "Comrades, don't look now," Lux said in a composed tone, "but I think Metro is behind us."

"Take it slow," I said evenly. Suddenly everyone was quiet.

As if it was some sort of cue, as soon as we crossed 108th Street, sirens were suddenly screaming at us and flashing red lights were assaulting us through the car windows. Calmly, Lux pulled over. Four or five cars had come from out of nowhere and now they surrounded us.

As we were sitting there, one of the pigs shouted, "All of you, get out of the car!"

We opened the door; they had their guns drawn. One of them reached in and started yanking us out one at a time as he barked at us: "Put your hands on the fence!"

We all walked toward the fence, then put our hands up, facing away from the cops. They grabbed our wallets and checked our IDs, one at a time. Apparently, the pigs had the office staked out, waiting for us. And they had one of the neighborhood dope fiends with them.

When they got to me, she pointed at me and said, "That's him. That's Wayne Pharr right there."

I thought to myself, *What the fuck?! Why are they looking for me?!*

"So you're Wayne Pharr?"

Things were happening too fast, so I didn't say anything; I just turned and looked at them.

"Put your goddamn face up on a fence!" one of them yelled.

As I did, one pig kicked me dead in my ass. Of course, my first reaction was to jerk back around, which I did. I recognized him: this was the pig called Hole, and I had seen him hanging around Panthers before. Hole pushed me off the fence, out into the street, and started waling at my head with his nightstick.

My immediate reaction when he started beating me for no reason was to try to defuse the situation. With my arms covering my head, I yelled, "Hey man, hold it; wait a minute! Stop! What's going on?"

His response was to amplify his efforts, busting me upside my head with even more venom. I had a big natural back in that day, so I think my hair cushioned the blows a little. But when he hit me with his stick again, I knew I had to fight back to stop this fool from killing me. I put my shoulder into his chest and pushed him back up against the fence. This pig was bigger than me, and he had his arms up over my head. For a split second, I thought about grabbing his gun and busting a cap in his ass, but I could hear the other cops behind me, jacking rounds into their shotguns: *yack, yack, yack*. I decided against that move and just went limp instead.

A group of them swarmed me and commenced to beat my ass. This was a time I was glad I had been on the gymnastics team in high school and had done the parallel bars. I'd also been the only one with a set of real boxing gloves in the neighborhood, which I'd used for what we called box-offs. My fitness and strength base paid off: the entire time the pigs were beating me, I never passed out.

After they swarmed me, one cop named Fisher put me in a choke-hold. I had on a pair of army boots, which delivered enough power that I was able to kick one of the cops off me. But Fisher still had me in a chokehold and was really trying to take me out. I felt like I might pass out, but desperate for air, I found the strength to reach back, grab his ears, and yank hard, which made him let go. He let go at the last second, and I sucked in a deep breath. Two cops were still on me, each one holding one of my legs. Fisher went at it again, try-ing to choke me out; these pigs were working me over pretty good. While all this was going on, I could briefly see Touré turn around, as if he was coming to my aid—but one of the pigs stuck a shotgun in his mouth and shouted at him, "Turn around and get back on the fence!" There wasn't a thing he could do.

A crowd of folks from the neighborhood had formed around us and began shouting at the pigs. Someone started to throw rocks, so the pigs put handcuffs on me and threw me in the backseat, as if they were taking me to jail. That was a good move for them, because it got them out of the neighborhood. I had no idea what was happening to Touré, Lux, Rachel, and Caveman.

I was sitting in the backseat, thinking that they were taking me to jail. But instead, they drove a few blocks down the street and started beating my ass again. Fisher was in the backseat with me, hitting me in my kidneys with his stick. Hole, who was driving, had one hand on the steering wheel and with the other hand was reaching back to strike me with his heavy flashlight.

There I was ducking and jumping, trying to protect myself as best I could, when Hole took a swipe at me and broke his flashlight. I thanked God for that, but with the flashlight broken, he pulled out his gun and stuck it straight at my forehead. "I oughta kill your black ass right now!" he exclaimed.

"You can't kill me. You already called it in," I replied.

"You ignorant bastard!" he laughed. "I'll kill you, they'll send me to the Valley for a month, they'll give your mother a nice write-up in the *Sentinel* newspaper, and I'll be back out here shooting the rest of your friends."

I couldn't believe that pig Hole had actually said that to me. I replied, "All right, you've got the power." *Asshole.*

They kept driving me around, kept beating my ass. At one point, we reached Will Rogers Park. One of the cops pulled me out of the car. "Run, you black motherfucker!" he yelled.

I stood there, frozen, with my head down.

He yelled again. "Run if you want to live!"

I wouldn't run because I knew that if I did, they would shoot me in the back. That wasn't going to happen.

Fisher pushed me back in the car, and Hole started hitting me with his stick again. I looked at him and realized that he was holding himself while he was hitting me. *This is a crazy, sick bastard*, I thought. *He's getting off on this shit.*

We began riding around again. They took me to different places: to the back of the Goodyear plant on Florence and Central and then on the freeway, where they acted like they were going to push me out of the car. After that, they started hitting me again.

I was getting tired, and they must've been tired too, because they finally drove me toward the hospital on Manchester and Denker. I wasn't sure if we were really going to the hospital, so I pointed out a homosexual club on Manchester. Since Hole was holding himself and got off on beating people, I wanted to give him somewhere else to go to possibly find somebody else to beat. That fool asked me, "Where? Where's the club of freaks?"

I said, "Right there!" with a nod in the direction of the club.

"All right," he said, and they took me to the hospital.

Back when I was low-riding, one of my friends had a neighbor who was a nurse at that hospital. When we pulled up, she came out, took one look at me, and immediately placed herself between the pigs and me to keep them off of me. Then she got word to my friend Lewis, who let my family know what had happened and where I was. I never knew that nurse's name, but she saved my life that night.

I let the doctor know that I was in a lot of pain. He examined me and found no broken bones or teeth knocked out. He gave me some pain medication and ice for the bruising and released me back to the cops.

The pigs put me back into their squad car and then took me to the jail over at the Seventy-Seventh Street police station. They shoved me into the interrogation room, behind one of those two-way mirrors, so that all the pigs could come and check me out. While I was waiting, I found the strength to do a few push-ups and sit-ups to show them I was still ready. Several of the undercover officers came to get a look at me. Pointing their guns, they tried to scare me. "We're gonna kill you, Wayne. Then we're gonna bury you with Geronimo, Blue, and Ronald."

That sadistic pig Hole came into the interrogation room. "How are you feeling, baby boy?" he sneered.

I gave him my middle finger. "Your ass-whipping days are over, you disgusting pig."

"What did you say?" he growled.

"If I see you on the street and I'm packing, I'm going to put one in you!" I replied coolly.

"Repeat that!" he challenged.

I repeated myself, and it was on between us.

They put me into a one-man cell with thick glass windows, away from the general population, so that they could see me at all times. They came into the room and told me with a laugh that they had a bounty on all of us. The bounty for G was $2,000, they said, and they might get $500 for me.

This was my first time going to jail, but I felt that I would be OK. I knew folks in jail from the neighborhood, like Floyd Bell, who would look out for me.

I was moved around to different places in the jail for the next couple of days. Eventually, my mother was able to bail me out. As we were walking outside, my mother could barely recognize me. She wanted to hug me, but she was afraid to touch me. "Wayne, have you seen your face?" she sobbed.

My head was lopsided, my ears were like cauliflowers, and my lips were puffed up and busted open. I had two black eyes, and breathing was still difficult. I had wounds around my neck from when they tried to strangle me.

"Yeah, Mom," I mumbled, not knowing how to console her. "But there ain't nothing I can do about it now."

If you weren't already an angry black man, an experience like that would make you one. I was charged and convicted of assaulting a police officer. I was given one year's probation. During the sentencing, the judge couldn't look me in the eye, seeing how brutally the police had fucked me up.

After I was released from jail, I stayed home with my mother, who had just purchased a home in Inglewood. Nanny came by the house, too, to make sure I was healing properly. They openly voiced their desire for me to get out of the Party. Sharon came by and brought Tammy. I was so happy to see my baby girl. And as much as Sharon wanted to support my work, she echoed my mom and Nanny. I pretended I didn't hear them.

I rested for about a week, and then I went right back to work at the Watts office. I walked in and immediately saw Lux. He came up to me with a bewildered look on his face. He wrapped his arms around my shoulders and we embraced.

"What happened to everyone else?" I asked.

"They roughed us up and let us go. We thought they'd killed you."

13

BLOOD AND GUTS

"Strap me up. I'll do it," I said fiercely as I stood up out of my chair. I got up quickly, and as I did, I sent it clanking against the wall before it collapsed on the floor. It was about two weeks after the beating; a few of us were at Central Headquarters talking, assessing, and strategizing. Of course, the topic of the beating came up—my face was still pretty busted up from the Metro ambush, still disfigured from the swelling and badly bruised. I'd had plenty of time to think about what those jackasses had done to me. I told G that morning if he wanted to blow up the Seventy-Seventh Precinct, I was the man.

G looked at me and laughed, shaking his head at my outburst. "This nigga's gone crazy," he said, giving me a quizzical look.

Maybe I was crazy. But I was also dead serious. As serious as Robert Charles had been, decades before me: Charles, an articulate, law-abiding activist from around the turn of the century, gunned down five New Orleans police officers in 1900 when they tried to arrest him while he was quietly sitting on a front porch with a friend. His crime? A black man standing up against racism.

I was even more serious than Mark Essex, a young black navy man who turned sniper in the early 1970s. Essex went on a killing spree in New Orleans after being subjugated, demeaned, and humiliated by his white commanders, and even his white peers, in the military. Although he was originally from Kansas, he received his military training in San Diego, California. He was surprised at how racist things were in California. It was around that time that he became a Black Nationalist. He took the racist abuse until he finally couldn't take it anymore. First, Essex killed five cops. A week later, he went to a Howard Johnson's hotel and starting shooting people— he said he was only after white people. He finally went to the roof of the building, where he went out in a hail of fire, exchanging shots with police helicopters from the rooftop. Afterward, they found more than two hundred gunshot wounds in his body.

I was, in fact, deadly serious, just like Tommy Harper, who also came after me. Tommy, a local student, got so fed up with the racist system that he tried to use explosives to blow up the Compton police station in July 1970. Unfortunately for Tommy, he made some novice mistakes and blew himself up instead. But I understood his sentiments. After his death, the pigs made up a nursery rhyme about him as a joke. They sang it to the tune of "Old MacDonald Had a Farm." *Sick bastards.* Drive somebody crazy and then laugh when he dies. I thought they were sworn to *serve* the communities where they worked.

In my anger, I decided to ambush either Fisher or Hole or both; it didn't matter much to me which one. Just thinking about them made my blood boil. They both continued to brutalize Black Panthers, having now made a regular habit of picking brothers up for no reason and driving around for an hour or two beating them, then making a stop at the hospital to get them a little patched up before hauling them off to jail—often on bogus charges or sometimes not even charging them with anything at all.

So I decided it was time to do something about it. I didn't really have a plan—just to get them. That was the plan. The morning I resolved to take action, my day at the office dragged. I couldn't focus on anything; I just wanted to get outside and move on it. Some of my comrades noticed I was distracted and, throughout the day, kept asking me if I was OK. "Yeah," I kept answering abruptly. "Over and out." *Leave me alone.* After what seemed like forever, it was finally time for me to leave. As I gathered my stuff, a couple of comrades invited me to hang with them and listen to some 'Trane.

"Naw, can't tonight. I got a meeting," I said, not really wanting to elucidate. "Can you dig it?" I finished curtly.

"We got you, brother, we got you," somebody said.

I already had the door open and wasn't even paying attention to who was talking. "I'll catch y'all another time," I replied over my shoulder as the door slammed shut behind me.

I went to the hospital, since I knew Fisher or Hole would eventually show up there with another comrade. It was a warm, starless Tuesday evening on what had been an otherwise quiet day. It was the day after my outburst at Central that had caused G so much concern. No matter. G would be glad when I reported back the news, I was sure of it.

I waited until dark and went around to where I knew they would enter. Off to the side, I noticed a big Dumpster. *From there,* I thought, *I could get a good view of the hospital entrance they would use. Perfect hiding place.* Those suckers would never know what hit 'em. I walked over to the Dumpster, pried open the heavy metal lid, and peered inside, trying to figure out the best way to climb into it without making a bunch of noise. Out of the corner of my eye, I noticed an old crate, so I pulled it over and propped it up next to the Dumpster. Stepping up onto the crate, I climbed inside and lowered the lid, leaving it open just wide enough for me to have a lookout. I squatted down in the darkness, settling in for the wait. *Hopefully it won't be long,* I thought to myself. As my eyes adjusted to the dark, I looked around me and decided it wasn't really so bad inside the trash bin; mostly, it was full of old hospital gowns and paper trash. So I stayed there, squatting inside the dark bin, from 10:00 at night until the early hours of the morning, my M-14 in hand, waiting for one of them to drive up with the next Black Panther in the car.

My mind wandered as I waited. I imagined the satisfaction I would get mowing their asses down. I imagined seeing the surprise on their faces as they realized they were finally getting their due. I kept thinking about their ugly threats, the obvious and perverse pleasure they had gotten out of beating me. And others. I thought about Hole holding himself while he was beating me, the disgusting image of him like that now burned into my brain. My legs ached from squatting for so long. I got tired of being stuck inside the dark Dumpster; the air was stuffy inside. I kept hoping no one would come with a new load of trash to dump. I wanted to move around, stretch my legs. But I couldn't. *Good thing I'm not claustrophobic*, I thought to myself. I waited and I waited. Neither one of them showed up. I went home that night exhausted.

But I wasn't done. I staked out the hospital again the next night, still determined to blast a cap in one of them. The second night was a little harder than the first, because I was already a little weary from my all-nighter the day before. This time I knew what was ahead of me for the next several hours, sitting in the bottom of a trash bin as the clock barely ticked. But I was unwavering in my commitment to give those sick bastards what they deserved. I imagined looking one of them square in the eye as he took his last breath. *Punk*, I would say. *Pig scum*, I would call him before I disappeared into the night.

But they were no-shows again. By the end of that second night, I was tired and discouraged. I decided that I was losing too much time and sleep hoping one of them might show up. I wondered if I truly was losing my mind, as G had suggested. I realized that I hadn't really thought it out very well anyway, so maybe it was a good thing neither of them showed up. I needed a better plan.

In the meantime, G moved me out of the Watts office to Central Headquarters. He came up to me at the office after my second all-nighter waiting for Hole and Fisher; I must have looked pretty washed out.

"Comrade Wayne," he said as he put a firm, brotherly hand on my shoulder, "I think you need a break from Watts. I want you to work out of Central for a while. We need a driver for the Central Committee, Elaine and Masai. I trust you to help make sure they get where they need to go when they are in Los Angeles."

"Right on," I answered automatically, dutifully. "Whatever the Party needs me to do."

I didn't really want to leave my home base. But actually, I was ready for a little change. I could already feel my shoulders start to relax, even as he told me the news.

He released his strong grip on my shoulder. "Use my GTO and the Party's yellow van. Ask Elaine and Masai what they need and I will make it available."

So just like that, I was operating out of Central and driving G's GTO. I loved driving that car—it was the hottest car in Los Angeles at that time. When he needed it or when we wanted to be less conspicuous, I would drive the van. G had been right—this was a much-needed move for me, at least for now. I started to feel rejuvenated.

I was now working for the Party exclusively, driving the leadership throughout Southern California, especially to areas where we had chapters, like Riverside, Santa Ana, and San Diego. I still maintained all of my college contacts, though, as well as my close association with the Black Student Alliance. They always provided me with a safety net and support. I didn't want to lose those relationships, even though my time was more limited than before.

I was cool with driving Elaine and Masai around too. Not only did it expose me to inner workings of the Party that I hadn't been aware of before, but also it kept me out of the office and on the streets, which I always enjoyed.

Elaine had been pulled into working with the Central Committee at the national level because David Hilliard needed help, so I drove her when she came down from Oakland. After spending so much time together on the road, we developed a mutually respectful friendship. We talked about office work, how to battle the police, and about our intimate relationships. Elaine met Sharon and my daughter, Tammy, to whom she was very sweet. She also tried to set me up with Gwen Goodloe, another sister. It was, after all, the sixties. I thanked her for the thought and then told her, with an appreciative smile, that I already had too many women, and it would be too tough to add another. Elaine just grinned back slyly and winked at me. We had a good laugh over that. But Gwen and I hit it off as friends anyway, and I made an extra effort to drive her to appointments.

And Elaine, she was one tough sister. When the pigs would stop us, she would get real indignant and challenge them. "Why the hell you messing with us?" she would chide in her smart bossy-girl voice. I always had to chuckle under my breath at her sassy reproaches to the pigs. But at the same time, I respected her for it.

Masai, though, was entirely different when I drove him. For one thing, he would get real quiet when the pigs vamped on us. His posture was to try to defuse the situation so that we could keep on moving. Unlike Elaine, he was still living in L.A. and traveling back and forth to Oakland. And because his home was in L.A., it was more dangerous for him to antagonize the pigs, especially the vicious L.A. Metro pigs, like Elaine did. They had more access to him. Overall, Masai was just a more even personality than a lot of comrades. He was always concerned that he had justification for what he did. And he was willing to learn from his mistakes. I compared him once to G while we were driving back to headquarters. Masai threw his head back and laughed at that. His bass voice resonated throughout the whole van. It was a good-natured laugh. He knew that G had a volatile nature and sometimes didn't think things through. He reminded me that G got mad at one of the captains one day and busted his head open with a lamp vase. Then he said that, as a matter of fact, he planned to talk to G about his temper, because if he didn't, "that Injun's going to get us all killed."

I chuckled, too. But I couldn't disagree.

Driving Masai was quite an experience, in fact. For one thing, he was a true ladies' man, so I often drove him to visit women he had

special relationships with—many of whom were very high-profile, like Angela Davis and actress Jean Seberg. Angela was easy on the eyes. I always enjoyed it when Masai instructed me to drive to her house. She was a striking beauty, tall and long-legged, with a big, beautiful Afro and a smile that wouldn't stop. When she walked into a room, you stopped whatever you were doing—she just had that kind of presence. But besides her good looks, the other thing you noticed about her right away was how intelligent she was, and yet she had a warm personality. At the time, Angela lived in a house near Vernon and Main. When we arrived at her place, we would all go inside and make small talk for a while until eventually it was me by myself waiting for them while they were in another room.

With Jean Seberg, however, I would wait outside. Jean lived in Beverly Hills. She was a stunning beauty, too, a blonde Audrey Hepburn and a real Hollywood type. I never saw her in any of her movies, but I sure knew who she was. She was svelte and petite and carried herself like a movie star. At the same time, she seemed real down-to-earth and sincere, and I got the sense that she truly understood that equality for blacks was never going to happen without revolution. She became a well-known supporter of and financial contributor to the Party.

Masai had a lot of respect for Jean's ability to move away from the comforts of Hollywood to support our work. But because of her support for us, she became a target of the FBI's COINTELPRO, which embarked on a smear campaign to ruin her. Based on a false story, "credible" newspapers and magazines reported that Jean was pregnant with a baby not by her husband but by an official of the Black Panthers, insinuating it was Masai. The incident was so upsetting to her that she miscarried shortly after the story ran. She insisted on a funeral with an open casket to prove that her baby was white. She was stalked and wiretapped and endured other forms of harassment. Then she stopped getting good roles in Hollywood. Jean eventually committed suicide; some say that it was after her relationship with Masai was exposed, while others related it to FBI bullying because she was raising so much money for the Party. She had been ruined for associating with us.

One day as I was driving Masai somewhere, the discussion in the car turned to my strategy for using the sewers, both to set up ambushes on the police and for protection. Masai already knew about my idea and seemed ready to pursue it further. He asked me all sorts of questions—*How would you do this, and what if that*? The conversation went on for some time, and then we moved on to another topic. But I was glad it had come up.

I pulled back into headquarters and went to turn off the engine. It was the end of the day, and we were ready to go home. Masai, however, wasn't getting out of the car. I turned to look, to see what was wrong. But there was nothing wrong. Instead, I could see that he was lost in serious thought. "Comrade Wayne," he said, "let's make a run into the sewers. I want to check your plan."

"Right on," I smiled. *Good*, I thought. *This is important.*

The plan was to drive Masai that night. We didn't want to arouse the suspicion of the pigs by riding in the GTO or the yellow van, which they would have noticed right away, so I got a car from a friend. I arrived at Masai's house after dark, and we left his place right away. Both of us were wearing army boots and military-style pants, ready for the giant rats and whatever else lurked below.

I decided to take Masai in at Central Avenue and 120th. The tunnels in that area were large enough to walk through, and from where we started, I was able to show him the main drain and then the four corner lines where the water ran in. We walked for a while and then crawled up the drainpipe so we could look out and see where we were in the city. We watched cars and a few people go by.

Masai turned to me with a frown. "OK, comrade, I'm checking this out, and I like it. But what's the plan?"

Good. He liked it. We needed to move forward on this. "From the four lines," I explained, "we can set up ambushes from different corners, and we can use it as an escape route from Central Headquarters."

"That sounds good," he said thoughtfully.

"Which part?" I asked. "The ambush or being able to escape from Central?"

He turned to me with a serious look on his face. "Both!" he exclaimed with a wide grin.

I didn't need to say a thing. I just smiled back and nodded.

"Comrade," he continued effusively, "this shit is major. You got to keep at this. I also think you need to draw some maps, so when the time comes, everybody involved can be ready."

"Good idea," I replied in agreement. But I knew as I said it that I wasn't drawing any maps. I was afraid they might end up in the wrong hands. I didn't want a paper trail.

As we continued walking through the underground, I showed Masai how to maneuver, and I fleshed out for him the possibility of the plan working. We stayed down there about two hours before we finally came back up, right where we left the car. Perfect.

From that point on, throughout my time as his driver, Masai and I would strategize about how and when to use the sewers. It almost became a reconnaissance adventure for him, but it encouraged me to continue pursuing the project.

In the meantime, I had to deal with that pig, Hole. He had a serious vendetta against me; he would look for me and then follow me. Each time he saw me in a car, he and his partner would pull me over and make me step out of the car. Usually they would surround me and put their hands on their guns. "Are you packin'?" he would growl.

"Not today," I would answer smoothly.

Always the same. Always lookin' for something or some reason.

Hole, in fact, continually tried to make some big scene and do some old cowboy shit as if he were going to draw his gun, like Wild Bill Hickok or O.K. Corral stuff. I sure wanted to take his ass out. But he had me at a disadvantage. He always knew where I was; he was everywhere. He was Metro; he didn't work out of one particular station. That meant the only way I could get at him would be to stay packed all the time, which didn't make sense, because they were looking for any reason to arrest me. Things got so bad, in fact, that unless I was driving for the Central Committee, I tried to avoid riding in cars.

I felt bad for the new crew in Watts. They had only been in the Party a few months, and already most of them had suffered three or more arrests: they'd experienced the wrath of billy clubs, saps, chokeholds, and guns shoved in their faces. The billy clubs hurt like hell and could do a lot of damage, but those saps were a real bitch. Those suckers could exact a lot of damage on flesh and bones. With all their government-backed weapons and resources, Metro was inflicting serious harm on the Party collectively and on most all of us individually.

The pigs at Metro Squad were determined to exterminate the Southern California chapter of the Black Panther Party, and they used all of the resources at their disposal: weaponry, intelligence, and city, state, and federal government. They hunted, chased, and confronted us day and night. They were willing to put themselves in danger just to get at us. They understood that when one of us was killed it was a big, devastating loss for us—one we could ill afford. They could easily replace their losses; we could not. And we weren't getting at the real pigs anyway, just their soldiers.

In July, some of the new Watts crew, including Lux, Touré, Craig Williams, and a few other comrades, were at the Watts office when the cops invaded, claiming they were looking for somebody. Of course, they drew their guns, forced everyone to their knees, and then arrested them all. Then in August, Chip, Hasawa, Virgil Smith, Tony Quisenberry, Bobby Davis, and Henry David Christian were at the Nickerson Garden Projects, working and singing with some children. The cops came and started busting them in the head with clubs and heavy-duty flashlights. They arrested Hasawa and Henry and beat them all the way to the hospital. Then they drove them to the Seventy-Seventh Precinct, where they were charged with resisting arrest and other made-up bullshit. These kinds of incidents didn't happen to the comrades just once or twice. They happened all the time.

The presence of danger was now our reality more than ever before. With the exception of Rachel, within two months of my getting jacked by the police, the four others with me that night were involved in police activity that cost them either their lives or many years in prison.

It also became obvious to us that Metro had assigned officers to each of us individually. We soon developed a common refrain: after walking outside in the morning, we reminded each other to "shake your tail." If we didn't lose our assigned officers, we could be harassed throughout the day, arrested, and even tortured for hours like I was. It was a game for the pigs but real life for us. All of us had the skills to kick their asses one on one, but they came in pairs, with weapons and the authority of the state. Armed with the knowledge that we were dealing with a bunch of punks, some brothers, especially in the rank and file, independently decided that it was time to make their own moves against the pigs. In fact, at the end of a hard day, that kind of thinking was becoming more and more common.

One night, a group of us were sitting around the kitchen table, talking and drinking, trying to calm our nerves after another stressful day of defending ourselves against the pigs. The dingy yellow light from the bulb hanging overhead was thick and hazy from all the smoke, and the mood in the room was just as heavy. The table was overflowing: empty bottles of beer, ashtrays spilling over with cigarette butts, half-empty glasses, and plastic cups full of Bitter Dog. I upended my glass, drinking down my last swig of the signature drink. Touré was sitting next to me. He slammed down his cup and cleared his throat. We all got silent, turning and looking at him.

"You know," he reflected somberly, "we'll never be able to focus on education and liberation until we stop these pigs. We're spending all our time on fighting them and defending ourselves against those bastards."

Bruce spoke up in a determined but quiet voice. We all strained forward to hear. "Yeah, I'm tired of playing defense," he proclaimed. "At some point, we need to go on the offensive."

We all nodded in agreement.

"I wouldn't mind taking the heads of Fisher and Hole," I added. "I actually went looking for them one night. G thought I had lost my mind."

Touré shot me an understanding glance. His voice was low but firm. "Sometimes, I think the leadership don't get it. They want us to let them handle it, but I didn't become a Black Panther to get clubbed and have guns put to my head on a regular basis."

He was referring to the orders from G, Ronald Freeman, and Long John that said we didn't need to engage in independent action against the pigs.

"The leadership can't handle all of the issues that are coming at us daily. Shit, they got their own issues," Bruce said resolutely. "They're constantly going back and forth to jail too."

"Remember," I added, "Huey said as a member of the Party, we must never let a pig take our guns."

A puzzled look washed over Bruce's face. "Does that mean we're supposed to go down if a pig stops us while we're packing?" he asked. I could tell he was frustrated. We all were, for that matter.

Touré stood up. "That means it's them or us."

Looking back now, I realize that our conversation that warm summer night in Watts foreshadowed the brutal months, soon to follow, of what some of us later called "blood and guts in Southern California." Beginning that summer of 1969, things started heating up everywhere, on both sides. First, the Party was continuing to grow rapidly. New members joined and became involved in our community programs. We were working on opening a revolutionary liberation school intended for elementary and middle-school children. Our goal was to create a new black consciousness to counter the oppressive ideologies of white racial supremacy and economic oppression being reinforced in mainstream schools. Schools were already being opened across the country, from San Francisco to Queens.

At the same time, David Hilliard, Emory Douglas, and Masai had recently joined Eldridge Cleaver in Algeria. In Chicago, Bobby Seale was being gagged and literally chained to his chair in court for trying to challenge his arrest for inciting a riot at the Democratic National Convention. And, of course, we were still reeling from the death of Sylvester Bell on August 15 and then the police shooting into Panther homes, both in San Diego. In Southern California, in fact, we were entering a period that was more dangerous than ever before. And in Los Angeles specifically, our worst fears were beginning to turn into reality.

It was the end of the first week in September, and Al Armour called the Watts crew into the office. I noticed right away that Lux wasn't there, and we were missing a few other brothers too. Al was leaning against the wall as we all settled into our chairs. He had a distressed look on his face; we knew what he was about to tell us was serious. I sat quietly off to the side, watching him closely. His body language did not bode well.

Al called us all to attention. "Norma gave me some news that I did not want to ever hear," he began. "She told me last night that Chip, Lux, and Caveman got into a shoot-out with the highway patrol," he finished somberly.

Norma was Al's wife, and she worked out of Central. We all respected her ability to get intel.

"There was some bloodshed," Al continued. "We don't know where they are or how they're doing."

"Where were they when it went down?" I asked dismally.

"Gardena," Al responded. "The police stopped them and there was a shoot-out. One officer was shot and Chip was hurt, but that's all I know. Everybody must be on high alert, because the brothers might contact you for some help. Make yourselves available in whatever way you can. We've got to pull together and find a way to help rescue them."

Damn! I thought to myself. The Gardena and Torrance areas were where the real redneck pigs worked. If one could imagine any pig worse than the ones in South Central, it would be those in redneck country. We were glad our comrades defended themselves and escaped without being killed, but we were worried about Chip, who we found out later had been shot in the head. We were receiving reports that Chip had made it to some members in the leadership, and G and Elaine helped to hide him for a while. But his head wound required medical attention and he had to be taken to the hospital, where he was labeled a fugitive and arrested.

Eventually, Lux and Caveman were captured and charged with assault and kidnapping. In the end, they were both tried and convicted by an all-white jury in Torrance and ended up doing major time, at least ten to fifteen years. Chip was also charged with assault on a highway patrolman, but he was additionally charged with murdering a security guard. He was convicted of all charges and sentenced to death. In 1972, though, when California overturned the death penalty, Chip's sentence was reduced to life in prison.

It's hard to describe how I felt about losing Lux to the pen. I became very emotional about it: he was one of my closest comrades, and he played a large part in my growth and development as a Panther. I felt his absence immediately. Al took Lux's conviction really hard too; he and Lux had joined together and led the Watts office. As for Caveman, I had known him since high school—we grew up together. Losing him to prison was like losing part of my history. Chip had recently joined, so we didn't share a lot of history, but I respected his talent and zeal, and I knew that we had lost a committed soldier. Out of the group that came from Tracy together, I knew his imprisonment would last longer than the others—the conviction of murdering a security guard meant that he would grow old and possibly die in jail.

Worst of all, the assault on the Party was still raining down on us in a fury. On the same day we found out about Chip, Lux, and Caveman, the cops raided the breakfast program again. It was September 8; I'll never forget that gloomy day, with all its bad news. Hasawa, Touré, Bruce, and a few others were there working and serving the children. The police came in armed, engaging in their usual despicable behavior, throwing the kids' food all over the floor, pushing and threatening. They were ordering the children around too, terrorizing them, shouting at them, and telling them to call their parents to pick them up. That shit is hard for a soldier to sit back and do nothing about. And there's such an irony in it all: yeah, we know terrorism very well. They've been terrorizing our people in America for hundreds of years. And now Hoover wants to label *us* the terrorists. We were just trying to fight back, fire with fire.

Then, four days after the attack on the breakfast program, we lost Nathaniel Clark; he was killed in a domestic dispute with his wife. I was at Central Headquarters when I heard about it. She said he was high at the time, and she shot him to death. He was only nineteen when he died. Clark was part of the original group who started the L.A. Party with Bunchy. It was a devastating loss for the organization but particularly for the Watts office.

And a few days after losing Clark, the Metro cops came to the Watts office, demanding entry. I was standing at the front entrance when they came. I quickly closed the door and then grabbed a pump shotgun, refusing them entry without a search warrant. "Haven't we been through this before?" I snarled through the locked door. "No warrant, no admission. You're not welcome here."

Fortunately, it ended without incident that day. The ministandoff went on for what seemed like forever, but it probably lasted about thirty minutes. We'd done this drill before: the pigs trying to threaten and scare us, yelling insults and obscenities, and then one of us hurling it right back at them, before they packed up and left. This had happened too many times for some of the comrades, and I knew they were itching to get back at the police. Things could have gone down entirely differently that day, but it still served to heighten the stress and agitation everyone felt.

September finally ended, and the beginning of October was a little quieter, so we had some time to catch our breath. Until, that is, October 18. It was a Saturday, clear and cool out. That was the day that Touré and Bruce decided to take offensive action against the pigs. I'm not sure what triggered the event—it could have been the latest trashing of the Free Breakfast for Children Program, or maybe it was the imprisonment of Chip, Lux, and Caveman. But obviously, the two of them finally made the decision not to wait anymore for the police to become reasonable human beings, human beings who would allow us to work in our community freely and defend ourselves, like free men should. They decided to no longer wait for the police to act like the "officers of the peace" they were supposed to be, who were sworn "to protect and to serve," as the LAPD's motto advertised in the official maxim they adopted in 1963.

I wasn't aware of what had gone down until the next day. I had been arrested; I was in custody at the Seventy-Seventh Precinct, on some trumped-up charge designed to keep me off the street. I was sitting on a bench in a jail cell when a Metro officer walked by. He saw me and kind of jumped back, a look of surprise washing over his face. "I thought we got you tonight," he said cryptically. "But I guess it was the other W.P."

I glowered at him, not saying a word, not moving a muscle.

"Yeah, we got on the ground and shot your boy in the head," he finished, emphasizing the word "head" with special relish, a perverse grin deforming his face.

What the fuck is he talking about? I thought to myself. *The other W.P.?* Question after question was racing through my mind. *Is he messing with me? Is he telling the truth? Could it be Touré he's talking about—Walter Pope? Is Touré in custody too? Or worse?* I shuddered.

I was in custody all night. The night dragged. It was torturous, wondering what had gone down and having no way of finding out. I was trying to stay positive, but worst-case scenarios were playing themselves out in my head. I couldn't sleep at all, couldn't even close my eyes and try to rest a little. By the next morning, I was exhausted, but they finally released me. I went straight to the Watts office, and it was there that I heard Touré and Bruce had been ambushed by an undercover Metro Squad car at Manchester and Stanford, sitting outside of a Jack in the Box hamburger stand. It was Craig who gave me the news.

I studied him. "So where are they?" I asked steadily. "In jail?"

Craig looked at me solemnly. "Touré is dead, man," he answered, as tears filled his eyes. "We heard Bruce got hit too," he went on, "but he escaped. He's in good hands though, getting help from the leadership."

The impact of his words pushed me back a couple steps, like I had just gotten walloped in the chest. I felt overwhelmed, distraught, and destroyed. I found a chair nearby and fell down into it. I sat in silence for a long time; this time I didn't even want to know what happened. I was trying to wrap my head around the loss of Touré. I broke down.

Later that day, Long John came to the Watts office. He clarified what *really* went down. His purpose in telling us, he explained, was to warn us against taking the offensive. He wanted to keep us alive.

"Comrades," he said firmly, "I know this has been a devastating time for you in Watts. The police are not letting up. But you *got* to hear me when I say that you cannot go on these suicide ventures against the police. It's too dangerous."

"What exactly are you saying, comrade?" someone asked.

"I know you heard there was an ambush yesterday, but I'm here to tell you the truth." Long John looked hard at each of us.

"So what really happened, Captain?" I pressed.

"Without telling anyone, Touré and Bruce had planned a surprise attack on the pigs," he replied straightforwardly.

My mind was racing. As he spoke, I flashed back to my ambush attempt against Fisher and Hole. I winced.

The attack had occurred, Long John expounded, at the Jack in the Box restaurant that had been robbed several times, so all of us knew undercover cops were staking out the place. Touré and Bruce spotted the police and parked out of view, then walked up to the back of the squad car and let loose. Touré had a .30 caliber M-1 carbine and Bruce had a double-barrel shotgun. Both of them got shots off. They wounded one of the officers, but then Touré's gun jammed, which gave the pigs an opportunity to return fire. Bruce had taken some bullets in the abdomen and was wounded badly, and Touré was killed. Based on what the police said to me earlier, they shot Touré when he was on the ground. I also heard later, through other sources, that they stomped him on his head too.

Somehow Bruce was able to get back to the Volkswagen they had driven in. He ended up at the apartment of Gwen, Elaine, and some of the other women. Long John and G came to help, and eventually they found a movement doctor who told them that Bruce had sustained life-threatening wounds and needed to go to the hospital. Bruce was arrested at the hospital, but his life was saved. He eventually did about seven years in prison.

The death of Touré devastated the Party in several major ways. Most of all, in losing him, we lost one of the most enthusiastic and committed future leaders of the Party. But for me personally, I had lost another friend. Glenda Josephs, who worked the breakfast program, was Touré's girlfriend. At the time he was killed, she was pregnant. At least I was glad to know his legacy would live on in his child.

Touré's death not only brought on more warnings from leadership about the rank and file taking independent action against the pigs, but it also created controversy throughout the chapter. Touré's gun had jammed, and it was a gun that Cotton Smith had worked on. By this time, everybody was looking at everybody else with suspicion. Comrades were on edge. Fingers were pointing to Cotton, because some thought he deliberately gave Touré a defective gun for the ambush. I completely disagreed with this, because I understood weapons and knew that the M-1 has a tendency to jam. They were good weapons, but I thought they should be used for defense as opposed to offensive assault precisely for that reason.

I didn't care about the controversy with Cotton or the critique of Bruce and Touré taking action as they had. I loved Touré like a brother, and I knew that I would miss him for the rest of my life. I was part of the honor guard at his funeral, and it was truly an honor. But it was also an overwhelmingly sad day for me. What was happening to the Party? What about the future? I came home from the services that day and sat down on my bed, my hand still clutching the wadded-up memorial card that someone had made up for him. I sat there for a long time. I needed a lift; I needed a reminder of why we were doing this. I wished more than anything in that moment that I could speak with my comrade just one more time. I opened the program still wrinkled up in my hand, smoothing out its pages, numbly reading and rereading the words inside. Then I reached over to my bedside table and grabbed the pen lying next to my gun. Inside it, I wrote Touré a little note, five simple words, a reminder.

ALL POWER TO THE PEOPLE.

"Arm Yourselves." Graffiti expressing the mood of the city in 1970. WAYNE PHARR COLLECTION

14

GETTIN' READY

From G to Long John and all the others, during the PE classes the
message was the same, urgent and clear: *The FBI has a mandate to
destroy the party! The head FBI pig, J. Edgar Hoover, has declared war
on us. You all know that he said we, the Black Panther Party for Self-
Defense, are the most dangerous threat to national security.*

And it was true: every chapter of the Party was under siege in
one way or another.

"We are at war, and we have lost many comrades over the last
year," Peaches declared as we sat in PE class one balmy October afternoon in Watts. All around the room, heads were nodding in agreement.

"It's not only us," she continued, "but our friends and family; all
of our people are catching hell and having their lives turned upside
down."

"Chairman Bobby Seale is on trial in Chicago," someone behind
me muttered angrily, "and the New York 21 Panthers are facing big
time for bullshit charges, like conspiracy to blow up the New York
Botanical Gardens."

"They even claimed that the New York Panthers were gonna kill Roy Wilkins, Whitney Young, and a bunch of old civil rights activists!" a pretty sister next to me added irritably.

"Panthers don't have time to think about tryin' to kill them ol' Negroes!" responded someone else.

The room filled with murmurs of agreement, in a unanimous acknowledgment of our new urgency. The frustration in the meeting room was now palpable.

By the fall of 1969, every chapter and every person dedicated to the Party was being persecuted for his or her political beliefs. Chairman Bobby Seale had been kidnapped by police in Northern California and taken to Chicago for his trial for inciting a riot at the Democratic National Convention a year earlier. During the trial, he was chained to a chair and gagged to prevent him from demanding his lawyer of choice. The Philadelphia office was raided, and the home of a Panther was shot up in San Diego. In Los Angeles, we had just lost several comrades from the Watts office—including Walter "Touré" Pope, Bruce Richards, Luxey Irving, Nathaniel Clark, Robert "Caveman" Williams, and Romaine "Chip" Fitzgerald—to death or imprisonment. Others in Los Angeles, like Ronald Freeman and Blue, were fighting murder cases, so they were locked up too.

In Watts, Al, Craig, James, and I led the office, but we also relied more and more on the few who were left of the crew that came from Tracy—Chris Means, Kibo, and Hasawa. I was pleased that the community was still with us, even though the mandate to destroy the Party was obvious and put a strain on the community too. Despite the attacks, we were able to recruit about twenty new members during that time, including Robert Bryan, a Vietnam vet and cousin of Craig Williams. Robert was hard to miss in a crowd: he liked to wear those great big Jackson Five hats, and he had a thick mustache. He was a little older than most of us, in his midtwenties, and I was happy that he came to us with military experience. Because we were under siege, having new blood like Robert was significant.

Although he wasn't new on the scene, Jimmy Johnson seemed to me to be trying too hard to prove himself. By late 1969, Jimmy was hanging around the Party on a regular basis. He was a pimp, but there was no comparison between him and Superfly. Frankly, I thought he was real low level. I met Jimmy at an apartment on Eighty-Fourth and Main where Panthers hung out. One of the first things I noticed about him, besides his wannabe pimp persona, was a long fingernail (which I believed was for snorting coke). After being accepted as a member of the Party, Jimmy operated out of the Broadway office. It was there that he worked himself up to captain, handling security. I never felt comfortable with Jimmy, though, because he didn't exhibit the same political commitment as others. When Jimmy, Ronald Freeman, and a few others went to San Diego to restore order after the Us killings, Jimmy got into an argument with one of the brothers and got shot in the mouth. I don't know exactly what went down that day, but he still stayed in the Party after that, to my surprise.

The high number of casualties we had suffered weighed heavily on our minds. Uncertainty was thick in the air. We never knew who would be available to lead our programs because the pigs took us off the streets so frequently. In fact, the police had spun us into a vicious cycle of repeat arrests, charging us with an endless list of made-up crimes and then dropping the charges when they couldn't make them stick. This meant we had to keep raising bail money, and keep going to court to defend ourselves, so that we could get back to our business in our community. The worst part was that we never knew what would happen to us from day to day.

But I wasn't waiting for the police to take me out: I was preparing for the war by making sure I knew the layout of the sewers and which ones we could access when we needed to. In fact, by this time, I had been going down into the sewers once a week. As the situation intensified, I went down even more often.

G had an informant inside law enforcement, so several of us learned of a planned police attack on the Los Angeles Panthers. But we weren't sure of when. I didn't know if G's informant was inside the FBI or the LAPD, but I did know that he was a black person sympathetic to the Party. G didn't share that kind of information with everybody, but it was essential information for those who would organize the Party's defense.

G gave the order that we needed to consolidate our people and resources. We found this out from Al Armour, who walked into the Watts office one day with a bundle of papers in his hands.

"What's up?" Hasawa inquired, looking up from the gun he was cleaning.

Al casually put down the Panther newspapers and asked us all to gather around. He said he had some news from Central. "In order to ensure the survival of the Party and its work," Al began, "we must defend our people and our resources."

"OK, comrade, but what exactly are you saying?" Hasawa asked, putting his weapon to the side.

"Consolidating offices, resources, and personnel will make the task of security easier and more effective," Al exhorted.

So far, he wasn't telling us anything we didn't already know. Those of us in the room were all looking at him now, still wondering exactly where he was going with all this. I leaned back against the wall, waiting.

Al continued. "The Broadway office is the easiest to close right now, due to Roland's situation."

He was referring to Roland Freeman, the section leader and driving force of the Broadway office, who had accidentally shot himself by sticking a gun down one of his pant legs before going outside. The gun went off and blew a hole in his foot.

"You all know that Roland's been out of action all year, so we are missing leadership there."

Hasawa looked at me and then back at Al. "Where are the Broadway comrades going to operate?"

"Some of the comrades will be assigned to Watts or headquarters. We're also closing the Adams office and reassigning some of those comrades to the Touré Community Center." Located on Exposition and Normandie, the Touré Community Center had been named in honor of our fallen comrade, Walter "Touré" Pope.

Then Al surprised us. He stood up, striding across to the other side of the room. He stopped and turned around. "I have been assigned to run the Touré Community Center, and Wayne will be running the Watts office," he declared.

I said nothing, instead nodding my head to acknowledge Al's revelation. It was time to get moving, then.

Along with reorganizing locations, we began to fortify Central Headquarters. It was October, shortly after Touré died. We couldn't fortify all of our offices because of the large number of resources it would take, but we absolutely needed to strengthen Central, since the leadership operated there. It was also where mass meetings were held, and most important, it was where G's informant said a hit might come.

As minister of defense, G led the fortification project. His war experience and military skills were critical for planning and execution. We were also fortunate to have Cotton on board, because he had the construction skills we needed to build structures that would hold. And as one of our most respected captains, Long John brought both leadership and a serenity that gave our soldiers the confidence necessary to keep moving forward. Long John managed the daily efforts of the rank and file, and he provided the team with an exceptional understanding of defensive tactics and strategy. Captain Omar brought important skills to Central's fortification too. His role in the Party expanded after Ronald and Blue were out, doing time. Omar had served in the military and, like G, brought those skills to the Party. And then there was George Young, whom we called Duck because of his voice inflection. He had been a marine before joining the Party. He worked out of Central, often serving as officer of the day. George's role was to help out in the office and dig in the tunnels when he had time. As for me, I participated in defensive strategy sessions, helped to devise our escape plan, and worked alongside Long

John organizing and working with the troops. I also made sure we had access to weapons. Even though some of us specialized in specific areas, a lot of our work overlapped.

Knowing that headquarters would be attacked with heavy forces, we made our plan: One, fortify Central. Two, resist and fight as long as possible. Three, escape through the tunnel we would build into the sewers. Four, while in the sewers, blow the office.

G never called for any kind of official large group meeting about our plan and the work involved; instead, he gave us our orders in small group settings or individually. The first order of business was to make sure we had the material needed for the fortification. We used our meager resources to purchase as many items as we could from hardware stores. Obviously, what we couldn't purchase, we liberated from construction sites.

Before long, we got pretty much everything we needed to begin our work. Everyone was busy; everyone had a task or role. G walked around, surveying the headquarters layout. "Cotton, where do we start digging?" he queried.

Cotton walked into one of the conference rooms on the northeast side of the building, toward the front. He pointed to a spot on the floor. "Right here," he said confidently. "This will give us the best line to the sewers." He knew the best route because Ronald had gotten maps of the city layout before he went to jail, and Cotton now had those maps. "We need to dig about thirty-five to forty feet to get to the sewer line," he finished.

G looked at Long John. "Comrade, I need you to begin organizing the soldiers into squads and get started."

Long John nodded his head. "Right on!" he grinned.

Within half an hour, we were tearing up the floors to access the dirt underneath and putting shovels into the ground.

Comrades worked in squads of four or five at a time; we were digging into the tunnel every day, all day, and sometimes all night. Everybody participated in the digging at one point or another. We passed the time talking and listening to music from the KGFJ radio station. The Magnificent Montague, Lucky Pierre, and the other DJs from KGFJ were playing Top 40 soul cuts for us, which made the work seem easier and go faster. We dug to B. B. King's "The Thrill Is Gone" and the soulful gospel hit "Oh Happy Day." The 5th Dimension invited us to a "Stone Soul Picnic," and James Brown shouted out, "Give It Up, Turn It Loose." And we turned it up and dug that dirt loose.

It was pretty warm in the tunnel, so sometimes comrades would take their shirts off to continue digging in comfort. There was no ventilation. Any air we had coming in came from the fans above the hole. Guys wore bandannas around their faces to keep the dust from getting into their mouths and noses; the work was exhausting and never-ending. But remembering our dead and the beatings we had taken kept us motivated. We also knew that we had no future in Los Angeles if the pigs maintained their posture and attitude toward us. We had a slogan to remind ourselves of why we were working so hard: "Off the Pigs."

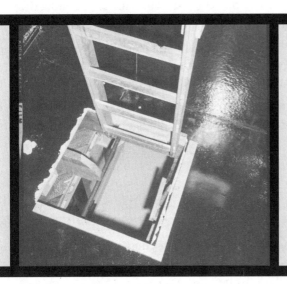

Entrance to the tunnel we dug from the Party headquarters at Forty-First and Central heading to the sewers. We had almost reached the sewers when LAPD SWAT attacked on December 8, 1969. UCLA CHARLES E. YOUNG RESEARCH LIBRARY DEPARTMENT OF SPECIAL COLLECTIONS, LOS ANGELES TIMES PHOTOGRAPHIC ARCHIVES

G came to check on the comrades, to make sure the work was moving at a good pace. At one point he looked at me. "Comrade Wayne," he said directly, "what's up with the sewers and artillery?"

The task that had been given to me was to map out escape routes through the sewers and determine how to dodge the police. "We have been checking for every possible way to make it out of here, and we are covered," I answered. "We got the heat covered too."

When it came to digging into the tunnel, Cotton was indispensible in making sure we did things right. "Comrades," he explained to all of us, "you have to understand that we can't just dig a hole in the ground. If we want success and want to live through this task, we have to brace the walls so the whole goddamn thing don't collapse!"

I don't know about the others, but I was a little nervous about the tunnel collapsing, so I was glad Cotton addressed the issue. He instructed us on how to shore up the tunnel as we used our picks and shovels, so it wouldn't cave in on us. We also helped Cotton run an electrical line into the tunnel for light, so we could see what the hell we were doing.

Another consideration was that digging the tunnel produced a lot of dirt. To handle that issue, G's military training kicked in: he had us use the dirt to make sandbags, and also pour the dirt into the walls, which would give the office some added protection against pig bullets. While some of the brothers dug, others poured the dirt into burlap sacks and tied them up for sandbags. Using a hammer, crowbar, or even an ax, brothers with more skills demonstrated how to break open the walls, find the empty spaces, and pour the dirt between the studs. We could hear it throughout the day: *Bam! Bam! Bam!* and then *swoosh*, as the dirt poured in.

The last area we had to deal with was the training room downstairs. It had a rear door that opened up to the backyard and rear alley, which created another vulnerability. For that, we used the tunnel dirt to secure the back door by piling it from the floor to the ceiling. It turned into a big mountain. No one, not the LAPD, the FBI, or the army, was getting through that door without going through two or three tons of dirt!

Periodically, someone would shout, "Man, I'm hungry!" which was a signal for a meal break. Then one or two of the brothers would make a run to the hamburger stand on the corner and bring back hamburgers, fries, and drinks. Other times, people brought in food, and sometimes we cooked. On the days when we cooked, mostly it was beans, rice, and spaghetti: something in a big pot that could feed a lot of people. Sometimes we ate stuff leftover from the breakfast program. We washed down the food with beer every now and then, but mostly it was RC Colas, Nesbitt's, or Cactus Coolers.

G was sure the pigs would try to throw tear gas in the office. "Long John, Cotton," he demanded, "you need to get some brothers to cover the windows with chicken wire. We need to prepare for tear gas grenades."

Cotton volunteered. "I'll hit up the hardware store tomorrow to pick up what we need."

Long John put the brothers on task when the supplies arrived. Things continued to progress smoothly.

As our fortification project began to take shape, G turned to Cotton and me. "You brothers need to make sure there are firing ports upstairs," he ordered. We assured G that it would be done.

Cotton built firing ports, which were rectangular holes cut in the wall or the wood, big enough for us to see out of. A metal hinge was used for the ports so that we could open them up to shoot and then close them to keep out bullets and tear gas, decreasing the chances of us getting hit. Cotton made two gun bunkers downstairs that had excellent fields of fire, meaning we could see everything that moved for one to two hundred yards. It gave us outstanding command of the street. These bunkers were reinforced with dirt and sandbags on top and in front to protect us in case the cops were shooting down. The bunkers had slats too.

We also needed to resolve the issue of the pigs coming at us from our office next door, as well as from the upstairs. Cotton built a trapdoor and a ladder to give us access to the upstairs without having to go outside. His idea for the trapdoor was genius. Luckily for us, the police didn't even know about it. We made sure that Party members didn't use the trapdoor either, because we didn't want to alert the police to its existence. Everybody was still walking up and down the stairs from outside. Even if the pigs found out about it, we needed to make sure they had no access to that door, because otherwise they would be able to raid downstairs and upstairs at the same time. So we reinforced the doors with big metal braces and wood. That way, the door of 4115½ South Central Avenue would resist even the pigs' handheld battering ram.

While we were fortifying the office, we continued our Party work, selling newspapers, feeding kids, holding political education classes, doing food and clothing drives, recruiting, training, and opening new locations. Carl Hampton was visiting us from Houston—he had been invited by G, came to Los Angeles in October, and spent most of his time at Central Headquarters. He was there to learn about setting up and operating a chapter. We explained the processes we used when selling the papers and collecting the money, setting up the office, recruiting, and holding political education classes. We worked with him about two days. He was serious about the Black Panther Party and didn't come to Los Angeles to go to parties and chase girls. I gained respect for him while he was here. He was intelligent but also demonstrated street-smarts. Carl Hampton never started a chapter but established a People's Party II modeled after the Black Panther Party. The Central Committee in Oakland refused to allow any new chapters because of police repression. Carl Hampton didn't even live a year after he visited Los Angeles. He was killed in July 1970.

Another project that was extremely important to us during this period was establishing the Bunchy Carter Free Health Clinic, a grassroots community operation to which physicians and nurses donated their time. It was located on the same block as our headquarters. Elaine, Gwen Goodloe, Norma, and Masai worked heavily on that.

One evening in November we held a meeting at the headquarters to discuss the health clinic. The physicians, lawyers, nurses, and volunteers attended, along with thirty members from other offices. The meeting began around 5:00 PM. As we moved toward 7:00, the meeting was ending, so the visitors started leaving. At some point, Will Stafford noticed some police activity while looking out of the window.

Will went over to G to speak to him. About two to three visitors were left, but G knew he couldn't wait any longer to take action. With serious authority, G said, "Attention comrades, everybody stop what you are doing."

We all stopped talking and started walking toward G so we could hear what he had to say.

"There are about a hundred pigs out front, blocking off the street."

The police had blocked off Central Avenue between Santa Barbara and Vernon Avenue and were diverting traffic away from the area. They cleared the streets so that no cars could get through. Then we noticed that they had surrounded the building; some of the pigs were on the rooftop, and police cars and vans were parked up and down the street. We saw some police running as they moved into position. The police were positioned to raid us.

G directed us. "Everybody move into position. Elaine, man the phones and let people know what's going on."

Elaine, Joan, and a few other women went upstairs to handle the communications. They contacted the news media, the national office in Oakland, and community activists. After the media was called, reporters, community leaders, and those from the neighborhood came out to see what was happening.

While the women were moving, G said, "Everybody else move into defensive position. Long John and Cotton, make sure everybody has a weapon."

Long John and Cotton went into the gun room on the first floor and quickly parceled out the arms. Of course, some of us were already packing, but having an additional weapon was not a bad thing. There were a variety of weapons in the gun room, but we had more people than guns. The guns were given to the most senior and most experienced in warfare. Those in leadership positions took the best guns, like the Thompson and M-14s. If a comrade didn't have a gun, then he was to stand by to take one from someone who had gotten shot or couldn't use it for whatever reason. Also, if a comrade didn't have a gun, he would be given a pipe bomb instead. As we received our weapons, G walked back and forth, issuing orders that ensured all of the entry spots were covered. Except for Elaine, who was on the phone, and G giving instructions, we all stayed quiet.

There were approximately eight rooms upstairs, which encompassed the newsroom, communications room, conference room, and others. The meeting room was in the center, with all the other rooms radiating off of it. I was positioned upstairs in a conference room, looking over Central Avenue, covering the window with an M-1 carbine. Will Stafford, Lloyd Mims, Long John, and Tony Quisenberry were upstairs too, spread throughout the other rooms. There were at least two people in every room, sometimes three. Paul Redd, Cotton, Duck, and Jimmy Johnson covered the windows and doors downstairs.

It became a cat-and-mouse game for the next two hours. Apparently, part of the negotiation with the police was that any women and children present could leave. G told the women to go, and they left gladly. About an hour later, the cops pulled out, but we stayed armed. We talked for hours about what had occurred. We knew we needed to urgently intensify our efforts after this.

The next day, G and I met and surveyed the situation. We noticed right away that the police did not leave anything behind that indicated they had been there. G said to me, "This was a reconnaissance mission. They were checking to see what kind of defenses we have."

I said, "Well, I think it was a pretty dumb move on their part. Coming in on us with that classic police shit of jumping out of cars and running toward the office. We could've easily smoked twenty to thirty of them in a few minutes."

"Yeah, I know. It would have been a bloodbath. They don't know our capabilities," G commented.

I concluded, "So many cops could've died last night. We would have never gotten out of jail."

But for the pigs, the dry run was successful because it provided them intelligence about our abilities, so they had to go back and regroup and strategize. Obviously, they decided that coming in on us when everyone was awake would leave them wide open. For them, it would make sense to come in the wee hours of the morning and try to catch us sleeping.

As we continued fortifying our headquarters, we were hit with some devastating news on December 4. During a predawn raid, at about 4:45 AM, the Chicago pigs had murdered Fred Hampton and Mark Clark, leaders in the Illinois chapter of the Black Panther Party. Chairman Hampton had been shot in his bed while asleep after being drugged by an FBI agent provocateur. Clark was shot while sitting in a chair on security duty. Clark was twenty and Hampton was twenty-one.

Upon hearing the news, I went to headquarters to get the facts. By the time I arrived, Black Panthers from all over the city were there already to get information, determine the Party's response, and mourn our loss. The scenario reminded us of Central Headquarters after Bunchy and John were killed. Like our two leaders, Chairman Fred and Captain Mark were effective organizers. They were bringing gangs together and establishing coalitions with them to support black liberation. It was no wonder the pigs wanted them dead. After hearing about Chicago, I knew that it was just a matter of time before we were hit. Were we ready to take on the added repression we knew was coming our way? We prepared for the worst.

On December 7, I took a break from Central Headquarters to spend time with Sharon and Tammy. We hung out at Sharon's mother's house, where I was able to get a good meal and wind down. It was a nice time for us. Tammy was about six months old and active for her age. She noticed me and smiled when I walked into the room. I talked with Sharon about what we were doing at headquarters. I left Sharon and Tammy late at night and went to Jerry's house.

This is the chair I was sitting in when the SWAT team burst through the door. UCLA CHARLES E. YOUNG RESEARCH LIBRARY DEPARTMENT OF SPECIAL COLLECTIONS, LOS ANGELES TIMES PHOTOGRAPHIC ARCHIVES

15

BUSTED

"You're losing a lot of blood, Mr. Pharr. We're going to give you some blood and some glucose to replenish what you've lost. You're quite a lucky young man," I heard a voice say.

It was coming to me from somewhere, but I wasn't quite sure who it was from or even where I was. It was dark, and then everything started getting lighter, but very fuzzy and surreal, like I was watching a movie underwater.

I realized I was lying in a hospital bed, and then I understood that I was in the jail ward of the county hospital. I must have been unconcious, I realized; as I awoke I wondered how long I had been in this place. The face of an emergency room doctor was hovering over me, peering at me with a serious look. I looked at him and took it all in but didn't really have it in me to respond. It was as if I was an outside observer, taking all this craziness in. The doctor told me that the wound in my forehead, responsible for the blood streaming down my face, was superficial. As soon as he told me that, I became aware of the blood all over me. The same was true for the pellets in my left arm—superficial. Gradually, I began to remember what had happened and why I was here. The pigs had ambushed us, and there had been a shoot-out. Right. I remembered Roland was here somewhere too, though I was too disoriented to know where.

The more serious issue was the buckshot wound located in a muscle on the left side of my chest, over my heart, the doctor told me. It was likely that my wounds came from a 12-gauge shotgun, he said.

"I don't expect those pellets to move, though, so we don't need to operate to try to get them out," he informed me.

I nodded my head. I was wounded physically, but now my spirit was soaring. The arduous work of fortifying Central Headquarters had paid off. We had survived.

While I was in the hospital, two detectives came by to question me. I was lying in a bed in a room with five or six other victims of gunshot wounds, including Roland. I immediately noticed the detectives when they walked in: they marched straight toward me and stopped next to my bed. I turned my head away from them.

"What's your name?"

Bleeding after the battle, I am being put into the back of a patrol car.
UCLA Charles E. Young Research Library Department of Special Collections, Los Angeles Times Photographic Archives

I looked up at them. "Wayne."

"Wayne who?"

"Pharr. Wayne Pharr," I answered feebly. I was too tired for this shit.

"Where did the guns come from?"

"I really don't know," I frowned weakly.

They were gruff and pushy, peering at me through contemptuous eyes. They asked me more questions, but I turned my head away from them again and closed my eyes, refusing to respond. That worked. They didn't stay long after that.

I stayed in the jail ward of the county hospital one day before I was transfered to the county jail in downtown Los Angeles. Two detectives woke me from my sleep about 2:00 AM and told me it was time to go. I was groggy and still weak, but I managed to sit up.

"Stand up and turn around," the big one said with real authority.

As I did, I heard the sound of handcuffs, and then I felt them tighten around my wrists, first one, then the other, pig number two taking obvious delight in tightening them until they were pinching and bruising my bones.

"Where are you taking me?" I mumbled.

"To the county jail, to join the rest of the club," pig number one spat sarcastically. They walked me outside, where their county van was waiting. It was cold as ice outside and not too much warmer inside the vehicle. All I had on was a skimpy hospital gown, which, besides being threadbare from too many bleachings, was drafty and too loose. I figured that since they hadn't been able to kill me with their guns, they were trying to do it by giving me the flu.

I was booked and fingerprinted and had my mug shot taken wearing only the hospital gown. After being processed, I was sent to a regular cellblock. I was still weak, but now I was alert. I needed to keep my head clear and my wits about me so I could deal with whatever might come my way. As I looked around the cell, I noticed immediately that I had been placed in the "snitch tank." I knew this because the jail housed predominately black inmates, but everyone in the cell with me was white. A few of the "inmates" tried to engage me in small talk, which I knew was really a search for information.

"How long have you been in the Party? What do you think about the student movement? Tell us what the rallies are like," they prodded.

Just like with the detectives in the hospital, I didn't have much to say and I kept to myself. Sure enough, I found out later that a couple of the white guys in the cell were trustees.

I considered myself a prisoner of war, so I had absolutely no expectations of being treated fairly by the state. As I sat mute in the cell, my mind was racing. *Will I ever see the light of day again? What happened to the other comrades?* I thought about my family: Mom, Nanny, Sharon, and Tammy. *Do they even know what happened? Do they know where I am?*

I was moved to a regular cell on the mainline after spending two days in the snitch tank. I figured they transfered me after they realized I wasn't ever going to talk. On the mainline, my cellmate, Sanford, was in for burglary. He was a few years older than me and very familiar with the criminal justice system. In fact, he explained to me, going in and out of jail was a way of life for him. I felt bad for him, but he said it so matter-of-factly that I believed he really had accepted that lifestyle.

The other inmates knew that I was one of the Black Panthers who had been in the shoot-out with the pigs. They were proud of us! And to show their gratitude and respect, they offered me their most prized items: cigarettes, candy, even money. I also ran into some of my homeboys from the 'hood, including Johnny McGill, whom I grew up with on Eighty-Seventh and Broadway. We recognized each other in the chow hall. He was sitting down eating and looked up from his plate; we made eye contact ever so briefly, and before he looked away he gave me a sign of recognition by nodding his head.

I never really got a chance to speak with him about why he was there or what he had been up to lately. But even though we didn't get the chance to talk, he let me know that he had my back. When the "bulls" would engage in their usual harassment of me, for example, by pulling me out of line or triple-checking my wristband, I noticed that Johnny and his crew were standing behind me. I was grateful for brothers like him.

My cellmate schooled me on the intricacies of prison life. Once, the bulls were yelling over the intercom, "Up against the wall, Blue! Stand still, Blue! Stop talking, Blue!"

I looked at him. "This Blue cat must be one bad son of a bitch."

"Nah, man," Sanford laughed. "We're *all* Blue!"

"What do you mean?" I frowned.

"All the inmates wear blue, and the trustees wear brown," he chuckled. "*You* are Blue."

I soon acclimated to cell life, the rules, and the daily regimen. At 5:00 AM, the bulls unlocked the cells for the "court line," which meant that all those who had a court appearance that day were to line up. The inmates used this opportunity to go from cell to cell to visit other inmates and trade, talk, or play games like chess and dominoes. Then at 7:00 AM, we would go to the cafeteria for breakfast, while those who were going to court got a sandwich for the bus ride. I was surprised to learn that there was a certain etiquette for eating in the county jail. For example, during meals, an inmate could cause a riot if he passed his hands over someone else's plate.

After breakfast, we would go back to our cells, or our "houses," as the inmates called them. We all cleaned our houses and took pride in having a clean and tidy space. The emphasis on being neat and clean was another surprise to me. Even as conscious as I was about stereotypes, I never stopped to think about the widely held view that cons don't care about hygiene and taking care of themselves. In jail, the truth was that people who were considered less hygienic were not tolerated. And we were supposed to have respect for others' property. Also, I learned that other than court line and mealtime, the only other opportunity to leave your house was to shower or to meet with visitors and lawyers.

One of the hardest things for me to adjust to, though, was being so openly exposed to homosexuality. I was sleeping one morning when I was awakened by a voice. "Kiss me, baby," a man murmured passionately.

Slightly panicked, I did a quick check and was relieved to confirm that no one was in my bed or coming at me. I looked over the side of my bunk, and underneath me, I found that my cellmate had this little Latino trustee in his bunk. They were fornicating.

Later that day, I asked the brother how long it took before people began to have homosexual tendencies.

"Three months," he said.

At that, my eyes popped open. "Three months? Damn, man, you must have been gay before you were locked up."

He didn't answer. I didn't pursue it any further.

After a few days on the mainline, the pigs tried to set me up. My cell was located on the ground floor, with a catwalk right above us. About 9:00 PM, a wad of newspaper was set on fire and landed in front of my cell. I heard something drop and looked up to see what it was. Startled, I yelled, "Fire, Fire!" I ran to the sink and got a cup of water, throwing it on the flames. But when I stuck my hand through the bars, a burly guard grabbed my arm. He had obviously been standing outside the cell, out of view the whole time, and waiting to pounce.

"You're trying to burn down the cell!" he bellowed.

"Utter bullshit!" I protested. "I was trying to put the fire out!"

Next thing I knew, that fuckin' bull had written me up and I was sent to the High Power Module 2500. High Power was where the high-profile and dangerous prisoners were kept in the county jail system.

When I got to High Power, I discovered that the majority of my comrades were already there: G, Paul, Will, Cotton, and Lloyd. Ike Houston, who worked out of the Exposition Boulevard office, was there too. Albert Armour and some others had been there, but they had gotten bailed out earlier. Everybody was in separate one- or two-man cells in the same block. Roland, I found out, was still in the hospital. He had gotten shot pretty bad in the arm during the shooting, and then when the roof blew, the falling wood had come down and smashed him in the head. He had been wounded pretty seriously.

The High Power section of the jail was different from mainline in several ways. For one thing, it was made up of tiny cells that were so small I could barely stand up. If there were two men to a cell, moving around was nearly impossible, considering that there was just enough room to lie down or sit down. Also, the cells were situated in such a way that the guards could see us all the time if they wanted to. Another difference from the mainline was that the bulls brought our food to us to eat in our cells, rather than allow us to go to the cafeteria.

The moves by the deputies to get us all into High Power had obviously been calculated; they wanted us out of the general population, isolated and confined. Our treatment was similar to mass murderers like Charles Manson; we knew this because Manson was an inmate at High Power during the time we were there. I saw him once when he was with his attorney. He was across the room, standing up as he was ending a legal visit with the lawyer. What I remember most about him was that he was a little bitty guy, which surprised me.

It was at High Power that I learned the full extent of the police mission to destroy the Black Panther Party of Southern California. G and Ike weren't even with us during the shoot-out at Central Headquarters, so I was taken aback when I discovered that they were in High Power. I had a ton of questions for them but knew I couldn't really talk freely with the guards around. If we did try to talk, there was a system: the guys on the end of the cellblock would look out for the bulls and warn us when they were approaching. Or we would just wait until we were in the shower.

I finally caught up with G and Ike for a few minutes when I saw that the guards were preoccupied with other things. We grabbed the opportunity to catch up with each other. "G!" I hollered in a hushed tone. "You there? Can you hear me?"

"Loud and clear, my brother," came his unmistakable voice. "What's happening man?" he asked, in a tone that told me he was glad to know I was there.

Where should I start? So much to catch up on! "Damn, G, how'd they get you?" I asked, still careful to keep my voice low. I was sitting on the edge of my bunk because there was no room for me to stand, and plus I didn't want the guards who could see me to get the idea to come check out what was going on. I was literally on the edge of my seat.

"Man, you don't know yet?" G sounded surprised. "The pigs set off three raids at the same time. They came into my home screaming for my arrest and shooting. They shot up the Touré Center that night too."

"And they hit us around the same time they hit you at Central Headquarters and G at his pad," added another voice on the other side of me. I could tell it was our comrade Ike. "I was there with Al, Craig, and Sharon Williams," he continued. "They came blazing in with guns and tear gas. We fought back and Al got some shots off. But Sharon is in bad shape. They kicked her in the chest so hard her lungs collapsed. And Craig got kicked in the mouth. It was brutal."

G continued the story. "While Saundra and me were sleeping, the fuckin' pigs broke into the house and put a gun to my head. What was so wild about it was that my girl lay across me to cover me, to stop the police from shooting me. She was willing to take a bullet for me," he said stoically. I could hear the emotion behind his words, though.

"That's love, man," I said.

I couldn't see G, but I knew he was proud. "I know," came the response. If I didn't know any better, I would've said he sounded a little choked up. "They arrested her, Kathy, and Evon," he continued. "The kids were there too. They were held at the station, but now they're with family." G lived on Fifty-Fifth Street in a house. It wasn't fortified like the office, so the pigs had no trouble getting in.

"Long John was in the back room," he went on. "It was dark. They knew he was there but really couldn't see him, so they fired on him a few times. I know they were trying to outright kill him, but he was able to dodge their bullets by jumping from side to side as they fired. When the pigs finally grabbed him, they kicked him in the mouth."

"Where is he?" I inquired.

"He was arrested, but they didn't charge him with any crime, so they let him go."

"What about you, Ike?" I asked.

"The pigs arrested all of us too," he said.

G added, "Man, Wayne, you really don't know what's been happening. Overall, eighteen of us were arrested."

"So, where is everybody?" I inquired, shaking my head at the thought.

"Different places," Ike replied. "Some comrades got different charges. The women are in Sybil Brand [an L.A. County correctional institute for women]. Elaine has been keeping us up to date. She said one of the biggest issues for the women is getting medical care. Sharon can't get her medicine for her injuries. Peaches is having some trouble with her stomach, and I hear she might have been pregnant. But Elaine is working with the lawyers to help them get what they need."

I got quiet as I thought about the movement sisters suffering like that. *Fuckin' pigs*, I thought to myself. On our end, Gil was dealing with a badly swollen hand and G was suffering from bad back pain from his injuries and also gastric problems. The deputies were refusing requests for medical treatment for them too. A few times, the physicians who volunteered at the Bunchy Carter Free Health Clinic petitioned the court to be allowed to come see us, but they weren't allowed in.

We talked about the shoot-out at headquarters. Ike asked, "So, when they came in, what did the pigs ask for?"

I replied, "They didn't ask for anything; they came in shooting."

Then G told us, "They claim they had search warrants for a few people, but I know they were looking for George Young, you know, Duck. You remember that day he pulled a gun on one of the pigs and told them to leave Central Headquarters."

"I see. Well, Duck wasn't even there. All they had to do was ask for him." I was thinking out loud now. "Man, the pigs went through all of that and didn't kill any of us. When we surrendered, we saw hundreds of cops. Their feelings must be hurt," I snickered.

Ike chuckled.

I continued, "The night of the shoot-out was the first time I had seen Roland in almost a year. But we pulled together as a formidable team. We were able to hold them off for hours, and I know we hit a few of them."

"Who all was at Central with you?" asked Ike.

"Roland just happened to be at the house because he was dropping Peaches off, so she could hang with Paul. They stopped at the office, got into a rap session, and Roland ended up staying. Will Stafford, Bernard Smith, Robert Bryan, Lloyd Mims, Gil Parker, and Cotton were there because they were working on the tunnel. Pee Wee was there too. I don't know if you know him, he's not a Panther, but he is from the neighborhood and helps out at headquarters from time to time. Robert and Paul Redd were serving as security. Tommye was there too."

All of a sudden, I was aware of a loud racket and a clamor of voices down the hall, and I realized it was our cellblock buddies warning us about the guards. Just like that, our conversation was over and we were back to doing nothing but sitting around in our cells.

Although I was confined, it felt good knowing I was with my comrades. We maintained our posture, and even our work, as Black Panthers. Through the bars of our cell doors, G led our activities, keeping us active physically and our spirits high. We talked about the support we were receiving outside. We applauded Elaine's organization of several mass rallies, with thousands of people taking off work to protest police repression. Civil rights organizations like the NAACP and professional groups like the Black Nurses Association came to our defense. There were meetings at black churches arguing that the police were silencing dissent by these kinds of raids. The Reverend Thomas Kilgore, pastor of the Second Baptist Church in Los Angeles, brought together community leaders young and old. People on the left side of politics, like Angela Davis, attended that meeting alongside people in the center, like an aide sent by Congressman Augustus Hawkins. While the community was organizing in our defense, our comrades used those opportunities to raise bail money too.

We also received reports of how the community had organized to clean up Central Headquarters after the raid. We heard there were all kinds of people who showed up to help, a real show of unity. Unfortunately, however, the cops showed up, too, to forcefully stop the community's actions. Police clubbed even state senator Mervyn Dymally in his effort to be helpful. It lifted our spirits, though, when we got word about how much our community understood what we had gone through and that they were fighting for us.

While in jail, we held political education and black history classes to keep ourselves sharp. G or I would lead the discussions, lecturing out from our cells, addressing the steel bars in front of us. Even though we couldn't see each other, the sense of camaraderie was thick in the air during the modified PE sessions. We even realized we didn't need to see each other—it was a good exercise in strength building. You could just feel the concentration, like those pin-drop moments. Periodically, a brother would holler out a question or a comment. Political education and black history were the kinds of things we didn't mind the guards hearing—in fact, we figured they might learn something!

"Now, we gon' let college boy lead the class today," G would say.

There would be a chorus of laughter as they encouraged me to speak. "Yeah, Wayne, give us some of them facts you gave the BSU!"

I was honored that G was asking me to help lead the discussions, and it was a good partnership too—the two of us balancing out each other's strengths and buoying each other's energies.

During one of my presentations, I brought up my family history in Gibson, Louisiana, to illustrate a point I was trying to make.

G cut me off. "I knew you were from Louisiana, but not Gibson! Do you know that my family lives not too far from there, in Morgan City?" he asked animatedly.

"What?" I exclaimed. "Yeah, I know that area; it's not far from Bayou Blue. My family isn't far from Bayou Black. For those of you who don't know, Bayou Black is a curve in the bayou."

It was an exciting discovery—knowing our families were in the same vicinity instantly made the sense of kinship between G and me even stronger. Now I knew why I was able to understand G so completely; he was just like all my relatives.

As I continued on with the point of my presentation, I noted that the military drafted lots of guys from the southeast part of the country: East Texas, Louisiana, Mississippi, Arkansas, and Alabama. I guessed aloud that they did this because the weather conditions in the Southeast were very similar to that of Vietnam and Southeast Asia, so therefore they thought we could withstand the heat better than others.

"Even though many of us came from some of the most racist areas of the country, we were still willing to fight—and *die*—for this country," G expounded.

"So many brothers felt that way," Craig chimed in.

"But we found out the hard way that the racism didn't end because we were overseas, fighting together," G finished. "In fact, I think Muhammad Ali summed it up quite nicely: 'Ain't no Vietcong ever called me "nigger."' "

"Yeah, that does sum it up pretty well," I agreed.

Eventually, Roland was released from the hospital and joined us in High Power. He had a cast on his arm, but he arrived in good spirits. Like the rest of us, he was glad to be around the people he had shared a life-and-death experience with.

Now we knew we had to focus on how to maneuver our legal situation. In fact, we expected serious charges to be leveled against us, like attempted murder. Thankfully, we had a powerhouse legal team who offered to work on our cases pro bono. As the others were, I was charged with a range of offenses: attempted murder, conspiracy to commit murder, possession of illegal weapons, and resisting arrest. Leo Branton, an outstanding African American civil rights attorney, served as our lead counsel; we didn't know how lucky we were. Branton was well known for his defense of so-called subversives or rebels, including the Hollywood Ten, the screenwriters and directors who refused to cooperate with government officials during their communist purge of the entertainment industry. Later, in 1972, he was also on the team that defended Angela Davis against murder charges, and it was his moving closing argument that famously helped convince an all-white jury to acquit her. Branton worked diligently on our behalf. He had a positive outlook and told us he would make sure we were not convicted of any of the serious charges. We were grateful for him.

Luke McKissack, a criminal defense and civil rights attorney, also worked with us for a while. Similar to Branton, he defended society's outcasts, rebels, and in his case even the notorious. Perhaps most noted was his legal work for Sirhan B. Sirhan, the man convicted of killing Robert Kennedy.

We met with our attorneys at the jail and before our court appearances. It was during our legal meetings that we learned more about SWAT, the Special Weapons and Tactics team, formed as a special unit of the LAPD to deal with subversive groups and high-risk situations. The LAPD was the first to organize this kind of unit, and, we learned, it had been formed specifically to deal with us! Considering all the other shit going on in society, we thought this obvious fear of us was laughable. We were feeding hungry people and giving poor and sick people medical care, things our government had promised but failed to do. In addition to that, though, we just weren't going to continue taking the undeserved beatings and murders the racist LAPD liked to dole out—and for that they formed SWAT.

We knew we were fighting an uphill battle. The judge even said in court that we were engaged in "armed anarchy" and that we needed to stand for attempted murder, conspiracy to commit murder, possession of illegal weapons, and a host of other charges. We were also aware that the weapons we had used had been confiscated, so they were now in the possession of the pigs.

Going to court required us to move first from High Power to the old county jail and then to court. We went for arraignments, bail, and preliminary hearings. After completing our business with the court, we were sent back to High Power, because they still wanted to keep us out of the general population. At High Power, sometimes we were moved to different cells or modules unexpectedly: the deputies didn't want us to get too comfortable, so they tried to keep us off-balance and confused. It was also a way they could keep us from trying to escape.

We arrived at the Los Angeles Hall of Justice for our preliminary hearings on Tuesday, January 6, 1970. There were demonstrators everywhere around the building, rallying to our support. People were shouting our slogan: "Power to the people!" Speakers, microphones in hand, cried out about the injustice we had suffered, noting that it was not separate from what was happening to black people everywhere. "The Black Panther Party is the party of the people," they said. People in the crowd, black and white, young and old, large and small, were holding up their placards of protest, black power fists in the air, and "eyewitness news" cameras were there to record it all. Elaine, we later found out, had organized the protests under the newly formed group Committee United for Political Prisoners. Masai, Elaine, and civil rights groups were stridently speaking out on our behalf.

While there was a lot of activity outside the courthouse, I noticed that the inside seemed dormant. It became obvious to us as we walked in that the courthouse was on lockdown, and security was extra tight. There were deputies all over the place, but very few people in the courtroom. I thought, *Is this really because of us?* Only one entrance to the courthouse was open, and the door to the stairway was locked so that people had to take the elevators with armed guards. The only people allowed in the building were employees and others on official business. Interestingly, it was at the preliminary hearing that the judge finally allowed a medical team in to see us.

The bulls hated us, of course. Fighting against the police had made us heroes to the other inmates, but we were targets to the bulls.

In the jail, we had gotten into a few scuffles with them over petty and not-so-petty issues, like trying to get them to deal with the rat infestation. We reported the rodent problem to the bulls, but they ignored us, so in court we reported it to the judge. The bulls told the judge we were lying and there were no rats on the cellblock. So, not surprisingly, nothing happened. After that, tired of putting up with the vermin and the lying guards, we took matters into our own hands. What we did was ingenious, I thought. We used the nasty red jelly that was put on our food trays to make rat traps. We called the jelly "red death," because we really didn't know what the hell was in it, anyway. Over the course of one weekend, we caught four or five rats. Roland, whose arm was still in a cast, put the dead critters in his cast before we went to court the next Monday. Claude Worrell, the lawyer for Pee Wee, complained to the judge again about the rat problem, and again one of the guards jumped up and called us liars in court. Then, in a dramatic showing up of who the liars really were, Roland stood up. He pulled the dead rats out of his cast, one by one, and held them out for all the court to see. Everyone in the room was stunned and disgusted. The judge immediately ordered us relocated. We considered that move a victory for the Southern California chapter of the Black Panther Party.

Finally, after we had been in jail for about two months, a court date was set for bail hearings. We were brought down from the holding cells to the court line, where we waited seemingly forever to leave for the courthouse. We were put in cells while we waited. In this area, prisoners were getting dressed for court, and some were coming and going from court back to jail and vice versa. There were probably two to three hundred people there at any given time; it was crazy and hectic. Sometimes there was food for us, usually sandwiches, which sat on a cart near the front of the room. If we could get to them before they were gone, we'd grab some up and eat them or tuck them away in our shirts for later.

While we were in the court line that day, we spotted Ronald and Blue on the other side of the room. They were there fighting a charge of attempted murder. We were glad to see them, and we started hollering—discreetly enough so as not to call attention from the guards but loud enough so that, we hoped, Ronald and Blue could hear us amid the chaos of the room. After trying for several minutes, we still couldn't get their attention. So G decided to get himself over to them; somehow he made his way into the section where Blue and Ronald were being held.

Then, out of nowhere, one of the bulls yelled out real loud, "Inmates! I have a cheese sandwich missing from the cart!"

Some of us stopped and looked at him, but mostly he was ignored.

But this deputy was not about to be disregarded. He became adamant about getting to the bottom of the so-called missing sandwich issue, and he started making a big deal over it. I couldn't understand why this chump was looking for a tasteless cheese sandwich, anyway. It didn't even make sense, because the food was for us. I knew he was just trying to start some shit.

The guard zeroed in on Blue, Ronald, and G and made a beeline for them. "Did you hear what I said?" he shouted angrily in G's face. "Who took the goddamn sandwich?" he pressed, his fat white face getting all puffed up and turning a bright cherry red.

G calmly looked him in the eye, and before anyone could blink, he hauled off and punched the fool, knocking him straight out. Not surprisingly, Ronald and Blue jumped into the fracas, kicking the shit out of this bull. Guards started coming from everywhere, yelling and shoving and grabbing inmates and hauling them out of the room. A bunch of the guards jumped on G and fought with him until they eventually subdued and handcuffed him. They brought him back over to our side of the room and threw him into the cell next to us. Before one of the bulls could get the door shut, though, G jumped back up and kicked him dead in the ass. The guard spun around on his heels, only to be greeted by a big, fresh dollop of G's spit—right in his face. Part of me loved it, secretly cheering G. *Right on, brother . . . get that bastard!* But part of me saw exactly where this was leading. "G! G! G!" I hollered. "Calm down, man! Cool it!"

G heard me and cooled out, thankfully, avoiding escalation and further provocation to deadly violence from them; they had guns, we didn't.

After the melee over the cheese sandwich settled down, the guards stayed on us, trying to goad us into a fight. The deputies were young like us; it was obvious they wanted to rumble.

As Black Panthers, we believed in self-defense; it didn't matter to us if it was on the streets or within the confines of a prison cell. So immediately after the incident, we set about doing what we needed to do: arm ourselves. We made jailhouse knives—called shanks—out of the clothes hangers that held our suits for our court appearances. First, we straightened the wire out. Then, quietly, we sharpened the tips by scraping them across the concrete floor. Then we waited.

As we knew would happen, a handful of guards eventually came and cleared the area of the remaining inmates, so all that was left were deputies and Panthers: about ten or eleven of us and maybe the same number of them—though who knew how many more lurked close by. We positioned ourselves in the holding cells, our hangers wrapped around our fists. The deputies had handcuffs and chains. We were braced for the next move from the bulls. The tension was high; no one was talking. We waited.

Next thing I knew, the watch commander was in the room, his big chest heaving as he barked at his deputies. Fortunately for us, he quickly sized up what was happening and immediately acted to defuse the situation. "Everybody hold it!" he roared.

As we watched, they all grudgingly came to attention, but they were still watching us out of the corners of their eyes. Things stayed tense. The watch commander continued to yell orders at them. He made the deputies put their chains down first. Once they had backed off, we gave up our shanks.

After the excitement of the morning, we still had to go to the courthouse. But because of the altercation, the deputies took extra precautions—designed, I guess, to further secure their safety but also to humiliate us. They shackled us from ankles to waist and chained us together, just like slaves. They brought us out of the cells one at a time, although we were still chained together. Then, we were led outside together, put on the bus together, and led into the courtroom together. Once we were out of the building and into the bright of daylight, I looked up and saw snipers standing along the roof and back into the hills. *Damn! I hope nobody trips and falls—they'll light us up like the Fourth of July,* I thought. Once we were in court, the prosecutors immediately asked the judge to raise our bail, citing the jailhouse fight that had started over the so-called missing cheese sandwich. Surprisingly, the judge granted us bail and told the prosecutor that he would need to file new charges.

It took half a year, but by the end of six months, we were all finally bailed out. My mother put up her property to use as bail for me. She even helped with G's bail. I was very moved that she would sacrifice so much for me and grateful that she loved and trusted me so much. My mom was hoping that this would be the last time I would ever be incarcerated.

I was released in March 1970, and as soon as I got out I went straight to Mom's house. It felt amazingly good to be home, sleeping,

In a scene reminiscent of slavery and Southern chain gangs, Los Angeles Black Panthers are led from the county jail to a bail hearing at the criminal court building at Temple and Broadway. Our hands and feet were shackled and we were chained together at the waist. Lloyd Mims is in front. UCLA CHARLES E. YOUNG RESEARCH LIBRARY DEPARTMENT OF SPECIAL COLLECTIONS, LOS ANGELES TIMES PHOTOGRAPHIC ARCHIVES eating recognizable and edible food, and being with my family—Nanny, Mom, Sharon, and my sweet little Tammy. I spent two days either in blissful slumber or sitting at the kitchen table with heaps of home-cooked food piled in front of me, soaking up the R & R.

But then I hit the streets again. I was, after all, still a Black Panther. First, I wanted to check out what headquarters looked like after the shoot-out. I was extremely curious to see what the police might have done to the building afterward. I had heard rumors that community members wanted to turn Central Headquarters into a shrine or a museum of resistance. But when I got there, I was disappointed to learn that because of the tunnel, the city had condemned the property. I would never enter Central Headquarters again.

16

TRYING TIMES

"Wayne, you make beautiful babies!"

I turned to see Peaches grinning at me, with a look that clearly told me she was *not* referring to my daughter Tammy. The women in the new office on 113th Street—Glenda, Peaches, and Brenda—saw them first. The trio was huddled in a group, leaning over, smiling and reaching out to the babies, as they cooed, oohed, and giggled.

I was momentarily dumbfounded, unsure of exactly what was going on.

I'd been out of jail for about a month, working nonstop to help rebuild the Watts office and, of course, my personal life too. I was at the new center for operations in Watts that day; we had closed down the office on 103rd Street and moved into a house on 113th and Anzac, right across the street from the Imperial Courts project. The switch from offices to community houses was in full effect, decreed by the Central Committee in Oakland. This way, the idea was, instead of attacking the Panther offices, the pigs would be attacking the community.

Pam was standing in front of me now, clutching the handrail of a doublewide baby stroller. The babies were small, yet so alert. Their skin was honey brown, like Pam's and mine, and they had light brown eyes. I looked at the twins in the stroller and knew immediately they were mine. And I had to admit, they were adorable.

I had been busy all morning working with a bright and eager young man, educating him about the work of the Party. "Excuse me, brother," I said to him abruptly as I pushed away from the table where we were working. He looked at me and nodded silently, a wide-eyed look flashing across his face.

I stood up and looked at Pam, still a little dazed, mumbling a curt hello. Then I asked her if we could go outside and talk. I could see that she was feeling as anxious as I was confused. "Of course," she replied, her beautiful brown face distorted by an awkward smile.

I followed her to the door as she pushed her overloaded stroller, which was burdened with blankets and diaper bags.

I had barely closed the door behind me when she spun around and looked at me. "I had them on April third," she blurted fretfully before I could say a word.

"Oh. So, so, what are their names?" I stuttered, unable to think of anything else to say at that moment.

"Aaron Dion and Darron Anthony Pharr." I watched the stress written across her face melt momentarily into joy, as she gazed proudly at the pair and pointed each one out to me.

I leaned against the house as I processed this new situation. I did some quick calculating: Tammy had been born in June 1969, which meant that she wasn't even a year older than her new brothers. We were both silent, staring at the twins, for what seemed like many painful minutes.

Finally, Pam broke the quiet, exclaiming, "Wayne, I need some help. I'm staying with my friend Cookie. But I need my own place."

"OK, sure, sure, I can dig that," I replied coolly. *What the hell am I going to do?* I thought.

We agreed to meet up later that night, to discuss the babies, the future, and to generally figure this new situation out. That would give me at least a few hours to recover from the shock of her news, even though I had no idea at the moment how I was going to make this work.

Pam was staying with Cookie across the street in the Imperial Courts project, a 498-unit housing project built in Watts in 1944. I went by their place after dinner and ended up staying and talking and negotiating with Pam through the night. Although I was still unsure how I was going to handle this, I had no intention of being an absent father to these boys, as my own father had been to me. I let Pam know that I would not abandon my children. We would work together to raise the boys, I assured her.

I left Pam and Cookie's just as the sun was beginning to spill orange across the sky. By that point, I was desperately feeling like I needed some rest; my head was spinning with questions, and especially what-ifs. I felt overwhelmed. But still pretty fresh out of jail, I didn't have my own place to stay, so as I stood on the sidewalk and squinted wearily at the morning sun, I wasn't immediately sure where I should go. I was pretty much living out of a duffel bag, shuffling between comrades and my mother's house. I was feeling conflicted and consumed with thoughts: *How am I going to support these newborns? Even worse, how in the hell am I going to tell Sharon about Pam and the twins? What's she going to do when I tell her? And what, exactly, do I want to do?* This was a predicament, for sure.

It took almost two months before I was ready to fess up to Sharon. The day I brought it up, we were at her mother's house, off Western and Seventy-Third Street, hanging together in the den. We were sitting on the couch, the TV going on and on, *blah, blah, blah,* but I was too distracted to pay any attention to it. This was about to be my day of reckoning; I felt as if I were getting ready to throw myself off a cliff or something, arms and legs flailing all the way down. The afternoon had actually been pleasant up to that point, the two of us sitting comfortably, holding hands, chatting on and off about noth-ing in particular. Finally, looking nervously into her eyes, I took a deep breath and then exhaled a jumble of words—words I had been dreading saying for two months now. "Uh, Sharon, I got this girl pregnant, and her name is Pam, and she just had twin boys, and yes, I'm the father," I blurted awkwardly.

I know I surprised her. Sharon recoiled, pulling her hand away from mine quickly as if she had just been scalded by hot grease on a stove. She put her head down for a moment and let out a silent moan, her whole body deflating. Then she looked up, straight ahead, refus-ing to look at me. In that instant, the mood in the room went from relaxed and quiet to tense and deafeningly silent. She didn't go off the handle or get emotional, and I hadn't expected her to; that just wasn't her personality or style. Instead, though, she just didn't react at all. We sat there, in thick silence, for what seemed like forever.

"What are you going to do?" she finally asked, in a voice so low it was almost inaudible.

I thought for a moment, choosing my words carefully. "Well," I said as gently as possible, "I have to put myself in a position to help take care of those kids."

"When did you meet her?" she shot at me next, accusingly. "How did you get involved with her?"

I breathed in again. "It was casual—a one-time thing," I said.

I knew I sounded lame. She didn't respond, remaining cool and composed, continuing to wait for me to justify myself.

"But, Sharon, I have to be a man about this and take care of these babies."

We were living in the late 1960s and into the '70s; it was the period of free love, and I wasn't sure if Sharon had fully expected monogamy—we'd never really discussed it. But monogamy was pretty much the way things had been between us—until Pam. I had never been out prowling, screwing all the college girls and movement women like I knew a lot of the other brothers were. I just got caught up that one time. I could tell Sharon was hurt, and I felt like shit.

There I was, a Black Panther, committed to liberating black people, but I had two women, three babies, no money, and no income.

Even before this news, Sharon and I were being pulled apart. She came from good people and a beautiful family, but they were uneasy about my commitment to the struggle and the violence that came with it. They worried that this could put Sharon and Tammy in dangerous situations. And I couldn't blame them for that. Also, I knew there was a general belief among her family members that my time on earth was likely going to be short because of my commitment to the cause. Those were some of the reasons why we had waited to get married, in fact. In the meantime, at least, both our families were committed to taking care of Sharon and our beautiful baby.

After I gave Sharon the news, my next stop was my mom's. I knew I needed to talk to my mother and Nanny about this unexpected development in my life, so it was time to get that conversation over with too.

Once I got to Mom's house, it was the same scenario: unsuspecting audience, uncomfortable moment. *Just get it over with, Wayne*, I told myself. We were all in the kitchen, and I just blurted it out. "I got twin boys," I announced in a flustered voice, my eyes fixed on my mother.

My mother stopped what she was doing and turned to look at me. "What did you say?" Her eyes were as wide as saucers.

I repeated myself. "I have two boys that I just recently found out about. Their mother's name is Pam and she lives in Watts."

What happened next, I couldn't believe. My mother fell on the floor and started crying. "What about Sharon and Tammy?" she sobbed.

I looked at her incredulously. *Unbelievable. She's more upset than me!* I thought. *Now what?* I turned to look at Nanny with pleading eyes. "Well, I've got to take care of them, Nanny. What else can I do?"

Nanny, who was always on my team, walked over to me and gave me a long hug. "Don't worry, son," she said, looking at me with warm, sad eyes. "Things will work out. And you know I'm here when you need me."

I smiled gratefully.

Then Nanny walked over to my mother. Moving slowly, she kneeled down on the floor at her side. She started to comfort her, murmuring soothingly as my mother wailed. I sat and watched the bizarre scene for a few minutes, still stunned by my mother's reaction. Finally, I got up quietly and left. There was nothing more I could do at this point, and I obviously wasn't going to get the support from my mother that I had been hoping for. But as I left the house, I couldn't stop thinking about the difference between the two and how they'd reacted. First, there was my mother's response, which was crazy to me. Then there was Nanny's reaction, which demonstrated her strong belief in me and which I felt consoled by.

My relationship with Sharon was pretty much over after my revelation to her that day. I was sad about that, but I knew I couldn't sit around and feel sorry for myself. I needed to move forward quickly, since I suddenly had two new babies to support. So I set about trying to do the right thing by these two infant boys that I had helped bring into this crazy world. And I knew, importantly, that my family and Sharon's family would continue to look after Tammy, even if her mother and I were no longer in a relationship.

Soon, however, I felt like I had jumped out of the frying pan and into the fire. The relationship between Pam and me was rocky right from the start. We were dealing with the pressure of trying to raise two boys while also trying to really get to know one another. And neither one of us was living in our own spot. To add to the stress, we were both suffering from a lack of resources. In fact, it didn't take long before Pam and I were regularly getting into arguments, especially about the way I was thinking about making money. And she wasn't shy about showing her feelings: we could easily raise the roof off any house when a row started.

After one of our "famous" fights at Cookie's house, Cookie's boyfriend came to pay me a visit at the office on 113th. He was a little older than me at about twenty-two, a tall, dark-skinned brother, with a strong build and a piercing gaze. He was also a dedicated activist with the Black Student Alliance, working alongside people like Baba and Damu, and he identified strongly with the local communists. We called him Ndugebele, but his given name was Tommy Harper. He was the guy who was eventually killed in 1970 while trying to blow up the Compton Police Department.

Ndugebele was a live wire. As he walked up to me, I could see he was agitated. "Hey, Pharr," he said as he looked at me squarely, placing his hand on the table in front of me. "You and me got a problem. You been disrespecting Cookie's house, and that shit is going to stop now."

I frowned at him. "What are you talking about?" I argued. "When have I ever disrespected Cookie?"

He scowled. "Whatever is going down between you and Pam is between you two; don't bring that shit to Cookie's house."

He finished his little tirade, and when I didn't respond the way he wanted, he started going ballistic. I stood up to meet him face-to-face, letting him know I wasn't scared and wasn't backing down either.

As I moved, Pee Wee and Will moved too, quickly getting up right in between us. "Everybody calm down," commanded Will as he maneuvered to keep us apart. "Tommy and Wayne, let's all sit and talk this through."

I did some quick calculating and decided to check my anger. I knew that because Pam was staying at Cookie's house, I was going to have to cooperate to alleviate any additional stress in her life. I certainly didn't want to make things harder for her—or me. I exhaled and let the tension in my shoulders go, looking at Ndugebele. "I meant no disrespect to Cookie, but I needed to talk with Pam," I offered.

He looked at me and nodded deliberately, earnestly considering what I said. "All right, brother," he said, reaching out his hand. "I accept that. You got to understand you are upsetting Cookie too, though."

Ndugebele and I both cooled off, and we continued to talk for a while longer. We ended the conversation expressing mutual respect for each other. A few weeks later, Ndugebele was dead. All power to the people.

On a bigger scale, while I was trying to manage my personal crisis, I was also working on our many legal issues related to the December shoot-out. After we had made bail, our legal team changed; although we'd established a close bond with McKissack, he was unable to work with us through the entire trial because of other commitments. Meanwhile, the court had ordered individual attorneys for each of us. Until we actually began working with our assigned attorneys, however, we met at Leo Branton's house, which was in Wellington Square. I liked Branton. Traveling to his house was an experience too: Wellington Square was a small enclave of wealthy African American families off Washington and Crenshaw, on the west side of town. Branton lived in a huge, two-story Victorian-style house. It was impressive to those of us who had never visited homes in that area, a whole different world.

My court-ordered attorney turned out to be a guy named Arthur Alexander. He was young and white, and, he told me, his father was a judge. I was immediately unsure about him.

"Hey, Mr. Pharr. Nice to meet you," he said casually, as he leaned back in his chair, tapping his pencil annoyingly on the table and trying to look too cool.

"Yes, sir," I replied briskly.

"We got a lot of work to do, so let's just jump right in," he pushed. "Tell me about yourself and what happened on December 8."

I wasn't a big talker, so I gave him the short version of the shoot-out and very little information on my background. I didn't know him, even if he was my attorney on record. I decided that I didn't need to be extra open with him; besides, he had the information he needed anyway to defend me.

The gut feelings I had about this guy were soon confirmed by his actions. I knew I was in trouble with him as my attorney when, during one of our subsequent meetings, he gave me the book *The Godfather*.

As he handed me the book, I looked at him quizzically.

"This is the way you got to do it," he said to me in a cryptic voice.

I thought that was odd, and it struck me as contrary to what a lawyer should say to his client. After that incident, what little regard I had for him was reduced even further.

On the other hand, I was very impressed with Will Stafford's young black lawyer, Johnnie Cochran. Cochran was flashy, and he had style, right down to his short and well-groomed Afro. I immediately knew this man was going somewhere in the world and would someday make an impact on society. He just had that self-assuredness about him and a sharp mind to go with it. He had an easy demeanor too. When we hooked up with Johnnie to discuss the case, he would take us to some of the trendy places in Beverly Hills and areas of wealth in Los Angeles that we had never been to. We appreciated the exposure we received from Johnnie and also his commitment to our defense. In fact, he believed in us so much that he continued to work with the Black Panther Party even after our trial ended.

Our trial began in May 1970. Of the variety of offenses we were charged with, the most serious were conspiracy to murder police officers and possession of illegal weapons. For me, the trial turned out to be an exhausting experience: not only was I required to show up to court frequently, but I also had to meet with attorneys, review endless documents, and respond to seemingly unending rounds of tricky questions. Then, in addition to the formal trial against those of us who were arrested during the shoot-out or in the other places raided the morning of December 8, other legal battles developed.

For one, the LAPD, via the City of Los Angeles, had the gall to sue the Black Panther Party for medical expenses, pensions, and compensations for the three officers we had shot, even though they were the ones who attacked us. Two of them had been shot in the legs, and the other one had been hit five times—in the chest, finger, and groin. They actually wanted us to pay them $5,000! That was laughable to us in the Party. It was so laughable to me, in fact, that even as a defendant, I never asked or wanted to know about the follow-up to the case. Even to this day, I can't fathom where the case went, but I do know that we had little internal discussion about the lawsuit.

For our part, we decided to countersue the City of Los Angeles for $57.6 million. The Black Panther Party charged the city with false arrest and imprisonment, assault and battery, and a number of other charges. We specifically named the three police officers, Edward Williams, Calvin Drake, and Richard Wuerfel, who came to our headquarters pretending like they were there to arrest someone but busted in with a battering ram instead. On top of this first lawsuit, we also sued the City of Los Angeles and all of its officials, including Mayor Sam Yorty and all councilmen, for harassment and depriving us of our civil liberties. We additionally named as defendants the LAPD, the Sheriff's Office of the County of Los Angeles, and Sheriff Peter J. Pitchess individually. None of the cases went anywhere, but we made it clear by filing suit that we would not be intimidated and would fiercely practice self-defense wherever necessary: in the courtroom, behind bars, and out on the streets.

A separate trial was held for the altercation with the guards in jail that had occurred on February 6, 1970, the day we were waiting for transportation to court and the guard pulled his cheese sandwich stunt. G and Paul Redd were both acquitted of the assault charges in that case.

The legal work took up an extraordinary amount of time for all of us, and it contributed to a decrease in productivity for the Party. All of us were acting and feeling discombobulated too, because we had lost several key people. Essentially, we were attempting to continue to meet the needs of a large city in the same way we had earlier but without an experienced crew. But those of us who were committed continued to push forward.

In June, I was working on tallying our newspaper sales in the Stockwell office. There were about seven people in the house when G called Roland and me into a small corner of the room for a more private discussion. He said, "You both have proven your commitment, dedication, and ability. So I am promoting you to the rank of captain."

I had never been interested in rank, but I knew that it was necessary to have order. "Yes, sir. What do you need me to do?" I should have foreseen this promotion, considering that Roland and I had put in a tremendous amount of work on behalf of the Party and our community. It was a good feeling to have our superior recognize our effort.

Becoming captain meant more responsibility but also more ideological and tactical training. G set us up to do extensive study and training at the Stockwell community house. Except to use the restroom and get some food, we were required to stay in a room and study for an entire week. We read Marx, Engels, Fanon, Mao Tse-Tung, and Eldridge Cleaver. Even if we had read those books before, we had to read them again. Dedon, one of the most astute members of the Black Student Alliance, stayed with us a few days and talked through some of the ideas in the literature. In the evening, we would take a break and go on night missions, which meant we had to travel throughout the community on foot, walk or run through people's backyards, traverse blocks, and avoid getting busted. We were required to stay together at all times. The goal was to show that we could maneuver in the streets and cover territory with knowledge and confidence.

During this period of training, Roland and I got to know each other even better than before. We engaged in long conversations about the meaning of the Party. I remember one night, as we were trekking through Compton, Roland said, "Man, I wouldn't do this, except that I love my people. Nothing will stop me from supporting the community."

"Right on man, that's real. I do it for the same reasons." I knew that Roland meant what he said.

Soon after that night, when Roland and I were serving the people as captains at a rally, G told us to take the guns being used for security back to the Stockwell office.

He said to us, "Captains, the police are all over this place, and we don't need anybody getting busted, so handle the weapons." So one by one, Roland and I approached Panthers who had weapons and gathered them in the car. We left the rally with about ten pistols. I was driving an old Buick then because the yellow van was too hot. The move we were making was pretty dangerous, and we knew that if we got stopped, we were going to prison.

While driving, I asked Roland, "What will you do if the police throw lights on us?"

He responded with all sincerity. "I'm gonna bail out of my side of the car shooting." That meant that I had to bail out of the car shooting too.

I said to myself, *Lord, get me out of this one.* I escaped narrowly again. We got the guns and ourselves back to the office without the pigs stopping us.

During the time we spent in jail and while we were out on bail, I also had the chance to get to know Cotton better too. I was seeing him and the brothers regularly now since our organization was working out of fewer places. Cotton was an easygoing guy, but I could tell that he had some strange tendencies. For instance, he loved hanging around Paul Redd. Wherever Redd was, Cotton showed up, and I thought it kind of bizarre. I had known Paul Redd since elementary school. His sister married Alex Bias's brother Ealy. So, I knew that Paul wasn't down for whatever Cotton was trying to sell.

My concerns about Cotton were solidified when we were at the 113th Street office. Paul Redd was sharing his art with us, which was similar to Emory Douglas's, so each page was filled with revolution, freedom fighters, and killing pigs. After that Cotton showed us his art, which took our conversation and thoughts about him to another level. He pulled out an orgy scene he had drawn and then started describing the scene for us. I thought to myself, *Well, maybe because he is older, he thinks this shit is OK*, but I thought the conversation was out of place. Certainly, Cotton knew of Paul's relationship with Peaches. Nonetheless, Paul didn't react to Cotton, so I don't think he caught on to whatever Cotton was suggesting by sharing that piece of art. As for me, I knew that I wouldn't be hanging with Cotton after-hours.

Although a lot had changed in the Party, the one thing that didn't was FBI and LAPD attacks and harassment. The FBI through COIN-TELPRO was trying to run the same game with the Nation of Islam that they had done with the Us Organization, writing notes to the two groups to stir up conflict. G sent me and Jimmy Johnson to speak to one of the lead ministers at the Nation of Islam to let them know that COINTELPRO was responsible for the messages. We set the meeting for a weeknight at the temple near Fifty-Fourth and Broadway. The minister and his security greeted us, and we had a very cordial meeting. I told them that we respected their organization and wanted no problems. The minister chided me for being in a ragtag organization like the Black Panthers. Then, on a more serious note, the minister said he understood the game the FBI was playing. We agreed that we were taking different routes, but we had the same goal of black liberation. At the end of the meeting, we all shook hands. There was no shooting between the Nation of Islam and the Black Panther Party of Southern California. The situation with the Us Organization had played out differently. I wonder why?

In the midst of averting a potential land mine with the Nation of Islam, Dedon stopped by the office in Stockwell and told me some terrible news. "Wayne, I just came to tell you that Melvin X has been killed."

Considering all of the trauma I had already experienced, I shouldn't have been perplexed, but I was. I just couldn't believe it. Melvin X was a student, the president of the Black Student Alliance, and I didn't think of him as being in danger. Of course, I asked the usual questions. "What happened? And why Melvin X?"

"He was found in San Bernardino in an orange grove, shot in the back of the head. Right now, we are not sure of who and why, but some are saying that it could have been the Us Organization or the police."

"Damn. Melvin was a good, strong brother," I said to Dedon.

He responded, "It's a major loss to the movement. He can't be replaced."

Melvin's murder not only affected the day-to-day operations of the Black Student Alliance, in terms of recruiting students for revolutionary activity, but it raised everybody's fears. It wasn't just Panthers under attack; it seemed like the entire movement on the left was in jeopardy.

As for the local pigs, they were still using the same ol' tired tactics of trying to intimidate the community, aptly demonstrated on a hot summer day at the Imperial Court project. I was there selling papers and recruiting for new members. It was about two o'clock in the afternoon, and I was rapping with a group of brothers: Alfred Fobbs, Lester Lucian, Ronnie, and another cat named Blue. They were aged nineteen to thirty and were always down to sit and discuss what was happening. As we sat on the gym field some pigs drove up next to us, parked, and walked up to our group. I wasn't familiar with these pigs, but I could tell by the scowls on their faces that some shit was about to jump off. They pointed to two of the guys that I didn't know. One said, "Hey you two, come with us."

Because we were sitting on the ground, we all looked up, but none of the brothers moved. "What do you want?" one of the guys said.

"We are taking you in for some questioning. Just come with us, so we don't have any problems."

The brothers still refused to move. Then both pigs reached out, and each grabbed one of the two guys, handcuffed them, and threw them in the backseat of the squad car. We didn't know if the cops had warrants or were just doing their usual rousting, but the other brothers on the gym field decided to challenge the pigs. Ronnie started yelling, "Leave them alone, you fucking pigs. Let them go!" While he was yelling, he was picking up rocks and started throwing them at the cops. The shit was on!

The crowd joined in and started throwing too—rocks, bottles, anything that wasn't connected to the ground. There was so much commotion that other project residents were opening their front doors to see what was happening. Of course, some of them joined the yelling and throwing.

One of the pigs called for backup, but he couldn't do much else but duck and dodge. Meanwhile, somebody opened up the back door of the police car and let out the two men who had been arrested. They started hauling ass. The backup pigs arrived in no time, and all of us began to scatter in various directions. As a member of the Party, I could easily see myself becoming a prime target of the cops, especially since I was selling our newspaper, so I was probably running the fastest. The project residents wanted to make sure that none of us got caught so they started opening up their apartment doors to us, enabling us to hide. I distinctly recall one kid who couldn't have been more than twelve opening his door and the two guys arrested running into his apartment.

Some of the kids in the project signaled for me to run in their direction. The apartment door was opened from the rear and they let me in. Some more kids in the next building allowed me to do the same, so I basically crept through the project, walking in and out of apartments.

By this time, the police were knocking on doors looking for the brothers who escaped. As I was traveling through the projects, I eventually joined up with them, because the young people directed me to where they were hiding. The brothers were still wearing the pigs' handcuffs, which was slowing down their movements. I had a small-caliber gun with me, so I wrapped it up to muffle the sound and tried to shoot the cuffs off. This was definitely a tricky move, and the brothers were a little scared of what might happen, so they turned their heads away from the gun as I shot.

After a few unsuccessful tries, I decided to take them to see Cotton, who I knew could handle the handcuffs. A brother in the neighborhood drove us to the Stockwell community house to find Cotton.

"Comrade Cotton, I got some brothers here who need your help."

"What's happening?" Cotton looked up from the table where he was eating. "Oh, I see."

"The pigs were trying to arrest them at Imperial Courts, but they got away," I told Cotton as the brothers nodded their heads.

Cotton checked out the situation. "I'll be right back."

Cotton returned with his tool kit. He got a hacksaw out and told the first brother to hold still. As he held his hands out, Cotton began to saw. It took more than an hour to get the handcuffs off, but the brothers left without getting arrested that night. I never saw them again, but the word got out about how the Black Panther Party had helped the brothers get away.

17

GANGSTA STYLE

On August 5 of the same year our trial began, Minister of Defense Huey Newton was let out of prison on appeal. Black Panthers and activists throughout the country were jubilant. Our true leader was back, and we would again have the leadership we needed. About ten thousand people showed up to see Huey released from the Alameda County jail and to celebrate the victory. G, Masai, and David Hilliard were present. G was there in his role as deputy minister of defense and security, making sure that no harm came to Huey. At one point during the celebration, Huey took off his shirt to show the strength of his upper body. I was glad he was out, but I thought to myself with some apprehension, *Malcolm X wouldn't have done no shit like that*. But still I was glad, willing and able to work with Huey to take the revolution to new heights.

Huey was low-key during his first month out, but the movement wouldn't let him maintain that posture for long. The minister's first order of business was to restate his commitment to the struggle against

Huey Newton and attorney Charles Garry in August 1970, on Huey's first day out of prison. Ducho Dennis, It's About Time Archives

racism, capitalism, and fascism during interviews and in his writings. I was down with Huey's letter to the National Liberation Front of South Vietnam, sent the same month he was released. In the letter, Huey offered to provide troops to help them fight against American imperialism. He wrote that black people in the United States are an oppressed nation living within an empire and that the Black Panther Party, as the vanguard revolutionary organization, was obligated to create turmoil in the oppressive state and divide its troops to help those in developing countries. Huey was also interested in making bigger moves inside the United States.

About two weeks after he returned, G and Red (G's wife, Saundra) stopped by my mother's house to talk to me about those moves.

"What's up baby girl? What's happening, G?"

"I've been talking with Huey about going south to organize our people into revolutionary forces. A few brothers from Los Angeles have agreed to go, and Huey is going to send some troops from up north. Are you down?"

"Let me think about it. What is Eldridge saying?"

"He's definitely down with it. We agree that my time will be better spent organizing the black nation for revolution, rather than going back to jail."

"Right on. I like the idea of carving out a black nation. We might even link up tighter with the RNA. But I don't know. Leaving might cost my mother her house. We won't get that bail money back if I don't show up for trial. Let me talk to her."

G and I spoke with my mother, while Red watched the conversation from the side. She responded as I had assumed. In tears, she pleaded for me not to go.

She said to G, "I love you, G, but Wayne is my only child, and I can't bear losing him. Please don't try to convince him to go."

A few days later, on August 18, G left without me.

Again, we were losing some of our most experienced cadre, this time to the underground. But the publicity around Huey's release also led to an influx of new Party members. The problem for us was that a lot of the members came into the Party believing that Huey was the black Messiah and didn't question his politics or those of the Central Committee the way some of the long-serving members would.

G was such a forceful presence, and after he went underground, the leadership in Southern California became real shaky. Jackanapes like Jimmy Johnson were now in command positions. Jimmy, whom I considered a chili-dog pimp and an ass kisser, somehow convinced Elaine Brown to support him. But in actuality, Jimmy really wanted to dominate people, and he was able to do it by forming a goon squad to beat and intimidate the rank and file. Jimmy liked hanging with me because I had rank and clout, but I didn't get off on beating Party members.

I remember when Jimmy wanted to discipline Ike. I had stopped by the community house on Seventy-Sixth Street. Jimmy said as soon as I walked in, "Wayne, we need to handle Ike. This nigga fell asleep on guard duty."

I wasn't interested, but I needed to see what he was up to, so I went with him to the bedroom where Ike was. On our way, Jimmy picked up a two-by-four from the floor, which was there because we were in the middle of modifying the house. I couldn't believe it. This fool wanted to hit Ike over the head with a board that could scar him for life or even knock him silly. Ike, who was from Alabama, was an army veteran. He was a short guy and easygoing. Jimmy was bigger than Ike and a bully. I could see what was happening. What the fuck! I decided to intervene.

"Jimmy, I've known Ike for long time, so I will discipline him myself." When we walked in I explained the situation to Ike and then hit him three times on his ass with a paddle. Ike took it like a man, but I could tell he had animosity toward me after that.

Later on we talked about the incident when I saw him in the Imperial Courts project. "Ike, man," I said, "I'm sorry about the shit that went down with the paddle. But Jimmy the Clown wanted to hit you with a two-by-four. I wasn't going to let that shit happen, but I had to do something to make the issue go away." I further explained, "That fool really wanted to brutalize you."

Ike told me he understood and was glad I came and spoke to him about it. "I will definitely watch out for Jimmy's bullshit."

Beating up comrades for minor infractions seemed to increase after Huey returned. People saw Huey use squads to do his dirty work, so they set up their own with young, impressionable members who didn't know how to question authority. As far as I could tell, we were not moving forward but backward. Instead of taking the party higher, Huey was taking us to unimaginable lows.

There were early hints that Huey was becoming a problem, but because the Party had built him up as a legend it was hard for us to accept what we were seeing, even though it was happening in front of our faces. For me, the first hint came from Roland Freeman. He went to Oakland to meet Huey about a week after his release. Roland wanted to spend some time with Huey and the organization in Oakland to see what he could learn. Huey was interested in meeting Roland, because he had heard stories about how he tried to cut a bullet out of his arm while in jail. Roland was also trying to make a bomb out of the playing cards we had. Back then, each card had nitroglycerin in the middle. Roland wanted to blow the cell door open to help his cellmates who wanted to escape. He wasn't successful, but people wanted to hear about the strategy.

When Roland left Los Angeles he was enthusiastic, but he returned sorely disappointed. I asked Roland, "How did it go?" I couldn't wait to hear all about Huey.

With a look of disgust on his face, Roland said. "Man, when I got with Huey, he acted like I was a nuisance. He invited me up there to meet him and then treated me like he wasn't interested in even talking to me."

With raised eyebrows, I said, "Are you serious?"

"Yeah. I think he was high the whole time," Roland continued. "And guess what else? Them niggas had an icebox full of food. They were eating real good. Nobody was hungry. Here we are, down here scrounging for the next dollar while they're up there living high on the hog."

"Damn, that shit ain't right," I said.

"Hell naw!"

Another reason I became disenchanted with Huey was the way he handled the situation with Jonathan Jackson, the brother of communist revolutionary and Black Panther Party field marshall George Jackson. Jonathan Jackson was a high school student in Pasadena who wanted to get his brother out of prison by any means necessary. Comrade George had gone to prison in 1961 for a gas station robbery. What was so cold about it was that George didn't even rob the station; he was just in the car when it went down. But the state gave him an indeterminate prison sentence of one year to life. In 1969, a racist prison guard was killed. The pigs blamed George and two other inmates for it, and they became known as the Soledad Brothers. If the Soledad Brothers were convicted of killing the pig—which seemed likely—they would be given the death penalty. Angela Davis became part of the Soledad Brothers Defense Committee.

During George's time in prison, he transformed into a revolutionary and joined the struggle. He worked actively to convince other inmates to commit to the revolution and bring unity to the prisoners. He explained to them that they were all being exploited and brutalized by the same enemy, regardless of race.

I met Jonathan Jackson in the middle of July, when the Los Angeles Panthers had a rally at a church on 108th and Grand. Roland and I were in the security detail, and Angela Davis was the featured speaker. I noticed a young man with a serious look on his face hanging in the back of the church. Of course, I noticed him because I could tell he was carrying a gun. It was Jonathan Jackson, and he was Davis's personal bodyguard.

A few months earlier, I had met Lester Jackson, George and Jonathan's father. My mother knew Lester from working at the post office, and she asked him to talk to me about my involvement in the struggle for black liberation. She knew of George's problem and Lester's concerns about his son's freedom and safety, so my mother drove me to Pasadena to meet him at the courthouse there. "Hello, son. I am so glad that we will have the chance to talk."

"Hello, sir. I am sorry to hear about your son."

"That's what I want to discuss with you," he replied. "Your mother is very worried and asked me to let you know the kind of trouble you can get yourself into working with some of these political organizations."

Lester Jackson asked me to go into one of the courtrooms, where we met one of his friends, a white judge. Sitting on the judiciary bench, Mr. Jackson and the judge spent about an hour talking with me about the politics of the "new left" and the real trouble I could get into if I remained in the Party. They told me that I needed to leave it.

I spent about an hour with them and respectfully listened. I told Mr. Jackson that I recognized his plight and that I appreciated the advice of he and the judge. Even though I had no intentions of leaving the Party, I remained deferential. I felt bad for Mr. Jackson. He was trying so hard to save his sons, and if he couldn't save them, he would save other young men like me. In this case, it was for the sake of my mother.

The day of the rally, I approached Jonathan Jackson. We had a brief conversation, during which I acknowledged my respect for him and his brother. I also let him know that I had met his father. It was obvious that he truly loved his brother. George told him it was important that he learn from Angela. I wished him well and he thanked me. Two weeks later, on August 7, 1970, seventeen-year-old Jonathan entered the Marin County Courthouse with guns to capture hostages to trade for the release of George. At the end of that day, the judge, the district attorney, and two prisoners were killed. Jonathan, whom George referred to as a man-child, was killed too, shot multiple times in the getaway van in the parking lot of the courthouse. It was a "shoot-in." All power to the people!

G had known of Jonathan's plans and told me he was going to the Bay Area to help. But at the eleventh hour, Huey called off all Panther support because he thought the move was suicidal and could have easily brought more heat to the Party. Jonathan moved forward with the plan by himself anyway. I felt that Huey could have talked Jonathan out of making that deadly move and offered him alternatives to support his brother. But instead Huey just stopped the Panthers from helping Jonathan that day.

James Carr, George's right-hand man while he was in Soledad, went to see Huey about what happened to Jonathan. Comrade George referred to James as "the Jackal Dog and the baddest motherfucker in the world." They founded a group called the Wolf Pack in prison. It was an ideological and warrior group they used to organize and politicize inmates, but it also taught and advocated self-defense. The rumors about the meeting between Huey and the Jackal Dog were floating throughout the Party. I heard that there was an altercation between the two and that the Jackal Dog punched or slapped Huey. In retaliation, Huey placed a hit on Carr. The Jackal Dog was killed eight months later, in April 1972.

Despite the disputes going on in the Party, I had three kids to support and no job. My babies needed milk, food, and toys, and I was providing very little of each. Obviously, the stress and strain of my situation was showing on my twenty-year-old face, because as I was walking by the projects one day, an old friend of mine stopped me and said, "Damn, Wayne, you look like you are broke." It was Lester, whom I had met organizing for the Party. He was a good brother but had a little man's complex so he was always getting into fights. Lester was sitting on the steps with another brother named Gary, drinking beer.

I answered Lester, "Yeah, man. I am broke."

Then Lester said, "Well, we broke too. So what we gonna do?"

I leaned against a wall. "I don't know. What's the plan?"

Gary, who I learned was a Vietnam vet, started talking then. "Hey, let's just start walking and find an opportunity."

As we were walking, we saw a couple of Mexican bars on Alameda and rolled over a few drunks outside until we were chased away. Then we took off walking on Imperial, westbound toward Vermont. Lester and Gary tossed up a brother and robbed him. I didn't take part in that. As I watched them, I could tell that these two brothers had heart but no sense. So I made myself the leader of this group.

I was ready to do what was necessary to feed my children. With the money I made hanging with Lester and Gary that day, I was able to buy some turkey, bread, milk, and other items for the house. I also bought a little weed and wine. I wasn't out of the Party, but I needed to carve out some time to make some money. I had learned from my captains about how to liberate what was needed for the Party, and it was time for me to use those skills for myself. We had a good Christmas.

I wasn't proud of it, but I knew what my short-term future would be like. I started a hustling and robbing crew, and we were making moves every night: stealing, robbing, and selling clothes and weed. We were doing it! As the leader, I showed the group how to use the freeways and efficiently plan our hits. I had given all of my guns to the Party and the pigs had confiscated the rest, so I didn't have heat. Gary made a solo move to help resolve that problem. He showed up one day with a 20-gauge double-barrel shotgun. He also had a bullet lodged in the middle of his hand because he had gotten shot while trying to get away. We cut the bullet out and patched him up, something else I had learned how to do from comrades in the Party. Now, we had Gary's pistol and a sawed-off 20 gauge, which allowed us to take more risks. For instance, we cased the Ace-Hi Motel. One night Lester heard a dope dealer's girlfriend say she was going to the store to get drinks and smokes. When she drove off, we made our move. The night was foggy with little visibility, which is not uncommon in Los Angeles. We knocked on the door and told the dealer that his girl was in a car wreck and to come at once. When he opened the door, Lester coldcocked him and he fell on the floor. I ran in and stuck the gun in his mouth. We demanded the money, and he gave it up without a fight. I didn't want to hurt him, and we didn't have to. A lot of our moves went that way. I became so bold that I would rent my guns out to people. They would take care of their business and return the guns. Of course people probably did all manner of things with those guns. We didn't care. We were stupid.

My clique was growing. James and Bon-Bon had just gotten out of prison, and they wanted in. Joe, Shaheed, and Richard were disaffected Panthers, and they wanted to work with us too. Richard, whom I had known since kindergarten, worked with the Black Panther Party on the Westside. He had married Pat Fredericks, a young lady who had helped to establish the BSU at Jordan High. Pam and Pat became good friends, so we used to see them a lot more than some of the others. It was a good friendship because they were both down with supporting our work in the streets. Sometimes Pat would even drive us. The original crew of Gary, Lester, and me had expanded to the point where we could go out with different crews with us as lead.

By this time, I had moved in with Pam. I felt better about myself because I was able to help us sustain our two-bedroom upstairs apartment in the projects.

One day, Lester answered a knock at my door and said some insurance men wanted to see me. I walked in the room and could tell right away it was the FBI. I couldn't believe it. I was committing crimes with a fool that couldn't tell the difference between insurance men and the FBI! There were two of them, and they were in my home. Of course one did all the talking, while the other did the looking around. The talkative one said they had been looking for me; they thought I was dead. I didn't say much. Then they looked around the apartment and offered to pay me $300 a phone call if I called them with information about the Party, especially details on a potential split that could be going down. With as much sarcasm as I could muster, I asked, "$300 whole American dollars?" Mr. Talkative said yeah. I told him that I could make more money than that in one day, selling weed if I wanted to. He said they'd see me again. Yeah, right.

Looking back, I believe that if I had been older or more mature at that time, I probably would have made other choices, but the people I trusted were no longer available to me to help keep me on the right path. If they weren't locked up, they were in Oakland, like Masai and Elaine. And I wasn't even sure of what I could say to them at that point, considering my feelings about Huey. I didn't even know if G had communicated to them that Roland and I had made captain. I was drifting away from the Party. Just like Huey, there was no one to challenge my decisions.

One of my neighbors in the projects was Mike Clark. He was recently released from Soledad State Prison and lived with his wife and two kids. We began to hang together because we both enjoyed boxing. He was a griot too and could talk endlessly about the history of the ghetto, inside and out. Mike was built like Joe Frazier and boxed with a lot of aggression, just like Joe. He taught me some of his boxing techniques as well as how to steal cars and trucks. We specialized in tires from Volkswagens because it was one of the most popular cars of the time. Once I got the technique down, we could take a tire in about thirty seconds. We frequently met our goal of stealing ten tires a night. We got most of them from the colleges, like

UCLA, USC, Cal State Los Angeles, or any one of the junior colleges. We sold the tires to a fence on Alameda. The money was good and coming in easy.

I was rolling in dough, and eventually Huey and the leadership in Oakland received word about my success. I don't know how they found out about the money, but it is possible that one of the guys in the clique was talking too much and to the wrong people. The Party decided that they wanted a piece of the action, so they sent Red, who had been going back and forth to Oakland, to demand some of the money.

Red was a fitting name for Saundra Pratt. She was light-skinned and wore a short red Afro; some would even call her a redbone. Red was about five foot six and had a well-put-together body. She wasn't lacking for attention from men. Roland and Ronald Freeman knew Red growing up, as a leader of the Westside gang called the Rebel Rousers. They all grew up together and used to hang out at the skating rink on Washington and Arlington. Red was down, an original gangster who would rob, boost, pull credit card scams, and sell dope and even herself.

I had first met Red at Central Headquarters with G. She was outgoing and dynamic in her own way. Although Red was in the Party, she wasn't a Party worker who sold papers and manned an office. She did things on the same level as G. She was his woman.

One day, Pam and I were at home when there was a knock on the door. I opened it to Red and five or six brothers. Obviously in charge, Red said, "What's up, Wayne? We need to talk."

I could tell she came to discuss something serious, so I sent Pam and my sons upstairs to a neighbor's house.

"The Panthers want to know: what are you doing these days?"

I answered, "Just handling my business."

"They sent me here to collect some of the money you're making."

I wasn't expecting to hear that. "I don't see why. The Party is not involved in what I'm doing. I'm not using Party cars, guns, Party nothing."

"If you don't support the Party, then we have been ordered to render discipline."

I knew I was going to have to fight when I made my next statement. "This is a shakedown. I'm not giving up any money."

The five or six chumps who had showed up with Red jumped me in the living room of the apartment. Luckily, I fell in a corner of the room, so they weren't all able to effectively get at me. If they had attacked me two or three at a time there wouldn't have been much I could do, but because they were all trying to get at me together, they jammed themselves up, so I was able to move quickly and strike a few blows for freedom every now and then. After a couple of minutes of this action, Red called them off. She even said they were getting the worst of this deal. "Wayne, we'll talk later." We exchanged a few more words and they took off.

To be honest, I knew the brothers could have really harmed me, but I think because of the respect they had for me because of my role in the shoot-out and in Watts, they went light. I had bruises on my arms and legs, but it could have been much worse. Really, I had my ass whipped previously by professionals, so I wasn't crying about that pretend beat-down. Still, I was pissed off—and Pam was wild with anger.

About a week after I had been jumped, Jimmy was driving Masai in Watts and stopped me in the street to talk. It was obvious that Jimmy had my previous job, driving Central Committee members when they were in town. Masai and I hadn't seen each other in a while, so even though I was hesitant because he was working in Oakland with Huey, I was glad to see him. We gave each other the black power handshake that indicated we were cool with each other.

Masai said, "Comrade, I'm glad we ran into you. I have been thinking about checking on you for a while."

"I'm doing good. Just trying to make it in these streets. What's up with you, brother?"

"Still working in Oakland, trying to save black people."

We started talking about my position on the Party. I was honest. "I think the Party is moving in the wrong direction, Masai. I hear G and the brothers underground are not getting the proper support." I also told him that Huey's people came down to "discipline me" as a cover to shake me down for some money. "I am going to be straight with you. I think Huey is an egotistical fool, and I don't want to see any more 'Huey-ites' in Watts."

Masai had always been straight with me. He agreed that what happened to me was wrong and echoed my sentiments about Huey's ego. I told him that he should think about getting away from them Huey-niggas. Masai told me, "I'm always going to do what's right."

We parted ways in good standing, and I had barely said a word to Jimmy.

A couple of weeks later, the smell of fire permeated the air. I looked across the street and saw the Watts office up in flames. It had been a dull green in the morning, but that night the color of the building was changed to black with gray smoke-like tinges next to the green that was left. I could see the firemen working to put out the flames, while the police were keeping people away from the building. The building was charred in big spaces and was burned so badly that the office could no longer be used. The rumor around town was that the police burned the office, but what really happened was that my clique didn't like that move made against me by national headquarters so they set fire to the office on 113th Street to ensure the Party had no access in Watts.

It became increasingly clear to me that Huey wanted to destroy the Southern California chapter of the Party. He had sent G and some of the brothers to the South with little money or resources for living expenses. When they called the national office for help, they were sent a pittance of what they really needed, and after a while no one with any authority would take their calls.

By this time, Roland Freeman, Cotton, Will Stafford, Will "Captain" Crutch from Oakland, and George Armstrong had joined G. Cotton, who was sent to join G, gave him the message that Huey would meet them in Marshall, Texas, to work everything out. But Huey didn't show up. Cotton then informed the group that Huey wanted them to go to Dallas to meet him. While all of this was happening, Huey and Roland were in contact with each other. As a result of those discussions Roland met the group in Dallas. He had only been there a few days before they all got busted. It was obviously a setup.

After being transferred to the county jail in Los Angeles, the next month, January 1971, G read in the Party newspaper that he was expelled from the Party. He didn't even know why. I don't know for sure, but it seemed obvious that Huey's intention was to destroy the militant wing of the Party. In this case he eliminated some of its most dedicated cadre. None of them could adequately fight back because they were all in jail. That was some treacherous shit!

Not surprising to me at all was Eldridge Cleaver's expulsion from the Party in February, a month after G's. The disagreements between Eldridge and Huey went back to the early days. They were ideological and tactical. When Bobby and Huey established the Black Panther Party, they worked within the confines of the law. But after Martin Luther King Jr. was assassinated, Eldridge, Bunchy, and G wanted to go on the offensive. Beyond that, the Party expanded under Eldridge's leadership while Huey was in jail, which I think contributed to a little jealousy on Huey's part. Instead of Huey being mad at Eldridge, I thought he should have been thankful. Eldridge did a great job maintaining Huey's image while he was in prison.

New York Panthers were also expelled—in particular, the Panther 21, a group of Panthers who had been arrested for various charges, including conspiracy to blow up department stores, railways, and police stations. New York members Michael Tabor and Dhoruba Moore challenged David Hilliard and Huey Newton in an open letter about what they believed were misuses of Party funds and abuse of power. In the same letter they praised the work of the Weather Underground. Dhoruba and Michael eventually resigned from the Party and went to Algeria to work with Eldridge. Other members in New York sided with Cleaver, and soon the entire group was expelled.

I truly believe that if the Party's strongest leaders had been able to meet and talk together during this crucial time, the dissension wouldn't have gotten so out of hand. But Bunchy was dead, Bobby was locked up, and G was in the South when Huey expelled him, so there was no personal confrontation. Huey had a few valid arguments, such as the enormous cost of bailing out members hurting the party. But his response was not to engage in dialogue, but to purge and attack. His behavior was so erratic that many of us were sure Huey was a drug addict and most likely was already addicted when he came out of prison. Huey didn't have to listen to anyone. He was unchallenged, in full control.

I really began to question Newton's sanity when he began calling himself the "supreme commander" and then "supreme servant of the people." These titles appeared in the Party newspaper, and Party leaders like Elaine were introducing and addressing him in public, emphasizing those titles. What bullshit! Somebody should've hit Huey in the mouth when he started referring to himself as supreme! Chairman Mao didn't call himself nothing with "supreme" on it.

Meanwhile, the problems between Huey and Eldridge were played out in public and out loud. The FBI had gotten in on the action by sending bogus letters and other information to both parties. It all came to a head during a talk show interview, with Huey live in San Francisco and Eldridge on the phone in Algeria to promote an Intercommunal Day of Solidarity. At the end of the conversation they got into an argument about the expulsions. Eldridge criticized David Hilliard's leadership and accused him of mismanaging Party funds. After that Huey called Eldridge a maniac and expelled his section of the Party. Not everyone supported Eldridge. Field Marshall George Jackson wrote to Eldridge and accused him of being a compulsive disruptor or agent provocateur.

But that didn't matter to Eldridge. During a telephone interview in March on KSAN Radio in San Francisco, Eldridge accused Huey of refusing to support acts of armed resistance. He expelled Huey and David Hilliard from the Party, and he reinstated G and the Panther

21. The Party would now be headquartered in New York under his leadership. Eldridge also called for the formation of a Black Liberation Army (BLA), which was to become an underground network of people committed to revolutionary activity.

I had buried myself in Watts, surrounded by my crew, when the split was going down. Because of the community work I had done in Watts, I was untouchable. But as a result of the internal Party war, Panthers were disappearing, turning up shot and missing, which was adding more police pressure. Robert Webb, a supporter of Cleaver, was shot and killed in Harlem on March 8, 1971, apparently by some pro-Huey Panthers. Sam Napier, distribution manager of the Party newspaper, was found dead in New York City on April 17, 1971. He was found bound, gagged, and shot six times. Considered a supporter of Newton, his death was blamed on the Cleaver faction. Fred Bennett, coordinator of the East Oakland branch, was missing for months before pieces of his body were found in the Santa Cruz Mountains. Rumors were spreading like wildfire about the reasons for his death: being pro-Cleaver or dating Bobby Seale's wife. I didn't know what would happen next.

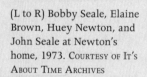

(L to R) Bobby Seale, Elaine Brown, Huey Newton, and John Seale at Newton's home, 1973. COURTESY OF IT'S ABOUT TIME ARCHIVES

18

TORN ASUNDER

Huey and Eldridge's rancorous feud not only affected the Party nationally and internationally, it caused great acrimony and divisiveness locally too. Some Panthers in Los Angeles sided with Eldridge, while others stayed with Huey. For those of us fighting charges related to the December 8 raids and shoot-out, the split in the Party had an enormous impact on our lives. We had come out of gangs, battled the Us Organization, and become hardened even more by war with the LAPD and its Metro and SWAT squads. We had learned military tactics and strategies and functioned together as a team to survive. Now, we were looking at each other with suspicion.

One day while the split was going down, Harold Taylor came by my spot in the projects. I was happy to see him; we knew each other from the neighborhood and our Teen Post days. He was underground quite a bit and constantly on the run, so having him come by the house was a special occasion, and we treated it that way. I invited him in and we went straight to the kitchen. "All I got is Schlitz or milk," I said to him with a laugh. "Which will it be, brother?"

Harold threw his head back and let out a laugh as I pulled two beers from the refrigerator. "Let's go on into the living room," he said. "I want to relax."

"You know the way," I replied as I handed him his beer. We both settled in, sitting back and relaxing, drinking brew, and catching up with small talk. Inevitably, the subject of our conversation finally turned to Huey and Eldridge.

"Which way are you going?" Harold looked at me. He had a mischievous grin on his face.

Actually, my choice didn't require any serious thought. "I know you're joking," I smiled coolly. "Shit. You know how I feel about self-defense. That alone requires me to join with Eldridge and the BLA. Plus, I'm going to be on G's side, whatever happens."

Harold grinned.

"From what I know," I continued, "only Al, Craig, Robert Bryan, and Tommye Williams are with Huey."

"Man, it's hard to believe that Huey has rejected the armed struggle." Harold shook his head, finishing his beer and getting up for another. "I never thought we would have a conversation like this."

I stopped and watched Harold walk into the kitchen, thinking about the split and everything else that was going down at the same time. I voiced my agreement: "You speak the truth, brother."

"Have you talked to anybody on Huey's side?" Harold called out from the kitchen.

"No, not really," I hollered back. "But I ain't mad at nobody as long as they don't mess with me. I just don't know if I can trust them like I used to."

Harold nodded. "Yeah, can we really be in the same room with them? I mean, Huey has done some foul shit. I can't ignore it!"

"I hear you man, but Al and I have always been tight. With Lux gone, it just doesn't feel right. I wouldn't mind talking with Al to clear the air, in fact."

Harold agreed. "Ain't nothing like knowing where you stand with somebody."

The BLA was a network of activists committed to self-defense, armed struggle, and appropriating what was needed for revolutionary change. Someone in the network approached me to confirm that I was down with the philosophy and the work. I assured him I was.

Shortly after this, a few brothers from the BLA came over and said G wanted me to go with them to hit a snitch. G was in jail, so I asked the brother about the specifics of the plan. After he explained it to me, I told him I couldn't do it.

"That stinks," I told him. "You guys can use my guns and whatever equipment you need, but I can't go with you on this one." I was always thinking about my children.

We talked a little while longer and they eventually left.

The brothers from the network were front-page news the next day. The operation had been a SWAT setup. Once they hit the scene, SWAT lit up their car. Luckily, no one was killed, but the car they rode in was shot up and the brothers got busted. My instincts were correct. I always felt that had I been there I would have been killed. Even though I had sided with the BLA, I wasn't going on any suicide missions.

The trial for the shoot-out started in February 1971. We were charged with conspiracy to murder police officers and possession of illegal weapons. No matter what the charges were, I understood that we were really being tried for defending ourselves against the SWAT team's assault on the Panther headquarters.

Going to court every day was exhausting. I dreaded getting dressed to go. In the mornings, I would throw on my Levi's or slacks and a pullover shirt and jacket and get in my blue Comet to drive to Superior Court in downtown Los Angeles. I was still running crews, making money at night and then making it to court in the morning. I realized I was hooked on the adrenaline from the robberies, and it gave me some relief from the stress of the trial.

Then one day I see Red in the courtroom. We hadn't spoken since the day she came to the house with Huey's thugs to shake me down. But the previous month, she had been expelled from the Party along with

G. Now, with G locked up, she was pretty much out on her own. Red wasn't showing too much, but it was obvious that she was pregnant.

After court, she walked toward me. "Wayne, I really want to talk to you and apologize for my role in what happened. I shouldn't have been involved in that situation."

I had no problem with Red. I knew she had been manipulated by Huey, David, or both and was acting on their orders. I hadn't been hurt, so it was cool. "I'm not holding any grudges. So, what happened?"

"It came from up the chain of command," she said.

"Yeah, I figured that." I changed the subject. "How many months along are you?"

She smiled as she answered, "About four months."

Red had gotten played just like Cotton and the others in Dallas. When she was going back and forth to Oakland with G she thought she had established some cool relationships with the leadership.

After that conversation, Red and I bonded. Since we were part of the outlaw faction, two of the few from the Southern California chapter that were out on the streets at the same time, it only made sense. Plus, Red was G's woman, and I wanted to help her out for his sake.

Red was traveling by bus, so I starting driving her home from court to an apartment way over on the Westside, off of Fairfax and San Vicente. We were hanging pretty tough because I had some action going with weed and red devils, and Red could move those pills. She needed the money, so it worked out for both of us. On a few occasions Red hung out with Richard, Pam, and me. We had a good time, reminiscing about the Party, laughing, drinking, and getting high.

One day, while we were in the car, we talked about the unexpected changes in the Party since Huey had gotten out of prison. "It's bad, Wayne. Huey's coke habit is dominating everything. He smokes and snorts up everything in eyesight. People spend more time feeding his habit than running the Party. He has severe mood shifts too. It's fucked up, really."

I said to Red, "The only way we can salvage what's left is to take him out. I say we hit him right now, make him a martyr—a hero to the movement before he completely destroys the Party." It was something to be considered.

Regarding the trial, I had no faith in the criminal justice system, so I didn't think we had a chance to beat the charges. Sometimes Pam and I would talk about what would happen if I were convicted. I let her know to get prepared, because I thought I would do some real time. One reason I was so fatalistic was the behavior of Judge Dell. He openly showed his disdain for us. For instance, G, Paul, and Roland wanted to replace their attorneys, but Dell denied their request, asserting that they really just wanted to make their attorneys errand boys. Then Judge Dell kept overruling the objections of the attorneys we truly believed were on our side. The goddamn judge even threatened to reprimand and lock up Johnnie Cochran under the guise that he was objecting too much. Equally contributing to my fatalism was the feeling Johnnie Cochran had that the prosecutors knew our strategy. Later we found that Cochran was right. He told us that one of the defense lawyers was an informant; it was Arthur Alexander, my

Weapons confiscated from LAPD SWAT raids of Geronimo and Sandra Pratt's home, the Walter Toure Pope Community Center, and the Panther Central Headquarters on December 8 on display by the LAPD in the Exhibit Room of Weapons. UCLA Charles E. Young Research Library Department of Special Collections, Los Angeles Times Photographic Archives

attorney. Cochran said that Alexander admitted to him that he was sharing information because he thought we might escape. Fuckin' traitor. He should have been disbarred for his actions.

The lead prosecutor was Deputy District Attorney Ronald Carroll. He relied heavily on the police officers as his witnesses and approximately two hundred exhibits. Most of the exhibits were of weapons, including ammunition, shells, ammo belts, the Thompson submachine gun, rifles, and others found at headquarters. If the actual weapon wasn't exhibited, then there were photos of weapons with one of us holding them, to convince the jury that we wanted to kill police officers.

To our benefit we had some skilled and kick-ass attorneys who were able to counter some of that bullshit the prosecutors were selling. However, we did have one major disagreement with our attorneys: we wanted to testify, and they didn't trust us on the witness stand! We had a message about police brutality against the black community and the Black Panther Party that we wanted to communicate from Los Angeles to the world. We also wanted to start a national discourse on the issue of self-defense, which the Party believes is a God-given right, and we were within our rights to defend ourselves on December 8. Our attorneys still refused to allow us to testify. Their concern, according to Cochran, was that our side might lose control of the trial during cross-examination. But I knew the real deal was that they didn't trust us on the witness stand, not even to answer questions with yes sir, no sir. The more I thought about it, I recognized that they were right in denying us the witness stand. Chuckling to myself, I thought, *Some of us could be hotheaded or not smart enough to spar with those professionals.* Eventually, we capitulated and relied on our attorneys to do their jobs. Plus, Ronald Freeman was a witness for us, and so we knew he could get our message out to the public. Johnnie Cochran and James Gordon made racism in the police ranks an important part of the trial, and we appreciated that.

The most unsettling aspect of the trial for me was when I found out that the star witness for the prosecution was Cotton! That chump made a deal to turn state's evidence against us in order to get the charges against him dropped. I was staggered when my attorney told me; at first I didn't even believe it.

I went home and told Pam. "Babe, I just heard today that Cotton turned on us! He is going to testify for the prosecution. That mother-fucka knows everything."

She looked at me, stunned, just like I was. "No, I can't believe that. What is he going to do, talk about how he shot those cops? Damn!"

"But, you know, the more I think about it, working with the feds is probably the only move that Cotton can see right now. He's scared as hell of G. People are still wondering if he set up the brothers in Dallas. And remember, Touré's gun jammed, and he was blamed for that. He probably thinks people are after him."

Pam and I analyzed it together. "Yeah, and if he was set up by Huey to take the fall for all of that, he can't trust them niggas in Oakland either."

I said, "If Cotton is innocent of setting up Panthers, then he sees himself as caught in the middle and doesn't know who to trust. To stay alive, at least a little while longer, he put his faith in law enforcement." Shaking my head, I said, "Shit. He can't trust them either. The nigga should have just disappeared."

Pam replied with her hands on her hips, "I'm wondering how much of what happened he is going to talk about. He can't tell the whole truth and nothing but the truth. Can he?"

"He is being protected by cops. All we can do is wait and see."

My involvement in the Party was rooted in Watts, so I felt that my exposure to Cotton was limited, compared to those based out of Central Headquarters. But I was partially correct.

Detective Raymond Callahan walked Cotton into the courtroom. A hush fell over the room. When I saw Cotton with Callahan, I knew we were in trouble. Callahan was the Panther expert for the LAPD's criminal conspiracy section, and he was committed to destroying us, whatever it took. I wondered what Callahan had gotten out of Cotton.

In his testimony, Cotton talked about being a handyman for the Party and someone who ensured that our guns worked. He stated that he attended classes on making bombs; he shoplifted bullets with the women and distributed literature on guerilla warfare. On the issue of children, Cotton said they were taught to hate policemen at the breakfast program and that we allowed little boys to play with pipe bombs. He also testified that the Black Panther Party was teaching him so much hate that he had to undergo psychiatric counseling.

On an individual level, Cotton accused G of telling him that a particular gun had killed three people and then asking him to store it, only for it to be found by the police. When it came to his testifying about me, I was wrong about our limited contact reducing my exposure. Cotton told the jury about how I took him down into the sewers, and that my goal was to ambush the police. Then, he called out Paul Redd and me as the two who shot the police officers who came to the front door when the shoot-out began. In that moment, he had implicated me as attempting to kill cops. I felt doomed to a life in prison. Motherfucka. I stared at Cotton during his testimony, looked him straight in the eye. Cotton didn't even blink. He stared right back at me, and at all of us.

"You goddamn liar!" Paul stood up and shouted at Cotton, which broke up Cotton's testimony.

"Fucking snitch!" yelled Roland.

G joined in condemning Cotton: "I knew you were a liar and a chump."

The judge went crazy and started yelling, "Defendants, be quiet!" And "Attorneys, tell your clients to sit down and be quiet!"

Of course, the judge's shouts just resulted in more Panthers yelling.

"You can't tell me I can't talk. You a racist dog!" Roland yelled back at the judge.

"Get them out of my courtroom, now." Judge Dell had the deputies remove Roland, G, and Paul from the courtroom. Some of the others left with them in solidarity. They were put into the holding cell next to the courtroom, but that didn't stop them from interrupting the proceedings. *Bang, bang, bang!* We could hear them banging on the door. The judge finally called for a recess until the next day.

Those of us who were still out on bail didn't join in the courtroom antics, knowing that they would have locked us up right away. We couldn't help our comrades by joining them in jail. We supplied them with things from the outside, like snacks, money, messages, and a few other items to help calm their nerves and relieve some of the stress.

Soon Red and I had developed a routine, moving pills and going to court. The baby in her belly was growing, making it harder for her to move around, and so she was relying on my rides more and more. Then one Monday morning I realized that I hadn't heard from Red about a ride, nor had she shown up to court. Tuesday and Wednesday went by and still no word from Red. This was strange because the last time I saw her, Friday after court, she was cool, calm, and collected. She had mentioned receiving death threats from the Huey-ites before, but that was a while ago. The judge issued a bench warrant for her arrest.

After court one day I decided to go by her apartment to check on her. I knocked on the door, rang the doorbell several times, but there was no answer. The rest of the week went by; still Red had not contacted me. By Friday, everyone was frantic. Pam came to court with me that day. After the proceedings ended, I grabbed Pam's hand and said, "Let's go to the morgue." It was downstairs from the courthouse. When we got there, the clerk started pulling out trays of unidentified bodies. Red was on the second tray. How far-fetched was that? While we were upstairs in court thinking about where Red could be, she had been downstairs in the basement. It was heartbreaking to see her like that. She had been killed—execution style, according to the police. She was nude and shot five times: twice in the arm, once in the leg, once in the stomach, and once in the head. She was found in a sleeping bag in Lynwood, eight months pregnant. I contacted G's lawyer so he could tell him.

Pam and I rode the bus home that day because my car was in the shop. I was extremely tense and feeling vulnerable to a possible attack. Even Pam felt that someone was watching us. I didn't feel safe until we got to Watts.

We had identified Red's body on Friday. Over the weekend, I received word through underground channels that when I got to court on Monday I should sit in the back row. So I checked into court and did as I was instructed, sat in the back with the spectators instead of going to the defendants' table. Those who had remained in the Party and were loyal to Huey were already seated in front of the judge's bench: Al Armour, Craig Williams, Robert Bryan, and Tommye Williams. The attorneys were also sitting in chairs at their tables, some in the first row and the others in the second. The jury was walking in and so was Judge Dell. As the judge sat on his bench, the deputies brought G, Roland, Will, Lloyd, Paul, and Ike out of the holding cell. I sat there and watched, looking at G, knowing that he blamed Huey Newton and David Hilliard for Red's death. A confrontation was coming, but I didn't know how far it would go. I expected a verbal assault, because we were in the courtroom.

Then G looked in the direction of the defendants' tables, locked his eyes on the Huey-ites, and went completely off! He ran toward the table where they were sitting and picked up somebody's briefcase, bashing it over the head of one of Huey's people. As he laid into Al or Craig (I couldn't tell which one), Roland, Will, and Paul started throttling the others. The defense attorneys started running and ducking under the tables for cover. It was sheer pandemonium in the courtroom.

Everything happened so fast that I didn't have time to think about what to do. But then I couldn't move anyway. I looked to my right to see that a towering muscular black deputy had put his hand on my shoulder; he was pressing so hard that part of my body was leaning to the side. The other hand was on his gun. Obviously, he was letting me know that if I moved, he would blast my ass. I quickly looked up at him and then turned back to see Judge Dell jump off the bench with a .38 revolver in his hand, backing into the judge's chamber! I didn't even know a judge would be packing like that!

By this time Al, Craig, and Robert were getting their asses kicked; G was running all over, chasing these fools. Al eventually ran into the jury box, and Robert Bryan and Tommye were fighting to get to the front door. A deputy grabbed them both and started beating them! Why, I don't know, because they were already on the floor. *Fuckin pigs!*

There was blood dripping on the courtroom floor. Al seemed to be bleeding from somewhere on his head and Craig was bleeding too. G was still out to kill. He grabbed a flagpole that had been in the corner of the courtroom, and a bailiff took out his gun and aimed it dead at him. I couldn't hold it in anymore. I started hollering, "G! G!" G and I had a system. Because I rarely yelled, he knew that if I did, then he needed to stop and hear me. G looked at me and put the flagpole down. By this time, the deputy sheriffs had their guns pointed at all six of them. My comrades were handcuffed and walked back into the holding tank. After all that, there was order in the court.

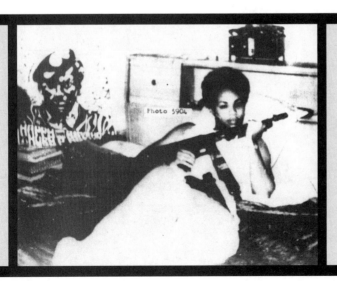

Saundra "Red" Pratt is holding a .45-caliber Thompson submachine gun. This photo was used as an exhibit during the trial for charging her with illegal weapons possession.
COURTESY OF VIRGINIA PRATT

The black deputy finally let me go and then just walked away. Whew! I just knew G was in trouble—you don't do that! He chased the judge up off the bench! Court was dismissed; we had the rest of the day off.

The rest of the trial was anticlimatic. G and the others coming from jail were separated and chained so the drama would be reduced. Seeing my partners like that made me furious. But there was not much I could do.

19

THE PROMISE OF TOMORROW

In the midst of the trial, I celebrated my twenty-first birthday. Pam and I had a party at our apartment in the projects. Anybody who was anybody was there: BSU friends from Harbor; BSA members like Baba, Jerry, Wendell, Jackie, and Yusuf; Party members who weren't locked up, like Richard and Tyrone; and the neighborhood folks. The party started at about 8:00 PM, and we danced, ate, talked, and drank all night.

A week later, I was talking to some friends on 103rd and Wilmington when I saw Cigar, the big fat pig who told me I would never make it to age twenty-one. He was driving slowly, passing by in his squad car, obviously perusing the streets. I taunted him, yelling and laughing, "Hey, Cigar, I made it to twenty-one last week!" He paused for a few seconds and yelled back, "You'll never make twenty-two!"

Our attorneys worked hard for us and made excellent closing arguments. With passion, they asserted our position: we had been provoked by the police and subjected to consistent harassment. Attorney Joe Reichmann made one of the best arguments on our behalf when he said, "The SWAT raid on the Southern California chapter of the Black Panther Party was like a Gestapo raid in Nazi Germany, so what were they supposed to do?"

On December 23, 1971, two years after the shoot-out on Forty-First and Central, the verdicts came in. The jury considered seventy-two counts against us, from conspiracy to murder police officers to possession of illegal weapons. We were found not guilty on all charges related to conspiracy to murder and not guilty on most of the other charges. In total, sixty-three verdicts were rendered, and the jury deadlocked on the others. We were also found not guilty of assaulting police officers.

Nine of us were convicted of conspiracy to possess illegal weapons: Geronimo Pratt, Robert Bryan, Renee Moore, Paul Redd, Willie Stafford, Tommye Williams, Al Armour, Craig Williams, and me. The jury was deadlocked on the charge of conspiracy to possess against Roland. Jackie Johnson (Pee Wee) and Ike Houston were acquitted of all charges. Bernard was a juvenile, so his case had been transfered to the juvenile courts. It was a seven-month trial with eleven days of deliberation by the jury. There were six black people on the jury. The People of the State of California versus the Panther 13 became the longest trial in Los Angeles history at that time.

When the verdicts were read I was elated! Some of the charges against us had carried life sentences. Although we were convicted of conspiracy to possess illegal weapons, the verdicts granted us an opportunity of having real lives on the outside. Richard and my aunt Mary Green had come with me to court that day to hear the verdicts. I looked back at them from the defendants' table and smiled. After it was over, I milled around with the attorneys and then left. I felt a little sadness come over me when I thought about Red. She would have been just as excited to hear the verdicts. With a new baby coming into her life, she would have been on cloud nine.

When I got home I called Nanny and Sharon to share the news with them. Sharon was happy for me, and Nanny "praised the Lord." The date for sentencing was set for January 13. I was still free on bail, so I had time to make plans and to get ready to do the time the judge would order.

Pam and I invited friends over that night to celebrate. Lester, Richard, and Pat came by. I had moved beyond drinking Panther Piss and beer to sipping Cognac. I found Courvoisier too sweet while Hennessey was much too bitter. My new drink was Martell VSOP. It was smooth. My man Joe Armistead hipped me to the brands. I purchased a bottle and went home.

As we partied, the women were sipping Tyrolia, Akadama, and Boone's Farm wine, and the men drank the harder stuff and smoked. Our music played loud that night. Songs that reflected the politics of the era played on the turntable. "Express Yourself," by Charles Wright and the Watts 103rd Street Rhythm Band, Marvin Gaye's "What's Going On," and the Isley Brothers' "Machine Gun" had us all grooving to their political and soulful messages.

The day of sentencing came. I had great misgivings about going to court. Could I do life in prison? I briefly considered going on the run but knew it didn't make sense until I at least knew what the sentence

My girlfriend, Pam, and I walking out of the courthouse after the trial verdicts were rendered. The smile on my face shows my relief after being acquitted of the most serious charge: attempted murder. WAYNE PHARR COLLECTION

This poster features the L.A. 13, those of us who prevailed against the predawn military assault by LAPD and successfully beat back their use of assault weapons, an armored vehicle, and explosives. COURTESY OF SOUTHERN CALIFORNIA CHAPTER, BLACK PANTHER PARTY

was. Judge Dell sentenced G, Will, and Paul to the state prison for the maximum time of one to five years. Four of us were sentenced to the county jail with probation after time served: Al, Craig, Robert, and me. During sentencing, the judge would render what he considered a life lesson to each one of us before he gave us our individual sentences. He said to me, "Well, Mr. Pharr, since you have been coming to court this last year, I have not figured out how to read you. You don't say much." I looked at him and didn't say anything. "I am giving you six months in the county jail with two months served, plus three years' probation. I don't want to see you again." I nodded. It could have been much worse.

The two women, Tommye and Peaches, were given only probation. For Peaches, not serving time was great since she was eight months pregnant. Except for G, who was twenty-nine, our ages ranged from nineteen to twenty-three.

I didn't want to do the time in jail, but knowing that I wouldn't abandon my boys and baby girl meant a lot to me because I had sworn that I wouldn't be an absentee father. I was the new black man, one who would stick around to raise my children. But life is filled with contradictions, I suppose. The path I took to provide for them could have easily added to my sentence.

Lester, Gary, and I planned one more hit so that I could leave Pam some money to live on while I was away. I called Freddie, the Mack Man, to find out about viable opportunities. Freddie always kept his ear to the ground, so he knew what was going on. He set up this guy who was a dealer. We caught him when he went to make his buy and took him out quick. We put him in the trunk of the car we were in and took off. We dropped him off miles away from Los Angeles. I let Lester and Gary keep the jewels he had on him, and I took my portion of the money. We also got a bunch of credit cards, which I gave to Freddie to fence off. We made $3,000 apiece for a few hours of work.

While I was on my way to Wayside Jail, G was just beginning the fight of his life. Caroline Olsen, an elementary school teacher, was murdered on December 18, 1968, in Santa Monica. G was at a Black Panther meeting in Oakland at the time. But he was indicted, arrested, and charged in February 1972 on the word of Julio Butler, once head of the Buckingham office and now informant. I guess Julio's crazy ass never got over G's appointment as deputy minister instead of him. The case was in Santa Monica, but somehow it was transferred to Los Angeles.

By New Years Day I was at Wayside. Before I left, I got some weed and pills and left them with Pam so she would have some money and I would also when I returned. The night before I left, I got blasted. I was apprehensive about going to jail, but I still had no regrets about the shoot-out and would do it again if the sheriffs showed up with guns drawn.

I did my time at Wayside Maximum Security up in the mountains. It's located about forty miles outside of Los Angeles. I put on some slacks and a pullover shirt and walked into the facility with clout and respect. I grew up a Broadway Slauson and became a Black Panther. The brothers inside knew how we had dealt with the pigs during the shoot-out, and they were impressed. The support gave me a good feeling, but that didn't last long. On my first night in jail, the guy in the bunk below me hanged himself. I went to sleep and woke up to the commotion. I saw him, with a belt around his neck. I never found out if he died, but he was unconscious when they took him out. There's nothing like seeing a brother with a noose around his neck to bring clarity. I had to be strong.

Wayside was organized by dorms, with about sixty people in each section. There were blacks, whites, and Mexicans all living together. I knew I wasn't in for long, so I wasn't trying to make any friends or enemies. My goal—do easy time.

The first week, I realized that I could make some money, so I purchased some candy, cigarettes, and Vaseline, all hot commodities in jail, and they moved quickly. Vaseline was important because brothers wanted to grease their bodies up. I opened up a little store from my cell. Soon, an old convict came by and said, "Young blood, I'm well connected on the streets. My people plan to put some money on the books for me soon, but I need some grease, cigarettes, and candy today. Can you help me out?" I thought, *How many times have I heard that story*? I gestured to him, as if I didn't have anything, but he kept talking.

"My name is Mills, and I worked for Bunk on the outside."

That piqued my interest. Bunk was the big dope man in Watts at that time. He sold all kind of drugs and specialized in heroin. He sold at the Front, which was on Wilmington and 120th, near Imperial. I said, "I know Bunk. We can work something out. I'm sure you are good for it."

Mills replied, "Thanks, man. I need to quit this heroin, cold turkey."

I gave him what he asked for and let him know I would help if he needed me. He instructed me on how to rub him down with the Vaseline and wrap him in the thermal blanket so he would sweat the heroin out of his pores. He said the sugar rush from the candy helped to alleviate some the pressure of quitting.

Sure enough, a few days later, he got a draw and paid me. I could tell he was doing much better.

After chow one day, Mills thanked me again. "The average brother wouldn't have done that for me."

I responded, "Sho' you're right."

"You're here for Black Panther shit, huh?"

"Yes, sir. Bunk used to help us out when we were short on cash."

Mills then said, "Come walk the yard with me and do what I do." He continued, "I know you are in for short time, but the bulls will try to set you up to get you more. Stick with me, so you can learn how to stay away from their traps." Mills took me under his wing and taught me how to survive Wayside.

Once a week, the inmates were given yard time. I loved to play basketball, so I was looking forward to it. But Mills told me to keep my ass in the dorms, because "if the shit breaks out, the guards will shoot you first." I followed Mills's advice and stayed in the dorms and got schooled. I learned how to play chess. Certainly, I had played before Wayside, but we played the game with real excitement; we used the language of war. The bishops, knights, rooks, and pawns got captured and killed. Everybody is there to protect the king, and my job was to break through the defenses. Mills and some other inmates also showed me some new boxing techniques, emphasizing the importance of using my left hand to maneuver a blind-side punch. And then there were lessons on the art of hustling and being successful in the dope game. I was educated on how to buy heroin, cut it up, and bag it. Heroin, as opposed to cocaine, was a physical addition, so an addict needed three shots a day: one to wake up, one to function throughout the day, and one to sleep.

Embedded in Mills's teachings were lessons on human nature. For instance, there was a fool in the joint who chased anybody he thought was susceptible to being bullied and then tried to turn him into a homosexual. A guy named Monroe, whom I knew from the streets, was being intimated by this lowlife, who would hit him in the chest and the arm. Monroe would retreat, not fighting back. One night after visiting hours a few young brothers were hanging around my bunk going through a deck of cards and doing push-ups. This fool is chasing Monroe around again, and as usual Monroe wouldn't fight back. So, I'm checking this shit out and decide I couldn't watch it anymore. I approached him and said, "Listen nigger, we're not turning out any more brothers. Stop that shit!"

Mills saw the play go down and said to me, "Young blood, now you need to watch your back. You saved a nigger that didn't want to be saved. A man will save himself." I knew that was righteous talk. That's the kind of education I got from Mills.

Jail wouldn't be jail if there weren't racial conflict and fights. When it happened, it was usually the whites and Mexicans against the black inmates. One day a playoff game was about to start that the black inmates wanted to watch. But some white boys had commandeered the TV early and were watching *Hee Haw*, a variety show about some white redneck farmers listening to country music. A riot broke out, and we whipped their asses. We didn't have weapons; we used our fists. We were turning over bunks and beating the white boys and some of the Mexicans who joined them. Those who didn't want to fight used their mattresses as shields. The guards came in and broke us up. That was the only major fight I had in Wayside.

Sometimes the guards would harass me or single me out for discipline. "Up against the wall, Blue!" they would say, while surrounding me and pushing me up against the wall. "Hands up. Let me check your pockets."

I would follow orders and put up my hands so they could search me. One time I had an orange in my hand. I got so damn mad—I squeezed it so hard that it burst in my hands. Mills was right there watching and supporting me, saying, "Be cool, young blood. Be cool."

Mills would work with me to turn down the noise in my head, so I wouldn't get in more trouble. Mills kept his word and made sure that I walked out of Wayside in one piece.

20

THE LIMITS OF FREEDOM

I walked outside, stopped, and took in a big breath of air. "Ahhhh," I said, to no one in particular.

It felt good to be walking out of Wayside Max. It was the springtime, and I was finally done with that place.

The jail time, legal battles, and especially the uncertainty that went along with both were all behind me. Standing outside the jail, looking up at the cloudless blue sky, I felt that a heavy burden had been lifted from my shoulders. I had been looking forward to the future and to reestablishing relationships with my family, and now the time had finally come. I couldn't wait to get started. The first thing I did was catch the bus to Pam's place.

No one was expecting me, and I was practically bursting with happiness at being free to go where I pleased. *It will be a great surprise*, I thought as I walked up and knocked on Pam's door.

"Who is it?" Pam called out from the other side of the door.

"Wayne," I said gruffly, trying to hide my excitement.

The door opened immediately. Pam smiled broadly as I walked through the door, immediately greeting me with the kind of hug that told me I had been missed and needed.

"Where are the boys?" I asked immediately.

"In the kitchen. Come on and see them," she replied happily.

I walked down the hall and around the corner to the kitchen and was immediately greeted with squeals. I looked at my sons and marveled at how they had grown in just those few months. Their first birthday had been in April, while I was locked up. I hadn't stressed about it too bad at the time, though, knowing that I would be coming home soon. Seeing them again was amazing. They had teeth, and they were walking and moving about.

Pam and I agreed to spend a quiet evening together that night; I wasn't in the mood to party. I was happy to be relaxed and reflective, enjoying the family life I had created.

The next day, I checked on Sharon and my daughter. Tammy was about to turn two, so she was running the show. She had my mother, Nanny, and Sharon all at her beck and call, demanding that all her needs were taken care of. As usual, whenever I went to see Nanny after being gone for a while, she cooked my favorite foods: red beans and rice, greens, and steak, in that order.

My mom and a few relatives stopped by Nanny's to see me and partake of the meal. I expected my mother to start pestering me about changing my life. I didn't have to wait long; she jumped right in. We hadn't even finished eating. "Wayne, I think this is a good time for you to think about going back to school."

I replied with as much sincerity as I could muster. "Yeah, Mom, I have been thinking a lot about that."

Nanny joined in, "If you decide that you don't want to go right back to school, you can always get a job. You're smart, Wayne; you can do anything you want."

I nodded. "I understand, Nanny. I'm trying to figure it out."

Of course, my mom couldn't help herself. "Son, I sure hope that you are not thinking about getting involved with that Black Panther

Party again. Being with the group hasn't helped you. And it's worrying the hell out of us."

I bit my tongue, because I was getting aggravated. "Things have changed so much with the Party that there is not much to go back to."

My family didn't really need to worry about the Black Panther Party. It was now a shell of its former self. Huey Newton had gone to China in September 1971. After his return, he ordered the Black Panther Party chapters across the country closed and relocated the leadership of various chapters to Oakland. Huey also formally announced that it was time for the Party to "put away the gun" to "serve the people." After the Watts office burned down, no other office was opened in the area. All other offices in Southern California were closed while I was in jail.

In the meantime, G's trial for the Olsen murder was coming up. He was being set up, because we all knew that he had been attending a Black Panther meeting in Oakland when Caroline Olsen was killed and her husband shot. His defense team tried to get Hilliard and Seale to go on record and declare that G was there, but they refused to help. I thought that shit was unforgivable. But I also knew that they wanted to see G locked up because they were afraid of him, even more so after Red was killed. Still, they should've talked things through and worked something out, rather than allow him to remain in jail.

Despite the Central Committee's refusal to affirm G's location during the murders, we believed he could beat the case. He had a winning legal team: Charles Hollopeter, a successful local attorney, was his court-appointed lawyer, and Johnnie Cochran served as cocounsel. Tyrone Hutchinson had already told the police that a couple of drug addicts from the neighborhood had committed the murder, so that information could be used to meet the criteria for reasonable doubt. Julio was a proven lying dog and an agent who had been snitching on the Panthers for years. And finally, Kathleen Cleaver flew to Los Angeles from Algeria to testify that she and G were in Oakland at the time of the murder.

The trial started on June 14, 1972. Less than two months later, on July 28, 1972, G was convicted of first-degree murder and given a life sentence. It was possible that he would spend the rest of his life in jail.

After the sentence came down, I stopped by Richard's place on Central and Eighty-Fourth. Richard had been recruited by Bunchy but worked out of West Adams with Julio, who was his section leader. "The way that shit came down on G is a crying shame," Richard said to me.

"I talked with Johnnie, and he said they are going to appeal," I replied.

"C'mon man, do you think G really has a chance?"

"I'm not sure. After G chased that damn judge off the bench, all the judges in California probably want to see him locked up. Considering all the reasons why he should have gotten off, it seems to me that to help G we might have to make some money and work it another way."

"I hear that. I still think that Bunchy should have gotten rid of Julio's crazy ass a long time ago. We knew he was sucker and a lowlife."

"Yeah, I know. But Bunchy could work with fools like that and get them to do the right thing."

Richard smiled, remembering times with Bunchy. "He put Julio in a box and watched him work."

I chuckled. "I love G, but he didn't have Bunchy's people skills and couldn't control his temper. Bunchy would instill a little fear in people, but they respected him nonetheless. With G, everybody is just plain scared. Julio was terrified of G."

Richard remarked, "G knew that Julio was a little off. Maybe he thought he needed to watch him, that's why he didn't just expel him. I'm glad I never had anything to do with Julio."

The sense of melancholy I felt was real. I hoped that the attorneys could really help G on appeal. But I was also feeling low because I had lost contact with some of my other homeboys. Baba and Wendell had gone to Canada, trying to escape a stint in jail for the attempted murder charge of Michael Lansky, a local communist leader. Then there was Billy Dean Smith, another brother we called "Duck," whom I had recruited into the Party. Duck was from Watts, and we were the same age. He had a green GTO, which he allowed the Party to use. I rode with Duck to Oakland for the United Front Against Fascism conference in July 1969. We had a great time, partying at night, attending workshops during the day, and hanging out with progressive young people of all races and colors. Duck had gotten drafted into the army and was sent to Vietnam. He didn't want to go, but he had no real options for refusal. He trained at Fort Ord and then was sent to Vietnam in October 1970. I heard through the grapevine that the officers were sending Duck to the frontlines every day, putting him on point, which meant that he could be the first to die. Duck fiercely protested his treatment, which led to several confrontations with his superiors in the army. Then a grenade exploded in the officers' barracks killing two officers and wounding another. After a grenade pin was found in one of Duck's pockets, he was arrested and charged with murder. Duck had been sent back to the United States and put in solitary confinement, where he remained. Luke McKissack, one of our attorneys on the SWAT case, was now defending Duck, which I was glad about because Duck would surely face the army's firing squad if convicted.

I was also mourning the end of my work in the Party. It had been my life for two years, and I was committed to our activism. I could still recite the Ten Point Platform from memory. But now there were no more political education classes and no more selling newspapers and no more organizing rallies. I couldn't deny it; I was still a Panther in my heart.

As sentimental as I was about the slow demise of the Party, I had to get my priorities in order, and making money was at the top of the list. Before I went to Wayside, I asked Pam to set aside some money for me. She kept her word, so I had a little cash in my pocket. I hit the streets to make sure I invested that cash into an opportunity to make more.

I turned my attention to the drug trade, full blast. Things had changed, and the black community was flooded with drugs. Weed and pills seemed primitive compared with the new drugs of choice: heroin, cocaine, mescaline, speed, and LSD. It seemed like everybody was using or selling drugs. Unbelievable to me, after participating in the black struggle, was that the pressure exerted on the drug dealers seemed nonexistent.

The abundance of illegal drugs in the black community signaled a change in Los Angeles, but there was also a new set of gangs. Crips, Bloods, Pirus, and others were taking over the streets. They were much more vicious than we were. When I was coming up, gangs boxed, wrestled, and sometimes used knives in fights. Periodically, a gang member would get killed. But the new crews were different; they wanted to see blood at the outset. It was nothing for them to pull a gun on somebody. In this new environment, I had to play just as hard.

At Wayside, Mills told me that robbery was a short-term game and that I needed to always remember that a wrong move during a robbery could be my last. Using that information, I looked for Freddie to hook me up with some action in a different arena. Freddie took me under his wing, and I started hustling with him all over the city. We sold weed, worked accidents, and played the horses at the racetrack. Because I didn't like the odds on winning at the track, I found a niche in loaning other hustlers money. Betting on the ninth race was a big deal, because it was the last race of the day. People would "baseball the bet," meaning that the numbers they bet equaled nine. But if a guy had been there all day, then he was usually broke. That's when I would step in, ready to help a brother out.

In return for my contribution, I didn't ask for money; I wanted to be paid back with the action—drugs I could sell. I would drop them off to one of my partners, like Slow Drag. I met him in the projects, and he was the person who introduced me to tooting cocaine. I had tried it before but really wasn't into it. But Slow Drag showed me how to take the rocks out of the cut, so that it was real pure and didn't ball up. One time Slow Drag made so much money he paid me twice in one day. Slow Drag was from Chicago, and the whole time he was in Los Angeles he wore coats, because he said "it didn't get cold enough."

Next, I needed to move my sons out of the projects. The county workers had recently come to make sure Pam was still qualified to receive welfare benefits, such as Aid to Families with Dependent Children and food stamps. When one of the workers asked me how much I made, I replied with $3,000 a month.

After they left, Pam went ballistic, yelling and screaming. "Wayne, why in the hell would you tell those people that you was making that much money? Now they are going to kick me off the county."

I yelled back at her, "I don't give a damn about the county! I was brought up hustling for mine and not playing the welfare game." I had no plans to be dependent on anybody's welfare. "Fuck that shit."

I moved us into an apartment on the Westside, on Ninety-Second off Normandie. It was the same neighborhood that caused me so much consternation when I was in middle school. It was a couple of miles from Henry Clay, the school where I had experienced racism. I can't explain why I went back there, except that I didn't want my boys growing up in the projects.

It was around this time that I got my wholesaler's license to sell clothes, which I sold out of the trunk of my car. Coats and hot pants made good money, but my staples were panty hose—off-black, coffee, and a little navy blue. Sometimes Pam would dress up in one of those nice hot-pants suits to generate interest, and then they would really sell.

While I was working my other hustles, Freddie came up with a good connection for Mexican Mud, which is brown heroin. Dealers liked selling it because they could sell one ounce for five hits. I sold to other dealers, rarely to individuals. The action from the Mud with Freddie not only helped me pay the bills and keep the lights on, but also contributed to my ability to pay for a few extras, like better TVs and electronics.

Then one day I took my boys to Rudy's Barbershop on Ninety-Eighth and Normandie for haircuts. I sat around jive talking with Rudy for a few hours with some of his other customers. Of the men Rudy introduced me to that day, Joe Armistead stood out from the rest. He was a tall, thin, light-skinned cat about ten years older than me. While we were shooting the breeze, I was checking out Joe's diamond rings and wondering what he was into. It was starting to get late, so I picked up my boys to go home.

As I was walking down the street carrying one son in each arm, Joe pulled up in a long, black 1970 Coupe de Ville and offered us a ride home. "Sure," I said, and Joe took us home. I invited him in. "Hey, Joe, I have a little blow in the house."

Getting out of his car while still talking, Joe said enthusiastically, "Sounds good to me."

Joe and I tooted some and then he split.

After Joe left, Pam came to me, livid. "You and this fool snorted up all the coke, and we need the money!" Blah, blah, blah.

I quickly forgot Pam's meltdown. I had a feeling earlier that day that I might get lucky, and I was right. A couple of hours later, Joe came back to my apartment with his girlfriend, Donna. Small world: Donna and I went to high school together at Washington. "Hello, Donna. It's good to see you. What have you been doing with your life?"

"Hanging with Joe."

Joe asked, "How do you two know each other?"

We both said, "Washington High" at the same time and laughed.

Donna said some good things about the work I did organizing the BSU at Washington.

Joe said, "Hey, brother, that was nice what you did this afternoon, inviting me to share your stash." While making conversation, Joe put an ounce of coke on an album cover and we consumed it. Joe and I started talking business while Pam and Donna got to know each other. Talk about being in the right place at the right time. I knew meeting Joe was a stroke of luck for me, and the fact that I knew Donna gave Joe and me a closer connection. He told me about his Mexican connection and said he would hook me up.

Joe introduced me to Homer, who would go to Mexico and get pure cocaine from the producers. Joe would come by weekly and drop a stash for me to move. Then Joe took me to Mexico with him to meet some of the players. I was ballin'. Freddie had given me the game, but Joe gave me my PhD in hustling. Now I was moving on the fast track. I put together a crew, and we began to sell to hustlers at the Gardena Casino. I had so much money, I bought about five cars in one year. But I didn't go Superfly. I made sure I gave Sharon some money, and Nanny. I bought a Mustang, a convertible El Dorado, and a Coupe de Ville. I would run the cars up and down La Cienega Boulevard, a long strip of highway on the Westside.

Pam and I were doing extremely well financially, but we couldn't get along. We decided to call it quits, so I moved out and into one of my mother's properties. It was a three-unit building on Forty-Third Street.

The breakup with Pam forced me to pause and look at my lifestyle. I knew what I was doing was against the principles of a righteous black nationalist, but I justified it. I was trying to make enough money to help get G out and take care of my kids. I knew my immersion in the drug culture meant that people without solid principles or morals surrounded me. It was so different from dealing with intelligent black people, who had a socioeconomic perspective rooted in nonexploitation. The contradictions were so great. I went from being a servant of the people to selling them drugs; I had succumbed to the money.

A few months after I broke up with Pam, I finally had the experience it took for me to change my lifestyle. Truly, a light went off inside my head. I needed a tester for some heroin, so I asked Chicken to participate. Chicken was a beautiful woman who was a dope fiend. I knew Chicken from high school. I will never forget the day she got into a fight with another girl on the gym field. She was beating this girl's ass, when her shirt flew open and those breasts of hers were flashing. That's when Chicken was looking good and in her glory. But years later Chicken was hooked and would do anything for a hit of heroin. She had just gotten out of jail and was walking down the street. I picked her up and asked if she wanted to go get a hit.

Before a buy, the dealer wants to know that the product is good, so I took Chicken to a see a guy we called Wolf, a big dealer who sold to the Hollywood set. As soon as we got there, Wolf pulled out the needle and stuck it in her arm. I didn't know it, but her veins were collapsed, so we had to keep digging and digging and digging.

It was then that I had an out-of-body experience. I was looking down at myself, digging a needle in a woman's arm. A voice—my voice—was saying to me: "Are you really that greedy? Do you really need the money this bad?"

The answer was no. Right then and there, looking at Chicken with a needle in her arm, and looking at the guys around me who, like me, were participating in a business that was killing black people, I knew it was over for me.

I didn't have to get busted. I didn't have to kill. I was making money, but I could no longer hold my head up high, like I had when I was in the Party. I wasn't the proud black man I once was. I decided, right then and right there, I would not be the scourge of my people.

21

FAMILY BUSINESS

I was sweating bullets at Floyd's Fish Market. My job was to cut, clean, and fry fish for eight hours a day, five days a week.

Floyd Metlock, a friend of my mother's, owned the joint. He had been pestering me to work for him for quite a while. At my mom's spot, Floyd had seen me and asked again. "Wayne, I'm still trying to get you to come help me out at the store."

I didn't have any other opportunities coming my way. "Sure, Floyd. What time should I be there?"

Floyd and my mom were playing cards, but they paused and looked at me, with their mouths open. "You can start tomorrow. Come about 9:00 AM, so we can begin to prepare the fish for the afternoon rush."

I said, "All right, I'll be there."

As I was leaving the house, Floyd shouted, "Hey, don't forget to wear comfortable shoes."

The fish market was located in the heart of the black community, on Vermont and 112th Street. Buffalo, perch, whiting, catfish, and red snapper sold all day and every day we were open. After taking the job at the fish market, my income immediately dropped to almost nothing. I went from making $2,500 a week to $120 a week. On top of that, I was wearing an apron stained with fish blood and standing over a deep fryer of boiling grease. Sometimes the perch had spines on the top that would stick in my fingers. I even cut myself a few times hacking away at a fish. But it was honest work, and it paid some bills. I sacrificed the money that selling dope gave me to do what was righteous for my people and my principles.

My running partners couldn't believe that I was working at Floyd's, so they came to see it to believe it. Richard had been in the Party, so he respected my decision. Even as I was filling the hot sauce and ketchup bottles, Richard nodded to me, saying, "That's all right brother. I'm proud of you, man." Joe was cool with it too, and every now and then he would come by so I could fry him a piece or two. There wasn't any shame in my game. I was for real. But some of the folks who knew how high I had been rolling couldn't accept that I was out of the drug business. There were even rumors floating around that I was selling drugs out of the fish market!

I was now out of the dope business and out of the Party. I worked, hung out with my friends, and was a father to my children. Periodically, the police would harass me, but it was nothing too serious. The most problems came from that pig Hole, who still had it out for me.

I was driving with Pam's brother in the car one day and Hole saw me going east on Imperial. He immediately hit the sirens and lights. I stopped the car in the middle of the street rather than pull over. This meant that I was blocking traffic and other cars had to go around me after that. As I suspected, Hole pulled up right behind me. I had hoped that he wouldn't be able to get around us fast enough and would run right into my car. But that didn't happen, so I had to deal with that fool.

Hole got out of his car and struck his cowboy pose, like he was going to do a big draw. "Get out of the car, and then slowly back away from it," he said. This was one of his tactics so we wouldn't be able to shoot his ass straight on, without warning; we'd have to turn around to aim at him. After we backed away from the car and turned around, Hole got up in my face, growling. "Wayne, if you got a gun, draw it."

I replied with a smirk, "I don't have a gun, Hole."

He walked around us, talking trash, and then eventually let us go. The asshole didn't ask for license or registration. He just wanted me to see his power. What a jerk-off.

Even though I had to deal with that kind of shit every now and then, the police weren't trying to beat my ass on a daily basis. I was making progress, or so I thought.

But then in May 1974, the pigs assured me that I was still considered a threat. At 3:00 AM, I was on my way home, driving through the alley in the back of my mother's house. I lived in one of the units over my mom's garage, upstairs, but not in the house itself. As soon as I pulled in and parked, the police threw the lights on me and lit up the alley like high noon. I noticed that five or six police cars had surrounded the place. There was also a police helicopter circling and surveying the scene from the sky. They had caught me off-guard this time. I had no expectation of an early morning run-in with the police, especially around my mother's house.

"Wayne, get out the damn car," one of the pigs shouted.

I got out slowly with my hands up. The pig then ordered me to lean over the hood of the car with my hands behind my back. While patting me down, he barked, "Are you armed or carrying any weapons?"

I answered, "No sir." Glad as hell that I wasn't. I didn't know what this shit was about. As usual, I told myself to play it cool.

The leader that night barked again, "Where is Patty Hearst, Wayne?"

I looked up at the cop talking to me. I was dumbfounded. *Are they really trying to hook me up with that craziness?* "I don't know where she is. I don't have anything to do with Patty Hearst."

Nineteen-year-old Patty Hearst of Berkeley, California, was the granddaughter of William Randolph Hearst, a rich white man who built a media empire. She had been kidnapped by an organization called the Symbionese Liberation Army (SLA) in February. After the media reported she was kidnapped, she went on the road with them, robbing banks. She even shot up a surplus store somewhere near Los Angeles.

"Wayne, I am going to ask you again. What do you know about the SLA?"

"Nothing," I said.

"We have information that you were involved with her kidnapping or that you are keeping her in one of your safe houses in Los Angeles."

I said emphatically, "I don't know what you are talking about."

"You are wanted for questioning; we may need to take you downtown."

"I swear I have nothing to do with that situation. I'm trying to mind my own business."

I looked toward my mom's home and noticed that she was looking out of her back window, checking out the situation. By this time, other neighbors had come out of their homes to check out the scene. I am sure that with so many witnesses, the police thought it was better to leave me alone, so they left. I walked upstairs, tired as hell, and went to bed, wondering if the pigs would come back.

Later that morning, I stopped by my mom's house to talk about what happened. I told her that I knew nothing about Patty Hearst and I thought the cops were just talking to anybody who had been an activist or had ties with militant groups. I told her I was glad that she had checked them out, because that stopped them from trying to harm me.

Because my mother had never seen me in danger before, the incident so unnerved her that she covertly called my father, Bill Pharr, and told him to get me out of town. In the meantime, the LAPD shot up and bombed the SLA's safe house on Fifty-Fourth Street on May 17, about two weeks after they questioned me. The SLA showed up for the fight and spent two hours going back and forth with the police. In the end, they lost a couple of members, including one of their leaders, Donald DeFreeze, who went by the name Cinque. My hustling partner Joe knew Cinque from way back. But there was no connection to me. The pigs were just still harassing me because we had blasted them out of headquarters.

Patty Hearst was eventually captured and prosecuted, but President Jimmy Carter commuted her sentence. Her lawyers said she was a victim of some bullshit called Stockholm syndrome, which supposedly makes you a slave to the beliefs of your kidnappers. That justification was absurd to me. If Stockholm syndrome could be used to justify crime, then all the damn activists I know should be out of jail.

Shortly after the pigs had questioned me at gunpoint about the SLA, my father got in touch with me. *What is this nigga calling me about after all this time?* I wondered. The last time I had seen my father was when I was about ten years old. I wasn't that interested in talking to him at that point in my life. But I guess curiosity got the best of me, so I decided to hear him out. After we exchanged a few pleasantries, my father said, "Hey, Champ, look, I am up here in Berkeley, and I'm hoping that you will come up here to spend some time with me."

At first I refused. "I'm not sure I have the time right now."

He continued, "Your mother said you are under some pressure down there with the police. She thinks it would be good for you to get out of town for a little while."

I heard him out and decided to go, figuring I had nothing to lose. I went to Berkeley to see him for a couple days. He was staying with my cousin Katy on Fifty-Fourth and San Pablo. He stayed there when he was in town and not on the ships, and had his own space in the downstairs area of her house.

I rang the doorbell and my father answered the door. I was hesitant and a little uncomfortable, not knowing what to expect. I didn't know what to do, so I just stared at him. He was about sixty years old, slightly shorter than I remembered and heavy around the middle.

My father wasted no time giving me a real generous hug. "It's good to see you, Champ. I hope it's OK that I still call you that." I could tell he was a little nervous too.

"Sure," I said, walking into the house.

He wanted to know how I was doing and told me that he always thought about me. *Yeah, but you weren't there*, I thought. "Champ, I had my partners check on you from time to time while you were growing up, and even when you became involved with those Black Panthers." That piqued my interest. He cleared his throat. "I have strong feelings about the Party. I like the ideas, but I got a problem with the whole gun thing."

I said, "Yeah, a lot of people do, but we have to defend ourselves."

Then he surprised me. "I knew John Frey's father—you know, the guy that Huey Newton shot. He was a merchant seaman; I met him on a ship a few times."

After he told me that, we both loosened up a bit, feeling that we had something more in common than just our last name. The next thing I knew we were talking about our family, laughing, and cracking jokes. Being with my father was surreal. I never expected that to happen.

I stayed with my pops for two days and then went to visit Aunt Dovey on my mother's side. In the meantime, he notified my mom that everything was all right and that he and I would be coming to Los Angeles together. My pops was ready to retire and in the process of deciding where he wanted to spend the rest of his life.

I drove Pops and myself the six hours to Los Angeles. It was a leisurely ride, but we talked about serious stuff along the way, like my half brother Druice Pharr. Nicknamed Dru, I had heard about him throughout the years but had never met him. Pops said that Dru had great animosity toward him because he didn't stay in Gipson, Louisiana, to raise him. My dad and Dru's mom lived on the bayou when they were married, but after they divorced, my father left because he couldn't find work. He saw a boat come down the bayou one day and jumped on it. He hadn't been back there since the 1940s. I am not sure why, but I didn't feel like Dru. I didn't hate my father.

I drove Pops throughout the neighborhoods in Los Angeles. I'll never forget how awestruck he was at the LAPD helicopter patrol and the way the pigs would light up a neighborhood. He said to me, "Damn, Champ, this is worse than Vietnam."

I was glad he saw it for himself. I told him, "Pops, this is what I have been trying to tell you. I been dealing with this shit my whole life."

"Now I understand your demeanor and style. Seeing you, son, makes me think of Robert Charles, the guy from New Orleans who fought the police in 1900." That's how I learned about Mr. Charles. "But I still don't like that Eldridge Cleaver. I don't know how you Panthers could follow a known rapist."

Pops hung out with Mom, and of course, they got into a fight. I know it had something to do with child support. He was ready to go after that. I am not sure how it happened, but we decided to travel to New Orleans to see Dru.

At the age of twenty-four, I finally met my half brother. He was a decade older than me. He had obviously taken after his mother's side in height and weight. He was big, about six feet, and more than two hundred pounds. But he and my father shared facial features and had the same laugh.

Dru was a self-made man. He had dropped out of high school to work in one of the neighborhood stores. After becoming an accomplished butcher, he opened up two grocery stores of his own in New Orleans. Soon after that he had opened a bar. Dru was one of the most well-known and respected black men in town.

When Dru found out I was coming, he threw a first-class party for me. The event was at his house, in a middle-class neighborhood. He greeted me with, "Hey, little brother, I haven't seen you since you was a baby."

I responded with a wide grin. "What's happening, man? I'm glad to see you. I've been hearing about you all my life."

"Little bro, I know you don't remember, but I met you when you were not even one year old, after your mom dropped you at our house. I was about ten and had to take care of you."

Dru introduced me to his friends and business associates, and we partied all night. I thought he was trying to impress me—and he succeeded. There seemed to be a clandestine plan to convince me to relocate to New Orleans. My father told me that Dru was experiencing some tax trouble and asked me to help him out. I was good with numbers, so they knew I could work on the problem. Dru also needed some help running his businesses. I agreed to stay a while.

My father decided that he was ready to go back to Northern California, so I drove him back across the country. When we got there, I dropped him off at the dock, and he went to the Philippines. He left me his Thunderbird and two grand in cash and told me to really spend some time in New Orleans and get to know my brother. On my way back to Louisiana, I stopped in Los Angeles to say bye to my mom, Nanny, and the children.

When I returned, Dru seemed a bit sentimental. With misty eyes and a smile, he said to me, "I'm glad you are back. I need to get to know my little brother. What kind of work do you do?"

"I worked in some liquor stores after I joined the Party. By the way, I used to deal in Los Angeles."

"I know you are not doing that shit anymore. You're a Pharr man; you're better than that. Hell, I can take two pieces of bread, lettuce, and tomato and make more money on that than a common dope dealer."

I laughed; I guessed he was right, especially if he was a serious entrepreneur.

"There is a lot I can hook you up with down here. But we don't hustle drugs."

Because Dru was the big brother, I gave him Pops's T-Bird, and I took Dru's Cadillac, which he had dogged out. I fixed it up so good, he wanted it back.

I found out that my brother had a reputation as a good ole boy. That meant he had relationships with the Italians and other white folks that allowed him access to liquor and cigarettes at wholesale. He introduced me to them, as well as to some beautiful women. I met even more women, because my job was to work at the bar. I settled into a relationship with Carmen, a woman whom I had seen passing by the bar periodically. She was so fine it would make a man cry. She was a cheerleader for Xavier College and athletic, and she wanted to be a flight attendant.

Now I had some stability. A relationship and a job and, of course, family. My only problem was that I couldn't keep up with the drinking lifestyle. People were drinking 24-7, all day and all night. When running a bar, the owner or employees are required to keep the party going, which kept the booze flowing. I ran the bar, but I did it without drinking all that liquor.

One night at the club, a brother in khakis and a nice jacket walked in. When I heard him ask for Wayne, I knew something was up. Everybody in the South called me Billy, after my father. He pulled me to the side and said, "I got a message from G."

I took him to a private spot in the club, served him a drink, and offered him some food. He was eating heartily as if he had not had a meal in a while: baked chicken, red beans, and greens. "How's G?" I asked.

"He's holding up well and still working on the appeal."

I wondered how G knew where I was or what I was doing, but it was likely just word of mouth. I was connected to Dru, who was well known throughout New Orleans, and people knew my history.

My guest then said to me, "I am here because the BLA is making moves in Louisiana and Mississippi and G needs a little help with something."

"Right on. I will do what I can to help." I was pleased with the offer, because it meant that I was still acknowledged as associated with the BLA, which kept me connected to the movement.

Being in Louisiana was working for me. I had never perceived a bond with my brother or my father. After I had been there for two years, I felt like I finally had a strong and very close relationship with Dru. But, I had to admit, I missed my children and I missed Nanny. My mother and Sharon were taking care of Tammy, and Nanny helped with the boys. I called and sent money, but it wasn't enough.

They needed my presence. I also missed Los Angeles. It was time for me to go back home.

Dru was sad to see me go but understood the need for me to raise my children. After being abandoned by our father, we agreed that I needed to be there for my own. I asked Carmen to go to Los Angeles with me and she agreed. I did the respectful thing and sought approval from Carmen's mom, promising to take care of her. We got the OK and took off. As soon as we got an apartment, she went to work. We eventually married.

The first place I worked after I returned was Smitty's Liquor Store. It was a nice gig, and I developed a reputation in the business of being an honest, hard worker. After a few run-ins, word got around that I didn't tolerate shoplifting and that if somebody got rowdy, they might get their brains blown out.

Soon opportunities from other store owners came knocking. Earl Livingston offered to pay twice as much as Smitty, so I changed jobs and started working for him on Seventy-Sixth and Compton Avenue. I was back on the Eastside.

I married Carmen after meeting her in New Orleans while visiting my brother Dru. WAYNE PHARR COLLECTION

Former members of the Black Panther Party started dropping by. The first one I saw was Roland Freeman. "Wayne, I heard you was back. It's good to see you." Roland looked like he had been taking care of himself.

"Same to you, brother. I was in Louisiana for a while, hanging with my brother and my father. What are you into?"

Roland said, "Insurance, man. It's not exciting, but I'm living."

Curious, I asked, "So, what's up with everybody else?"

"Long John went to school and got a bunch of licenses to do plumbing and electrical work. He is also a licensed mechanic."

"That's cool. So you both are entrepreneurs, running your own businesses."

Roland answered, "Yeah, you know it's hard for us to get jobs, or even work for somebody. By the way, Ronald got involved with some church and moved to San Francisco. Masai is doing work for the Communist Party. He's married to a Filipino woman."

I was finally able to get together with my old comrades when Harold Taylor threw a party. A lot of the comrades showed up: Ronald, Long John, Masai, Roland, Jerry, and others. Richard wasn't there because he was doing time for a robbery, but Tyrone contributed to the fun. We had a blast being together again, reminiscing.

After the event, all of us remained in touch. We were still each other's comrades and tried to keep each other on the straight and narrow path. This was especially true when it came to dealing with the temptations of drugs or continued confrontations with the police. One of the most important issues my comrades worked on together was the Free Geronimo Pratt campaign. Roland, Ronald, Peaches, and Long John took the lead. They proved to be tireless and dedicated warriors, raising money and awareness.

Working for the store owners was cool, but a dead-end job for me. I didn't want to kill anybody for money, and the liquor store business could be dangerous, with the characters and clowns who sometimes came through. Like my brother Dru and Roland and Long John, I wanted my own establishment.

I would eventually start my own business, and I did it in the arena that had been a part of my life since I was a child: real estate. I had watched my mother engage in the business of real estate and property ownership all of my life. Two of my cousins, Gloria Prescott and Sue Pharr-Smith, were also successful in real estate sales. I was checking out my cousins and realized that my ability to hustle would be an asset in the business. I expressed my interest to a guy named Paul Baker, who worked for Charles Williams's Century 21 office. He brought me a bunch of brochures on attending real estate school. Then, I asked Uncle Henry Green for a loan to pay for school, and he came through. I finally got my real estate license in 1978. I was worried about my criminal record, but all I had were assault cases and the possession of weapons conviction from the SWAT case. I had no fraud, drug cases, or anything that was considered moral turpitude. I was given a restricted license, which meant that if I was convicted of any crime, the real estate board could take my license without a hearing.

Charles Williams hired me to work at Century 21 as an agent. He was a sharp broker and taught me what he understood about the business. I loved the real estate game. It was a hundred percent better than working in liquor stores. The harder you worked, the more money you could make. Plus, I was also able to purchase my own property.

With Charles Williams's assistance and the help of my family, I was able to grow my business. Soon, I had enough resources to hire an agent to work with me. Joe Armistead became that agent. Joe had gone to Liberia and invested in diamonds, but things turned sour and he lost his ass over there. Joe had given me the dope game when I really needed some money, so I gave him the real estate game. I loaned him some money and gave him the books and information he needed to work in real estate. He took the exam and passed it.

I worked for the Charles Williams Century 21 Agency for two years. In 1981, I moved to Citizen's Realty with Jim Hobbley, a broker who was located in a more integrated area on the Westside of Los

Angeles. That was a great move for me because it gave me access to a whole new clientele. Jim was a good guy, but he was a poor money manager. After he neglected to pay a few important bills, we received an eviction notice. Jim and the staff collectively agreed that I had the skills and ambition to head the office. I became the head of the Citizen's Realty franchise. By then, I had four agents working for me.

I had found my niche: the business of real estate. I participated in professional development programs throughout the city. One of the best was the broker development business run by Century 21. I learned how to recruit and train more agents and expand the business overall. I was a good trainer because I had great organizing and people skills, skills I learned from my comrades and mentors in the Black Panther Party. Over time, I grew my business to a staff of sixty people, including my mother, who became one of my secretaries. We moved again, staying Westside, to Pico and La Brea because we needed more space.

Fortuitously—and ironically—it was the business that had caused me so much misery as a kid that ultimately provided me with a legitimate avenue to wealth and prosperity. It has also been the engine that

By the 1990s I had become one of the top-producing real estate brokers in the Los Angeles area. I am in my office pleased after closing another big deal. Wayne Pharr Collection

allows me to make a meaningful contribution to black people, especially gaining access to a home and land. Even when people experience financial crises, I can use the tricks of the trade to help save their homes or use that resource to pay for their children's college education or finance other important needs. I know from experience that real estate is one of the best ways for a poor person to obtain wealth. I see my work as a way to fulfill one of the tenets of the Ten Point Platform of the Black Panther Party for Self-Defense. *We want land, bread, property . . .*

EPILOGUE
HONOR AND SACRIFICE

It was, unfortunately, just a matter of time: Huey's love affair with crack cocaine ultimately proved too great for him to overcome. Huey Newton, the cofounder of the Black Panther Party for Self-Defense, died on August 22, 1989, gunned down by a drug dealer outside of a crack house in Oakland. The Party's minister of defense was only forty-seven years old when he was murdered. The killer wanted to score points with the Black Guerilla Family—a prison group that began as political before some members turned to criminal activity—by offing Huey.

Before Huey's death, the Party leaders most loyal to him bore the brunt of his out-of-control, drug-induced, violent, and paranoid behavior. Among other things, he expelled David Hilliard, viciously assaulted Bobby Seale, and had one of his goons pistol-whip Masai. Before he was expelled, David Hilliard developed a crack cocaine habit that had become just as bad as Huey's. David had started calling me for cash. "This is Chief of Staff David Hilliard. I need you to send money to the Party," he would say. But I wouldn't do it. Other than being desperate to feed the demands of his addiction, I'm not sure why David would call me anyway, considering that I had sided with Eldridge and not Huey. David did at least finally sober up, joining a substance abuse treatment program.

It took years for me to get over it, but I wasn't mad at Huey or David anymore. Addicts do crazy things, and those with power are worst-case scenarios because their subordinates will aid irrational behavior. After Huey was released from prison, the contradictions were apparent to anyone who bothered to look. The Southern California chapter of the Black Panther Party was labeled by Huey as a bunch of "out-of-control gangsters," and *that* part of the lumpen that couldn't be saved; but at the same time, our national leaders had goon squads beating people on a whim. Then, after our entire chapter had been expelled from the Party and our offices shut down, Panther leaders in Oakland started shooting prostitutes and pistol-whipping tailors. It was ironic that the Los Angeles Panthers proved our commitment to the revolution while the leaders of the Party, who were calling themselves revolutionaries, were acting like gangsters. We in L.A. put in serious work, and that is what vindicates us.

In 1975, a few years after the Southern California chapter was shut down, Eldridge Cleaver returned to the United States. He did a year or so in prison for his involvement in ambushing the cops when Bobby Hutton got killed. I never learned what Eldridge had to do or say to get back into the country, and it didn't really matter to me. Eldridge, like many of us, did what was necessary to stay alive and hopefully avoid living his final days in prison. As with Huey and David, I held no grudge against Eldridge, although many of us in the Party had risked our lives to support his leadership instead of Huey's.

After returning, Eldridge went through a lot of changes, ultimately metamorphosing into someone I didn't recognize. First, he started using crack cocaine, and then got busted in Northern California. He cleaned up his act and then publicly committed to Christianity. On the issue of Eldridge's drug addiction, he was no different than so many other black people trying to survive while living on the edge. At the time Eldridge returned to the United States, black communities were being flooded with hard-core drugs—a planned assault intended to quash the black liberation struggle. At the same time, jobs for blacks were scarce, which made it all the more easy to succumb to those dangerous substances.

Every black leader, if not every individual, would be well-served to read the "Report of the National Advisory Commission on Civil Disorders," written in 1968 in response to the urban uprisings in the 1960s led by black people. The study called for jobs and better education in the cities as solutions to the crisis. But, despite what the report advised, little changed: few opportunities for employment appeared, and the educational system went from bad to worse. Crack cocaine and heroin distracted many in our community, and we stopped pushing the system to negotiate our demands for opportunities, rights, and respect. Tragically, the dope trade filled the economic vacuum and became the provider of some economic opportunities, which were so lacking in the inner cities. Then a "war on drugs" was instituted throughout the country and included harsh penalties, such as "three strikes," which locked up our people.

The so-called war on drugs has been a veiled war on black people. I truly believe that drugs were put in our neighborhoods to destroy leaders like Huey and Eldridge, along with thousands of young black men. Drugs destroyed our will to fight as a community against oppression. Imagine how many Malcolm Xs have been locked up or killed because of the drug trade. The highly addictive nature of crack cocaine began destroying our family structure: black men were in jail, black women hooked on the drug began selling their bodies and sometimes their children for a hit. Those of us living in the cities in the early 1970s witnessed the transformation.

In the 1980s, Congresswoman Maxine Waters exposed the link between the Central Intelligence Agency and the international drug trade. When right-wing groups in Nicaragua, called the Contras, sold cocaine in black communities to fund their war against the Nicaraguan government, the CIA and the Reagan administration turned

At the premiere for the movie *Panther*, written by Mario Van Peebles and starring Marcus Chong as Huey P. Newton. Chong's strong resemblance to Huey was noted by many Panthers. WAYNE PHARR COLLECTION

a blind eye. Ricky Ross, a Los Angeles dope dealer, purchased the drugs at cheap prices and trafficked them in major cities, thus contributing to the crack cocaine epidemic. Drugs were so plentiful and lucrative that the local gangs became major players in the dope game. The next thing I knew, community youth had gone from aspiring to be the next Malcolm X, Bunchy, Huey, or Eldridge to bragging about living a thug's life. Becoming a gangster became more prestigious than being a freedom fighter.

It's obvious even today that the police are not interested in ending the scourge of drugs that is ravaging our community. Going back to when I was selling, I knew then that the police weren't putting much effort into trying to bust me, because slinging dope is not a threat to the capitalist system. What a contrast to my Panther days! I truly believe that if the police had put the same intensity into ending the dope business that they had put toward destroying the black liberation struggle, there would be no dope business today.

I'm proud of the sacrifices the Black Panther Party made for our people. And I recognize that so many others who came before us suffered tremendously and gave even more of themselves. We should know about the efforts of our freedom fighters so that young people might gain the will and strength to fight another day.

Geronimo ji-Jaga Pratt should not be forgotten. As one of the L.A. 18 arrested on the morning of December 8, 1969, G waged war above-ground and underground until he was framed and wrongly convicted of murdering of a white schoolteacher in 1972. Even behind bars, G never stopped fighting. It took twenty-seven years, but with the skill of his lawyers, the work of the community, and his commitment to be free, the courts eventually had no other choice but to release him. Johnnie Cochran, one of the attorneys who represented G in that case, later said that overturning that conviction was the greatest victory of his career.

In 1997, hundreds of people waited outside the courthouse in Santa Ana. Eldridge and Kathleen Cleaver, Roland and Ronald Freeman, Long John, me, and so many others who made up the Free Geronimo Pratt Committee, were all there to greet him on the day he was released. As usual, Peaches sang a freedom song. Looking strong

Geronimo and Romaine "Chip" Fitzgerald in captivity together in San Quentin during the 1980s. By this time, both had served more than a decade. Geronimo's murder conviction was overturned and he was released in 1997. Chip remains in prison today, making him one of the longest serving political prisoners in the United States.
COURTESY OF VIRGINIA PRATT

and vibrant, G walked out of the courthouse. The crowd applauded, shouted, and cried. He said a few words and then drove off in a black Jeep that had been purchased for the occasion. That night, the Free Geronimo Pratt Committee held a banquet in his honor at a local church.

Eldridge and G reignited their friendship, and from time to time during the late 1990s I would hang out with them and Kathleen. We went to bars or restaurants, spending long hours holding court wherever we were, rearguing Panther history and politics. After Hugh Pearson's biography of Huey Newton, *The Shadow of the Panther*, garnered attention, we had a lively discussion about the book. I remember G saying that Pearson's description of his relationship with Huey while they were in San Quentin together was so accurate that it seemed like Pearson had been in the room with them. It was eerie, we all agreed.

Eldridge and Kathleen had divorced in 1987, and it became obvious that G and Kathleen had more in common with each other than G and Eldridge had at that time. Kathleen had become a lawyer, and she had worked with the legal team for G. Eldridge was elated that

Geronimo and my daughter Dana at my home on Bronson Street after his release from prison in 1997. WAYNE PHARR COLLECTION

G had gotten released from prison, but he had little involvement in revolutionary politics.

Eldridge and I were never close, but we engaged in plenty of conversation and debate when we were together with G. He knew about the shoot-out and the role that Los Angeles played in the Party. We agreed that Huey Newton destroyed the organization, along with COINTELPRO. On May 1, 1998, at the age of sixty-two, Eldridge died of a heart attack in Pomona, California. I drove G to the service. It was a revolutionary funeral, in honor of his revolutionary past. Another chapter in Panther history ended.

In those days, G was in and out of town quite a bit. He traveled to Northern California to spend time with his wife, Asahki ji-Jaga, whom he had married while in prison, and their two children, Shona and Hiroji. He came to Los Angeles to work on his civil suit against the FBI and the City of Los Angeles for false imprisonment and violation of his civil rights, and to visit family and friends. Sometimes I would meet him in Hollywood at one of the swank hotels where he stayed. Other times, he would stop by my crib in West Los Angeles and hang out. He also traveled to Louisiana to check on his property and visit his people there. One time, when we were both in Louisiana, I toured his property. He had one of those nice Victorian framed houses; it was a pretty yellow with white trim and a quaint country backyard. At one point, he took me on a tour to the back of the house and into the garage. I immediately noticed that it had no windows. G told me that he spent a lot of his time in the garage whenever he was in Louisiana. He had spent eight years in solitary confinement, and I understood that his affinity for his garage was related to being institutionalized. I'll never forget when he said to me, "When I was in the hole, the ants used to talk to me and bring me food." I said to him, "You've got to break this habit, G. Brother, you are not in prison anymore."

Because he had an interest in living in Africa and a desire to stay off the radar in the United States, G left America and emigrated to Tanzania, in eastern Africa. I was happy for him; I thought it was a beautiful transition and always wished that I could have made a move like that. In Tanzania, he worked with the local population to get fresh water pumped into the village and also helped them gain access to electricity. After courting Joju Cleaver, the daughter of Eldridge and Kathleen, the two eventually married.

On June 2, 2011, fourteen years after he had been released from prison, G died of heart failure while still living in Africa. The following month, we memorialized him at the Agape International Spiritual Center in Los Angeles, which was founded by Dr. Michael Beckwith, a famous new age spiritual leader. The service was packed, overflowing with supporters who admired and loved G. Lawyers, friends, and family spoke, and a moving video of his work in Tanzania was played. I was one of the three Black Panther Party members who gave a tribute to him at the service, along with Kathleen Cleaver and Ronald Freeman. As I spoke, I observed that G had become very humble after his release from jail; he had even forgiven those who were responsible for his serving all those years in prison. I talked about his work in Tanzania and about the strong love he had for black people. G was cremated in Africa, and his ashes were spread over Lake Victoria.

On that fateful morning of December 8, 1969, along with G, four other individuals had been arrested at the Pratt residence: Saundra Pratt, Kathy Kimbrough, Evon Carter, and Long John. Although none of us is really certain, G had heard that Saundra was killed by some mobsters she had previously worked with in New York. Long John, Kathy, and Evon were not charged with a crime. After Kathy and Evon were released, I lost contact with them. Long John remained loyal and committed to the Party. Against his lawyer's advice, he came to our trial and bail hearings to support us, and he worked with the Free Geronimo Pratt Committee. Long John is now working as an independent contractor, specializing in automotive, plumbing, and electrical work. The bond we established back then remains to this day. I have the utmost respect for Long John's dedication and hard work as a captain in the Party.

Captain Long John Washington of the Southern California chapter worked out of Central Headquarters. He worked hard to keep the rank and file out of danger. COURTESY OF JAMES SIMMONS

Two of the four Party members arrested at the Touré Center that morning, Sharon Williams and Craig Williams, disappeared from the Los Angeles scene shortly after the trial ended. They had elected to remain in the Party under Huey Newton's leadership, and to this day, I am not sure what happened to them. Al Armour sided with Huey too. He and his wife, Norma, moved to Oakland, and Norma went to work alongside Ericka Huggins at the Panther Liberation School. At some point, Al moved back to Los Angeles and enrolled in college, earning a bachelor of arts degree from California State University, Long Beach. After he returned to Southern California, I would see him every now and then. I finally decided to stop by his house so we could talk things through and work out our differences. We discussed the good times at the Watts office and at the funeral home where he worked. We had supported each other through some difficult times as well. Those memories and the trust we had for each other was enough to let sleeping dogs lie.

Al eventually developed multiple sclerosis, a degenerative disease that attacks the nervous system. I continued to visit him every now and then after he was diagnosed in an effort to support my former comrade and give him company. I watched him deteriorate as his disease progressed, to the point where he was bedridden for the last ten years of his life. He and Norma had divorced by then, so his family took care of him at home, at least until he needed more medical attention. He died on April 12, 2013, in a convalescent home.

Ike Houston was also at the Touré house on the morning of December 8. After the trial and his acquittal, Ike eventually left California and moved to Detroit. Ike had some difficulties with substance abuse, but the last time we talked he told me that he had joined a recovery program and was trying to stay committed to sobriety.

After doing time in prison for the shoot-out with the highway patrol, Lux became a restaurant manager in West Los Angeles and is now busy raising a family. Bruce Richards did his time after his conviction for the police ambush that included Walter Touré Pope's death. Bruce eventually moved to New York and is heavily involved in union organizing there. He and Lux are both involved with the Committee to Free Chip Fitzgerald. To date, Chip has served more than forty years in prison.

The five-hour shoot-out with the LAPD and SWAT at Forty-First and Central bound the rest of us together in history. We have carried the weight and trauma of that event throughout our lives. We were each affected differently, however; in part, it's likely that our ability to manage and move forward was related to the support we received from family, friends, and other supporters. A few of us were able to live productive lives, while others suffered from myriad problems and psychoses.

Gil Parker was beaten severely on the roof that morning when SWAT first attacked. The police continued to brutalize him even after he was arrested. Despite the beatings, Gil managed to create a life for himself. He now works in Northern California, where he lives with his wife and children. Periodically, we call each other on the phone to check in. It's always good to hear from Gil, and I'm so glad he survived the storm and is living a healthy and productive life.

Enjoying a meal in 2012 at the monthly Black Panther Party for Self-Defense Breakfast. The breakfast serves as a regular gathering place for us to maintain our camaraderie and to raise funds for political prisoners and those still suffering from the effects of the state war against us. We also honor our martyrs and engage newer activists.
WAYNE PHARR COLLECTION

After the Party was shut down in Los Angeles, Roland Freeman became an insurance agent for a time. He left that industry to become director of a community youth-and-sports group home for at-risk boys. It was a good move for Roland, and it allows him to mentor and support young people, something he loves to do. Still committed to community organizing, Roland also became president of the local Universal Negro Improvement Association for a time. Currently, he is the primary organizer of the Black Panther Party Breakfast, a fund-raising and informational event held monthly at a soul food restaurant in Los Angeles.

Those of us who remain, and are able, gather regularly with other activists and supporters at the event to memorialize those we've lost and to raise money for political prisoners and prisoners of war. Roland has been gifted with a wonderful, supportive family who respects his commitment to keep the memory of the Southern California chapter alive.

Bernard Smith became a Muslim and changed his last name to Arafat. At the age of seventeen, Bernard was the youngest of the group who battled SWAT that morning. He served time in a juvenile

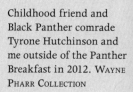

Childhood friend and Black Panther comrade Tyrone Hutchinson and me outside of the Panther Breakfast in 2012. Wayne Pharr Collection

correctional facility. He currently works with me at Citizen's Realty as a real estate agent. He also drives big rigs when he is not selling property.

After the split in the Party, three of the crew who fought SWAT on that long December day ended up staying with Huey: Tommye, Lloyd Mims, and Robert Bryan. I haven't spoken with any of them since the verdict. I heard that Tommye became a lawyer, and I am not sure what happened to Robert Bryan. Of those three, Lloyd Mims may have had the most tragic experience, considering that what happened to him was foolish and unnecessary. During the trial, he skipped bail to go to Oakland and work with Huey. Apparently, he became one of Huey's hit men. He was charged and convicted, with a guy named Richard Rodriguez, of killing James Carr, the "Jackal Dog." I felt bad for them both that they had gotten sucked into Huey's craziness. Mims was a cool cat who had helped us dig tunnels at Central. He was a relatively new member of the Party and had gotten spellbound by Huey's mystique. He and Rodriguez were both sentenced to life in prison.

Like Roland and Lloyd, Paul Redd maintained his involvement with black liberation politics, and like Lloyd, his activism took a wrong turn. In 1971, Paul shot at two officers in a police car and jumped a fence as he ran to get away. The gun in his belt buckle went off and the bullets hit him in the jaw. After being taken to the hospital for treatment, Paul was arrested and sent to prison. He did about six years in Soledad. When he came back to the community, Paul was never the same. His wife claimed that while he was imprisoned, doctors performed a lobotomy on him to reduce his tendency for violence. Whatever happened in the joint, Paul never recovered from it. He became reclusive and hard to get a hold of. At one point, he was homeless. His parents are doing their best to take care of him.

Premature death took the lives of Will Stafford, Jackie (Pee Wee) Johnson, and Peaches. Will became involved with the Black Guerilla Family and got killed in Oakland in the 1980s. Before Will's death, he and I talked periodically, and he told me he was working with Doc Holiday, who was a big dope dealer. Pee Wee became a handyman and an alcoholic. He died in the 1990s of cirrhosis of the liver. Renee

Members of the Black Panther Party at Roland Freeman's house after a monthly Party breakfast. These original Panthers demonstrate their continuing commitment with a power to the people salute. Left to right: Hank Jones, Joe Rice (Communist Party), Wayne Pharr, Roland Freeman, and Minister of Culture Emory Douglas. WAYNE PHARR COLLECTION

"Peaches" Moore, a mother of two, died a few years ago of cancer. She remained a community activist until the end. She was most passionate about legalizing marijuana.

As with G, Melvin "Cotton" Smith's life became steeped in controversy. After turning state's evidence against us, Cotton was in some kind of witness protection program. Two decades had passed and I had not heard much about Cotton, except that he was living down south. Then I read in the newspaper that Cotton had killed two guys, whom he thought were members of the Black Liberation Army. He was convicted and sentenced to life in prison and eventually died locked up.

I suspect that Cotton was paranoid, considering his role in the trial and the rumors about him being a snitch while he was in the Party. Cotton had turned on us in the end, but I don't believe that he was a snitch while we worked together for two reasons. First, when the raid jumped off, Cotton was the only person in the house who was awake. I was asleep; it was Cotton who woke me and told me that the police were out there. If Cotton had been a police agent, he could have just let them in and hit all of us—it would have been much easier and a much more successful operation for them if done that way. Second, Cotton got the Thompson machine gun and opened up on the police while he was behind me. If Cotton had been an agent at the time, he could have shot me in the back instead of shooting the police. He handled himself like a comrade, not an agent. What I believed happened is that he was afraid for his life after Huey set him up in Dallas. He thought G was going to kill him because he led G, Roland, and the other brothers in Dallas to the area where they were arrested under the direction of Huey. Knowing that he had been set up by Huey and then was under the suspicion of G, Cotton probably thought the safest route was to work with the cops. He wanted to stay alive.

As for me, after leaving Louisiana, I returned to Los Angeles, married Carmen, and had another baby girl, Dana. I focused on building a strong business and strong family. My real estate business prospered until 2007, when I had a stroke and lost my ability to hustle like I used to. Pam, Sharon, and I raised our children as brothers and sisters who love and support each other. In the early years, after my sons were born, Pam would babysit Tammy if Sharon needed help. We made sure that the children spent time with each other. Now, Tammy and the boys have their own families, and I am a grandfather many times over.

One of the saddest moments in my life was when Nanny passed away in 2009. She was born in 1909, so she lived one hundred years. She saw a lot in those many years. She was a strong and patient woman. She knew how much I relied on her love and support and that I didn't want her to leave this earth. She said to me right before she died, "Let me go now, Wayne." Although I didn't want to ever lose her, I don't have the right to complain, because I was truly blessed to have had her in my life.

Nanny always got a chuckle when she thought of Uncle Edwin and me being in jail at the same time. When I was in jail for the shoot-out, Uncle Edwin and I actually saw each other in passing. He had been thrown in jail for a drive-by shooting—I often say he committed one of the first in Los Angeles. While at a gambling shack, Uncle Edwin believed the proprietor was trying to take advantage of him. So he left the joint and had his wife drive him back to the place, where he shot the guy from his car while the guy was coming out the door. After his release, I would see Uncle Edwin at family events. He died in the late 1970s from a stroke.

I lost my father in 1994 to diabetes and my brother Dru in 2000 to cirrhosis of the liver. In 1999, I went back to New Orleans to work with Dru, at his request. I appreciated my brother more than he ever knew. He gave me enough moral incentive to stay out of the dope business, and that put me on the track to righteous and dignified prosperity.

All things considered and relatively speaking, I have lived a fairly good life. Any real sadness I feel is related to the loss of friends and comrades, those who died very young, did or are still doing long

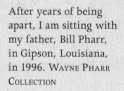

After years of being apart, I am sitting with my father, Bill Pharr, in Gipson, Louisiana, in 1996. WAYNE PHARR COLLECTION

stints in prison, or those suffering from post-traumatic stress disorder. Sometimes I think that I should have done more or that if I had been morally or spiritually stronger. Maybe I could have been a better resource for my friends, comrades, and partners.

Of the Black Student Alliance, Jerry Moore changed his name to Morri Bey. He, perhaps, is the one who suffered least from direct repression from the system and also became the most educated. He joined the Moorish Science Temple and became an entrepreneur. On the other side were Baba (Ronald Preston) and Wendell, both of whom did eight years in San Quentin. They were convicted of the attempted murder of a local Communist Party leader in December 1969. They fled the country and were captured in Canada. I didn't see Baba again until the 1990s. He is now a practicing chef and remains a community activist. Wendell was paroled to the San Francisco area and passed away fifteen years ago. Julius became an activist around food programs. He died about three years ago of stomach cancer. And then there was my homeboy Duck—Billy Dean Smith. He beat his fragging case, which turned into one of the biggest legal cases out of the Vietnam era. Not only was Luke McKissack his lawyer, but the whole antiwar movement fought for his freedom. Now he is back in prison, I'm not sure what for. But trouble seems to follow him.

Like Duck, trouble followed Harold Taylor. He became a telephone repairman in Miami, Florida, but was pulled back into the vortex of COINTELPRO in 2007 when he and seven other activists, the San Francisco 8, were arrested and charged with the 1971 murder of a police officer. Although Harold had been charged with the crime more than thirty years earlier, the case had been dropped due to insufficient evidence. After they were rearrested, Harold and the other defendants were viciously tortured by the police, who even used cattle prods on their genitalia, in order to force a confession out of them. After spending months in jail and raising bail money in the millions of dollars, all but two of the defendants were set free.

The treatment of the San Francisco 8 is a testament to the continued injustice inherent in this country. Like LAPD cops Cigar, Hole, and Fisher, who never had to pay for the beatings, harassment, and attempted murder of Party members, those cops who tortured Harold

Druice Pharr, Gale Madison (Dru's half-sister), and me in New Orleans.
WAYNE PHARR COLLECTION

Taylor and his comrades will never be charged of a crime. I am not afraid to say that at this time, on this day, on this earth, an organization similar to the Black Panther Party for Self-Defense is still necessary.

I have no illusions about a postracial society that supposedly came into being after Barack Obama became president. It is during this time and era that Oscar Grant, a young black man was shot and killed while lying facedown on the ground at Fruitvale Station in Oakland. The shooter, a police officer, was convicted of involuntary manslaughter and served less than a year in jail. The shooting and murder of the unarmed seventeen-year-old teenager Trayvon Martin by racist community watchman George Zimmerman is another example of the frailty of black life in this country. In the Zimmerman case, the attempt by the local government in Sanford, Florida, to avoid arresting Zimmerman by covering up his crime shows collusion and racism. It was only after weeks of protest and nationwide attention that the police in Sanford arrested Zimmerman. After going to trial, Zimmerman was found not guilty by a jury of women, mostly white. No black women were chosen to serve.

The environment that we live in still cries out for the need of organized self-defense to protect the black community. Christopher Dorner, perhaps more than anyone, highlighted the unequal justice in this country. Taking a page from Mark Essex, Robert Charles, and even Tommy "Ndugebele" Harper, Los Angeles police officer Dorner went on a killing spree to protest the LAPD's racism and ultimate termination of his employment. Dorner, who hoped to be accepted as part of a team of police officers sworn to protect and to serve, found out that he wasn't after accusing another officer of excessive force. Like O. J. Simpson, Dorner thought that he had become one of "them," but when he found out he really wasn't, he suffered psychosis or a mental breakdown.

In addition to self-defense, there is still a need to fight for affordable housing, jobs, a living wage, and adequate food and health care. Embracing Black Nationalism by advocating control of our own neighborhoods and cities could be a step in the right direction.

Imagine if we were in control of a state, county, or even our city. Ronald Freeman might be a police chief or Long John a professor. Even Duck could have been a general. But people of color are still fighting for a fair chance at success. Sure, those people of exceptional ability can be incorporated into mainstream America, like Oprah, Magic, or Obama; they would be successful no matter the odds. But the real truth is revealed by how society treats the masses and those without exceptional talent or wealth.

Although I am not advocating violence, I know that sometimes you've got to be ready to fight. It is better to battle and lose than to run away while telling yourself you've won. From my experiences, I know that life can be up and sometimes down, but either way, we must keep our eyes on the prize.

"WAS IT WORTH IT"

All power to the people.

Many times over the years I've been asked, "Was it worth it, and would you do it again?" The answer is yes on both accounts.

"If you don't stand for something you will fall for anything."

I believe the Black Panthers and other militant organizations did more to ensure our human and civil rights than all the marching and praying of the last 100 years.

What the power structure realized with the urban riots and the growth of the black militant movement of the late '60s was that there was a new black man and woman in america.

One who was willing to fight and die for human rights and black liberation.

Huey Newton, Bunchy Carter, Field Marshal George Jackson, Joanne Chesimard, Kathleen Cleaver, Elaine Brown, Geronimo Pratt, Walter Pope, Tommy Lewis,

Steve Bartholomew, Robert Lawrence, Fred Hampton, Mark Clark, Carl Hampton, Melvin X, Tommy Harper, and the architect of the movement Malcolm X;

there are countless others who paid the price with their lives and freedom.

This new black man would *fight* no matter what the odds.

Was it worth it to start a breakfast for children program, which shamed the gov't to start the Head Start Program and inspired Operation Push?

Was it worth it to start free medical clinics?

Was it worth it to test over 10,000 people for sickle cell?

Was it worth it to start liberation schools?

Was it worth it for Eldridge Cleaver, Masai Hewitt, and Stokely Carmichael to put our struggle on the international stage and make contacts with revolutionaries all over the world?

Was it worth it for us as black human beings to practice self-defense?

Was it worth it for Marcus Garvey to try to buy ships so we could travel to Africa?

Was it worth it for Elijah Muhammad to start economic programs to feed and clothe ourselves?

Hell, yes, it was worth it.

The 10 Point Platform and program as so eloquently put by Chairman Bobby Seale and Minister Huey Newton is still a viable piece of work,

and for this we were viciously attacked by all the force of the power structure, as organizations and as the black community as a whole.

By the same token we have to clean up and take charge of our own house and go back to the teachings of Malcolm X and international Black Nationalism.

Everybody in the world sees our true power but us.

Would I do it again?

HELL YES!

Power to the People.

INDEX

INDEX